Japan and China

Japan and China

Cooperation, Competition and Conflict

Edited by

Hanns Günther Hilpert
Stiftung Wissenschaft und Politik, Berlin

and

René Haak
German Institute for Japanese Studies, Tokyo

First published 2002 by
PALGRAVE
Houndmills, Basingstoke, Hampshire RG21 6XS and
175 Fifth Avenue, New York, N.Y. 10010
Companies and representatives throughout the world

PALGRAVE is the new global academic imprint of
St. Martin's Press LLC Scholarly and Reference Division and
Palgrave Publishers Ltd (formerly Macmillan Press Ltd).

ISBN 0–333–97038–1

This book is printed on paper suitable for recycling and
made from fully managed and sustained forest sources.

A catalogue record for this book is available
from the British Library.

Library of Congress Cataloging-in-Publication Data
Japan and China : cooperation, competition, and conflict / edited by
Hanns Günther Hilpert and René Haak.
       p. cm.
    Includes bibliographical references and index.
    ISBN 0–333–97038–1
       1. Japan—Foreign economic relations—China. 2. China—Foreign economic
relations—Japan. 3. Competition, International. I. Hilpert, Hanns-Günther.
II. Haak, René.
    HF1602.15.C6 J357 2002
    337.51052—dc21   2002017697

10   9   8   7   6   5   4   3   2   1
11   10   09   08   07   06   05   04   03   02

Printed and bound in Great Britain by
Antony Rowe Limited, Chippenham, Wiltshire

Contents

List of Tables

List of Figures

List of Abbreviations and Acronyms

ADB   Asian Development Bank
AFTA   ASEAN Free Trade Area
APEC   Asia-Pacific Economic Co-operation
APN   Asia-Pacific Network for Global Change Research
ASEAN   Association of Southeast Asian Nations
ARF   ASEAN Regional Forum
CDM   Clean development mechanism
CO_2 Carbon dioxide
COP   Conference of the Parties
DAC   Development Assistance Committee
EFTA   European Free Trade Agreement
ET   Emission trading
EU   European Union
FCCC   Framework Convention on Climate Change
FDD   Floppy disc drive
FDI   Foreign direct investment
FIEs   Foreign invested enterprises
FSU   Former Soviet Union
GATS   General Agreement on Trade in Services
GATT   General Agreement on Tariffs and Trade
GDP   Gross domestic product
GHG   Greenhouse gas
GNP   Gross national product
GTAP   Global trade aggregated
HDD   Hard disc drives
IBRD   International Bank of Reconstruction and Development
ICT   Information and communication technology
IDA   International Development Association
IGBP   International Geosphere-Biosphere Programme
IHDP   International Human Dimensions Programme on Global Environmental Change
IMF   International Monetary Fund
IPCC   Intergovernmental Panel on Climate Change
ITA   Information Technology Agreement
JBIC   Japan Bank for International Cooperation
JEXIM   Export and Import Bank of Japan
JI   Joint implementation
JICA   Japan International Cooperation Agency
JV   Joint venture

LDP	Liberal Democratic Party
METI	Ministry of Economic, Trade and Industry (Japan)
MFA	Multi-Fibre Agreement
MFN	Most-favoured nation
MITI	Ministry of International Trade and Industry (Japan)
MNE	Multinational enterprise
MOF	Ministry of Finance (Japan)
MoFA	Ministry of Foreign Affairs (Japan)
NIE(s)	Newly-industrializing economy(ies)
NTB	Non-tariff-barriers
ODA	Official development aid
OECD	Organization for Economic Cooperation and Development
OECF	Overseas Economic Cooperation Fund
OOF	Other official flows
PMO	Prime Minister's Office (Japan)
PPP	Purchasing power parity
QELROs	Quantified Emission Limitation and Reduction Objectives
R&D	Research and development
RMB	Renminbi
SITC	Standard International Trade Classification
SOCB	State-owned commercial bank
SOE	State-owned enterprise
SPC	State Planning Committee
SRES	Special Report on Emission Scenarios
START	Systems for Analysis, Research and Training for Global Change
TAR	Third Assessment Report
TFP	Total factor productivity
TQC	Total quality control
TRIMs	Trade-related investment measures
TRIPS	Trade-related aspects of intellectual property rights
TRQ	Tariff-rate quota
TT	Technology transfer
UN	United Nations
WTO	World Trade Organization

Notes on the Contributors

Deepak Bhattasali is Chief of the Economics Unit and Lead Economist for China in the World Bank and is currently posted in Beijing.

René Haak is Senior Researcher and Economics Group Manager in the Economic Section of the German Institute for Japanese Studies (DIJ) in Tokyo.

Hanns Günther Hilpert was Senior Researcher at the German Institute for Japanese Studies (DIJ) in Tokyo from 1999 until 2001 and is now Senior Research Associate at the Stiftung Wissenschaft und Politik (SWP) in Berlin.

Juichi Inada is Professor at the Senshu University in Tokyo and adjunct Research Fellow at the Japan Institute of International Affairs (JIIA) in Tokyo.

Masahiro Kawai was Professor for Economics in the Institute of Social Science at the University of Tokyo (1986–98), and Chief Economist of the World Bank's East Asia and Pacific Regional Office, Tokyo (1998–2001), and is currently Deputy Vice Minister for International Affairs at the Ministry of Finance, Japan.

Yasuko Kameyama is Senior Researcher at the National Institute for Environment Studies (NIES) in Tsukuba.

C. H. Kwan has been working as Senior Economist at the Nomura Research Institute (NRI) in Tokyo and is now Senior Fellow at the Research Institute of Economy, Trade and Industry (RIETI) in Tokyo.

Tomoo Marukawa has been working as Researcher in the Institute of Developing Economies (IDE) in Wakaba, Chiba, and is currently Associate Professor in the Institute of Social Science at the University of Tokyo.

Katsuji Nakagane is Professor in the Graduate School of Economics and the Faculty of Economics of the University of Tokyo.

Markus Taube is Professor for the East Asian Economy and China at the University of Duisburg.

Yan Zhu is Research Fellow at the Fujitsu Research Institute (FRI) in Tokyo.

Foreword

Japan and China are Asia's two largest national economies, and economic relations between them have been the centrepiece of a recent research programme of the Economic Section of the German Institute for Japanese Studies (DIJ) focusing especially on foreign trade, strategic management and human resource development. This publication brings together up-to-date research by a number of renowned Asian and European scholars and presents a documentation, an analysis and an evaluation of the various microeconomic and macroeconomic aspects of the Sino–Japanese relationship. By elaborating comprehensively on trade, investment, economic cooperation, management activities and strategies among other topics, this book closes a gap in the landscape of Sino–Japanese literature, which is usually more concerned with history, politics and security. It will certainly prove useful as an essential tool for academics and those doing business in Asia.

The German Institute for Japanese Studies is one of Germany's most eminent foreign research institutes and is concerned with academic research on contemporary Japan. Founded in 1988, the Institute is funded by the Federal Government, but maintains its independence in matters of research. The German Institute for Japanese Studies is thus a manifestation of the awareness in Germany of the need to obtain a better understanding of East Asia and Japan in particular. To this end, the German Institute for Japanese Studies conducts research in the fields of the humanities, the social sciences and the economy of modern Japan, as well as in the area of Japanese–German relations (www.dijtokyo.org).

In January 2001 the German Institute for Japanese Studies organized jointly with the Fujitsu Research Institute an international conference in Tokyo with the title, 'Japan and China: Economic Relations in Transition'. We would like to extend our thanks to Mr Toshihiko Fukui, Chairman of the Economic Research Centre, and Mr Dennis S. Tachiki, Senior Economist, both at the Fujitsu Research Institute, for their hospitality and friendly cooperation in the course of this conference. The event has been supported by the Friedrich-Ebert-Foundation and the German Embassy, and this is gratefully acknowledged. The majority of contributions in this volume is based on presentations of this conference.

I would like to thank all those who contributed to this volume and made its publication possible, first and foremost the authors for writing their contributions and cooperating efficiently with the editors. Professional proofreading was provided by Anne Heritage and Dr Paul Kremmel. Last, but not least, special thanks are due to Dr Hanns Günther Hilpert and Dr René Haak, both from the Economics Section of the German Institute for Japanese

Studies, who not only organized the conference (together with Dennis S. Todiki), but also conceptualized this book and oversaw its speedy and efficient editing.

Tokyo, January 2002   IRMELA HIJIYA-KIRSCHNEREIT
                                        Director, German Institute for Japanese Studies

Introduction

Hanns Günther Hilpert and René Haak

All through the 1990s Japan and China experienced diverging courses of economic fortune. The economic superpower Japan, following the collapse of its stock and real estate markets, went through a decade of enduring economic stagnation and most of Japan's industry has not been able to keep pace with the high growth and rapid productivity gains of its main competitors in the US. In contrast, China has sustained high economic growth rates of around 10 per cent per annum and Chinese firms have gained dominant world market shares in an increasing number of industrial sectors. As a result, China's developmental gap to the leading industrialized countries narrowed substantially, and China has achieved the stature as a centre of regional political and economic power.

Both in international business and in international economics, it is widely recognized that the current rise of China has wide implications for the international economic and political order in general and for the East Asian region in particular. From this broadly accepted assessment the obvious conclusion follows that Japan, more than any other major industrialized country, is facing the challenge of an economically and politically successful China. China's industry with its low sales prices and its improving product quality, is set to become a major competitor in global manufacturing products' markets, including the Japanese domestic market, which is quite a worrying prospect for Japan's economic and political elites. On the macro level, China is challenging Japan as East Asia's centre of economic gravity in terms of production and markets. Considering the increasing economic and political importance of China, the crucial question arises: What kind of relationship between Japan and China will evolve? Will it tend to be cooperative or conflictive?

An inquiry into the structure and dynamics of the Sino–Japanese relationship is a major task in itself. Economically and politically, Japan and China are not only the two foremost important countries of East Asia (see Table I.1) in terms of the size of the economy (Japan) or their future potential (China), they are also major international players. Considering the repercussions the Sino–Japanese relationship has on the political stability

1

Table I.1   Japan, China and the USA compared (1999)

	Unit	Japan	China	USA
GDP	bn./US$	4349	991	9256
GDP per capita[1]	US$	34375	782	33889
Share of East Asian GDP (1998)[1]	%	66	15	n.a.
GDP growth 1980–90[1]	%	4.1	9.5	2.0
GDP growth 1990–99[1]	%	1.2	10.3	3.0
Foreign exchange reserves	bn. US$	287	158	6.0
Foreign trade volume	bn. US$	727	487	1779
Share of world trade[1]	%	6.4	4.3	15.6
World competitiveness (2000)[2]	score points	57.52	49.53	100
Population	m. people	127	1267	255
Land area	sq. km	377829	9560770	9372614

Notes: 1.   Own calculations from IMF figures.
  2.   USA 100 (Ranking by IMD).

Sources: IMF (*International Financial Statistics, Direction of Trade Statistics*), IMD (International Institute for Management Development), own calculations.

and the economic development of the Asia-Pacific region, this examination is even more important. It is certain that the state of the Sino–Japanese relationship will have a major influence on the investment environment and the business confidence in the region as well as on the regional flows of trade and investment. It can even be maintained that the process of regional economic cooperation may be contingent on the right balancing of Chinese and Japanese interests. Both Japan and China, which are aspiring to leading roles in East Asia, must deal with the influence of the US in the region. Therefore, the state of Sino–Japanese relations, along with the major political role of the US in this security triangle, will have a major impact on the region's interstate political relations and security environments, and possibly even on the preservation of peace in East Asia.

The historical and political setting

The contributions in this book are focused more on the economic side of the Sino–Japanese relationship than on political and security issues. History and politics, nevertheless, are highly relevant for economics in general and also for practical daily business. They form the background environment in which the interplay of economic forces and of individual business actions takes place.

The past 2000 years of Sino–Japanese relations have been harmonious and mutually beneficial, at times, and antagonistic and conflictive at other times. On the positive side, Japan appreciates the Chinese historical contribution in the realms of religion, philosophy, culture and technology. China, in turn, is pursuing an economic policy partly inspired by the developmental success of

Japan and its followers in Asia, such as Taiwan, Korea and Singapore. On the negative side, however, the fierce political military conflicts and the atrocities of war in more recent history weigh heavily on the mutual relationship.

To understand the current mistrust and the uneasiness in Sino–Japanese relations, a brief recourse to the modern history of Japan and China is necessary. The two countries reacted differently to the challenges imposed by the imperialistic advances of Western powers into East Asia in the nineteenth century, and partly as a result of this they became opponents in politics and war. Japan, following the example of Western imperialist powers, tried to colonize China. As a consequence of the Japanese military advances of the nineteenth and twentieth centuries, China lost parts of its territory and the Chinese people suffered heavily under the Japanese occupation and aggression. After the end of the Second World War, China and Japan remained adversaries, being in opposite camps in the Cold War. Although a kind of Sino–Japanese rapprochement took place in the 1970s and 1980s, when China distanced itself from the Soviet Union, an earnest Sino–Japanese reconciliation has not yet occurred. An unfortunate historical legacy of mutual mistrust and suspicion still remains. Many Chinese are seriously concerned about a possible revival of Japanese militarism. On the other hand, there is fear in Japan of an increasingly political and militarily assertive China.

The mutually negative images place a heavy strain on the relationship, but the more serious concern lies in security matters. Japan's and China's former common strategic interest of containing Soviet military threats has virtually disappeared in the post-Cold War's new strategic settings. For the future, it cannot be ruled out that both countries' strategic reorientations may lead to a renewal of Sino–Japanese strategic rivalry. Therefore, the potential prospect of political confrontation between Japan and China has to be taken seriously. Bilateral political conflict flared up already in the 1990s in various contentious issues such as the border conflict over the *Diaoyu/ Senkaku* islands, the revision of the US–Japan security treaty, the dispute over Taiwan's sovereignty, China's nuclear testing, and the unresolved legacy of Japanese acts of war and aggression in China. The political uneasiness of the relationship has its negative repercussions on bilateral economic relations, as can be seen by the numerous cases of discrimination of Japanese investors by Chinese authorities, by the linkage of Japanese ODA to China's nuclear policy and human rights record, and by the emergence of the Sino–Japanese trade conflict in 2001.

It is somehow assuring that a solid diplomatic framework for official state relations is firmly in place. Bilateral diplomatic relations were resumed in 1972, soon after the normalization of Sino–US ties. In 1978 Japan and China, recognizing their common strategic interests, signed the Treaty of Peace and Friendship with the deliberate objective of promoting peaceful and friendly ties. The Long Term Trade Agreement, concluded also in 1978, served as a kind of economic underpinning of the Sino–Japanese political rapprochement and provided a political and legal framework for the increasing trade between the two countries. However, Sino–Japanese relations came under increasing strain in the 1990s, when the Cold War era ended and the international political and economic environment changed accordingly. As already mentioned, Japan and China clashed politically on various occasions. To overcome the structural frictions and to set up a more solid basis for the bilateral relationship, the Joint Declaration on Building a Partnership of Friendship and Cooperation for Peace and Development was announced in 1998, during an official visit to Japan of China's State President Jiang Zemin.

In addition to the basic political agreements mentioned, both countries are linked in a web of bilateral contracts on specific issues, and by common membership in a number of regional and multilateral organizations. Most significant among the latter are APEC (Asian Pacific Economic Co-operation), the ARF (ASEAN Regional Forum), the WTO (World Trade Organization), the UN (United Nations) and their sub-organizations, and the Bretton Woods institutions (IMF and the World Bank). These regional and global institutions have an important role to play, as they can offer a generally agreed institutional framework for conflict solving, and may help accommodate the political rise of China. International institutions of this sort are giving China the opportunity to gain international prestige by staging great events such as the 2001 summit of the APEC forum in Shanghai or the 2008 Olympics in Beijing.

The solid integration of China into the international economic and political system is indeed a major objective of Japan's China policy. Japan's political and economic elites widely hold the belief that a China gaining political stature and economic wealth as a result of peaceful interaction with the outside world by means of diplomacy, trade, investment and economic cooperation is a more stable and more predictable China. Therefore, Japan is actively promoting China's economic development and integration into the international division of labour. A stable and economically thriving China certainly advances the political stability in all Asia and thus promotes Japan's comprehensive security, which traditionally encompasses various non-military issues like economic and social stability, environmental safety, as well as access to energy and other strategic resources.

Also, China ought to welcome unreservedly Japan's China engagement policy, which is serving well China's own objective of promoting economic growth, domestic development and modernization. However, there are reservations because of other – potentially conflictual – Chinese policy objectives, such as the maintenance of China's national independence and sovereignty as well as the national concern for its standing in the regional and international order. China seeks to avoid being entangled in a web of economic and political dependencies, drafted and directed by Japanese institutions and suitable to Japanese interests. China is wary of becoming just another 'flying geese' within a Japan-dominated 'Greater East Asian Co-Prosperity Sphere'. These Chinese caveats notwithstanding, there is ample scope for pragmatic political and economical cooperation between Japan and China in which Japan pushes for integration, engagement and pacification of China, while China tries to extract the maximum of concessions in return for its willingness to cooperate.

Cooperation, competition and conflict

In contrast to politics and security, the economy can be considered the bright spot in China's relations to the outside world. The generally well-developed integration of China into the world economy is mirrored by large and steady flows of goods, services, capital and information between the two countries. Presently Japan and China are running one of the world's most extensive trading relationships, amounting to a total of around US$ 90 billion in the year 2000, if Hong Kong entrepôt trade is included. Whereas China is currently Japan's second most important trading partner, being surpassed only by the US, Japan is China's most important import source and second largest export market (see Chapter 2). Japan is also, after the trade and finance entrepôt Hong Kong and the US, China's third most important investor country. Moreover, although investment in China accounts for only a minor share in Japan's total FDI by value, China is a prime location for Japan's overseas manufacturing plants (see Chapter 3). Besides setting up its own subsidiaries by outright direct investment, Japanese business is committed to the Chinese market in various other ways, such as capital lending, contract manufacturing, sales commissions or licensing agreements. Further to its far-reaching private business relations, Japan and China are also running a close ODA relationship: Japan is China's top donor and China has been Japan's top ODA destination for over 20 years (see Chapter 6).

As the above list shows, Sino–Japanese economic relations are extensive, well advanced and solid. The cooling down of political relations during the 1990s obviously did not harm economic relations. On the contrary, business is seemingly booming across the waters between China and Japan. In both countries the preconditions for a continuation of this economic boom are in place. China is still at an early stage of its economic and industrial development and the country's accession to the WTO is likely to further boost its domestic growth and open up its markets. Japanese business is eager to exploit these opportunities in its neighbourhood, as is shown in regular company surveys in which respondents usually name China as the most promising country for foreign investment and market development. Recognizing the divergence in the development of political and economic relations between Japan and China in the 1990s, this book deals explicitly with their economic relationship, which at the same time is marked by elements of cooperation, competition and conflict.

By strict economic reasoning, cooperation is certainly the prevailing element in Sino–Japanese economic and business relations. It may be a trivial fact, but nevertheless important, that virtually all Sino–Japanese business actions are voluntary, not coercive. China's transformation to a capitalist market system is so far advanced that Sino–Japanese economic relations are widely based upon free choice interactions of the marketplace, which only take place if profits can be earned and the general business environment is favourable. In the Sino–Japanese case, the necessary conditions for free enterprise business are basically met. Thus, the mere fact of booming business relations is reason enough to characterize the Sino–Japanese economic relationship as cooperative rather than as conflictive.

A convincing reason for the cooperative nature in Japan and China's economic relations is the economic complementarity of the two countries' supply structures. Whereas Japan is rich in capital, technology and highly qualified people, the comparative advantages of China are the inexhaustible reservoir of low cost labour and its natural resources. In striking correspondence to neoclassical predictions, these differing factor endowments cause natural differences in income, in productivity, and in the respective comparative advantages in the international division of labour. They are the essential source of mutual beneficial business and trade between Japan and China.

Further to the difference in supply structures, a comparison of the macroeconomic and the institutional dimensions suggest that the often-cited notion of economic competition between Japan and China is still more a future vision than present reality. At the moment, Japan is the economic superpower and (coastal) China is only an upcoming and potential challenger. In the year 1999, Japan surpassed China by a factor of four to five in economic size and by a factor of 44 in economic income per capita (see Table 1.1). The more fundamental difference is that Japan is endowed with a full range of technological capabilities and also with the kind of economic and political institutions of an industrialized economy and a modern democracy. Beyond that, Japan over the past 100 years has displayed an astonishing capacity to absorb and to manage social, industrial, technological and demographic change while maintaining social and cultural cohesion. Since Japan started the process of catching up with the West already at the end of the nineteenth century, now, at the start of the twenty-first century it possesses a significant 'institutional' lead. China, on the other hand, is still negatively affected by a number of serious institutional obstacles, in particular the weak foundation for the rule of law and the general lack of transparency. Such shortfalls will be a heavy burden as China, in the course of its further development and modernization process, struggles to overcome the legacy of overstaffed, loss-making state enterprises and to cope with the increasing social inequalities and poverty in rural areas.

The theoretical reasoning for the basic cooperative nature of Japan–China economic relations notwithstanding, practitioners from business and trade policy will quickly point to the numerous cases of severe business competition or to the various bilateral trade and investment conflicts. These objections from real-world experience are well founded and show why the general cooperative nature of Sino–Japanese economic relations needs to be complemented by additional competitive and conflictive elements. This modification is necessary because the strict assumptions of the economical (essentially neoclassical) model apparently do not apply to the real world. In particular, two qualifications are necessary in our deliberations.

First, Sino–Japanese business relations are not entirely free-market based. In many instances, political power supersedes the free interplay of market forces. To be sure, the role of the state is important in setting up an efficient legal and regulatory framework, in particular in the domain of transborder business exchange. However, policy interventions in Japan and in China go much further. To start with, tariffs and non-tariff barriers are impeding the access to the respective import markets. Moreover, Japan and China's domestic markets are highly regulated and domestic business is often subject to public-private collusion. In many cases, political interference leads to discretionary, non-market-based business actions and/or discriminatory policy decisions. State interventions are one of the root causes for trade and investment conflicts and business discrimination. They can be held largely responsible for the fact that the large economic potential of the bilateral relationship is not fully utilized.

Second, the economic relationship between Japan and China is not only static in nature. Dynamic forces also shape the relationship. It must be acknowledged that both the increasing industrial competition at the microeconomic level and the gradual shift of economic weight at the macroeconomic level are dynamic phenomena and that they occupy a central position in both countries' bilateral economic and political agenda.

Owing to successful industrial upgrading, Chinese manufacturing firms are catching up in quality and technology in a growing number of industrial sectors and thus are threatening the Japanese 'incumbents' with displacement competition. To the chagrin of Japanese industry, the Chinese 'challenge' is not confined to the area of light, labour-intensive manufacturing industries and agriculture, but increasingly includes capital-intensive and even technology-intensive industries as well. Thus, for Japan, China is not just a partner to be helped by economic aid and industrial investment but also a tough competitor in world markets. On the other hand, China has to deal with foreign competition, too, since foreign firms, notably Japanese firms, will be increasingly active in China's domestic market as a result of China's import liberalization in the wake of the WTO accession.

The Sino–Japanese business competition mentioned above is supplemented by macro-level conflicts. If China and Japan keep growing at the same rates as they did in the 1990s, China will surpass Japan by the year 2020 and become the second largest economy in the world. Although it is quite unlikely that the long-term growth rates of Japan and China will be the same as the 1990 averages, it is sure that the size of the gap between Japan and China will narrow considerably and eventually disappear. Then the centre of economic gravity in Asia will gradually shift from the Japanese islands to the Chinese continent. This sea-change will have tremendous repercussions on international trade and international trade policy. For example, China will gain and Japan will lose purchasing power in the international markets for energy, raw materials and food, which are all considered by Japan's economic and political elites as strategic supplies. Eventually, there will also be a shift of bargaining power in international trade negotiations. Since China aspires to build a 'prosperous and strong great nation' (*fuqiang daguo*), ensuing conflicts between the ambitious challenger China and the incumbent leader Japan are to be expected.

To sum up, cooperation, competition and conflicts all characterize the economic relations between Japan and China. These three elements are not mutually exclusive, but coexist and interplay. In the absence of political shocks, it is not unlikely that the current state of Sino–Japanese economic relations will remain unchanged, as outlined above, for a considerable period of time. As China's accession to the WTO will advance the liberalization and the deregulation of the Chinese economy, Sino–Japanese trade and business relations should also expand substantially. Thus future Sino–Japanese economic relations can be expected to deepen and to broaden further, and become increasingly complex. However, as long as the mutual relations remain ambiguous and unresolved conflictive elements linger on, the full potential of the economic relationship will not be realized. The current blockage resulting from mutual mistrust and discomfort cannot be overcome by market interaction. Rather, positive government intervention is needed. For certain, the Japanese and the Chinese governments have an important role to play to prevent hostile relationships, to build up mutual confidence and trust, to promote bilateral trade and business ties and to enlarge the scope of economic cooperation.

Economic assessment

As outlined above, the Sino–Japanese relationship is important for the two sides as well as for the region. The economic relationship itself is rapidly expanding, thus becoming even more important. Furthermore, Sino–Japanese relations are marked by elements of cooperation, competition and conflict. This publication takes a closer, analytical look at the inherent nature and the structural features of Japan–China economic relations. The following chapters concentrate on the various economic interfaces in both countries' relations, such as trade, investment, economic cooperation, Japan's role in China's economic development, and business activities and strategies of Japanese enterprises. They look at the economic forces and the longer-term trends shaping the relationship. This economic assessment occurs at a critical time, just ahead of China's accession to the WTO, which is expected to be a milestone in China's relations to the outside world.

The contributions start with **C.H. Kwan**'s presentation of the neoclassical analysis framework of Sino–Japanese economic relations in the context of China's emergence as a major player in the world economy. As a consequence of the difference in factor endowments and the gap in the level of industrial development, bilateral economic relations can be characterized as complementary rather than competitive. China's entry into the WTO should prompt a further division of labour between China and Japan according to comparative advantage, with the former specializing in labour-intensive products and the latter specializing in high-tech products. Japan will benefit largely from the rise of China as an economic power through the incurring improvement of its terms of trade. However, Japan's income distribution will change, as the share of capital will increase at the expense of labour. The chapter also explores the prospect for more bilateral intra-industry trade in manufactured goods as the income gap shrinks and for additional Japanese investment as China's investment environment liberalizes.

The analysis by Kwan is extended by a quantitative analysis of Sino–Japanese trade by **Hanns Günther Hilpert**. The chapter presents (1) trade volumes in absolute values, (2) relative trade shares, and (3) bilateral trade interdependence indices. As China's foreign trade data is distorted as a consequence of asymmetric accounting for Hong Kong entrepôt trade, the necessary corrections are made. The quantitative trade data analysis shows the dynamic development of bilateral trade over the last 20 years resulting in unusual high degrees of trade interdependence. These results not only imply that the trade relationship is more complementary than competitive, but also that the overall economic relationship is cooperative rather than conflictive. The chapter also investigates the different causes of the rapid trade growth.

Subsequent to trade, investment is the second principal economic link between Japan and China. **Katsuji Nakagane** presents absolute volumes, relative shares and main characteristics of Japanese foreign direct investment (FDI) into China. His comprehensive stocktaking is followed by an investigation into the contributions of (total and of Japanese) FDI to China's domestic growth. For this purpose, estimates of growth and of FDI functions are set up. The resulting estimates show that Japan has contributed substantially to China's economic development. The author foresees the continuation of the dynamic relationship between trade, investment and growth in spite of a difficult business environment in China and the frequent Sino–Japanese investment conflicts.

The accession of China to the WTO is often considered a watershed in China's economic relations to the outside world. **Deepak Bhattasali** and **Masahiro Kawai** examine this claim by employment of a quantitative global trade model. They assess that the WTO impact on China's economy and foreign trade is modest in the short and medium term when compared with the resource reallocation that is already taking place due to the ongoing transformation process. Only the agricultural sector will suffer some disruptions in the medium term. Industrial growth can either stagnate or grow rapidly, depending on foreign direct investment, local protectionism and the private sector. In all scenarios, Chinese trade with the Asian region will grow rapidly, especially in agriculture, and there will be a boom in domestic services. China's share of world trade may double. Whereas the overall impact on Japan's total output and trade will be negligible, Japanese manufacturing exports to China are expected to expand across all sectors, and to be especially strong in the area of textiles and electronics. Japan's agricultural imports from China will increase.

Markus Taube examines Japan's role in China's industrialization process. Five interfaces are identified and further scrutinized: (1) industrial policy, (2) official development aid, (3) transfer of technology, (4) foreign direct investment, (5) corporate governance structures and business concepts. The chapter concludes that Japan certainly played an important role in China's industrialization process over the last two decades. The Japanese influence has been exerted over various channels, however, none of which played a dominating role just themselves. Japan's impact on China's industrialization rather has to be understood as the combined effect of various influences.

There have been substantial official development aid (ODA) transfers from Japan to China over the last 20 years. Apparently, ODA lies at the core of the Sino–Japanese relationship and it has strong political, diplomatic and economic implications. **Juichi Inada** shows the large dimensions of Japanese ODA to China and he describes its macroeconomic, sectoral and social impacts. Further on, the political environment and the political problems related to the Japanese ODA in China are discussed. The key future issues are identified, namely the implications of recent institutional changes in Japan, and the shift in focus to social development, development of the poorer interior regions, agriculture, environmental protection and institutional capacity building.

Environmental policy is a major part of Sino–Japanese economic cooperation. **Yasuko Kameyama** examines how global environmental problems, especially the global climate change problem, have changed Japan's China policy in recent years, which has been traditionally based on its traditional comprehensive security concept. It is concluded that the international regime on climate change has influenced both Japan and China in a positive way, that the Sino–Japan relation may improve by utilizing institutions established under the climate change regime, and that success for such improvement lies significantly in the hand of China.

René Haak takes an international management theorist's look at the activities and strategies of Japanese companies in China. He discusses the role of China as a new and important business operation base for Japanese companies, and his analysis focuses on the question of why Japanese companies are attracted to China. Starting from the existing academic literature, a new summarized framework for further analysis and discussions about the various forms of Japanese business strategies towards China is presented. Six strategic options are discussed from a theoretical perspective. They are the export strategy, the international strategy, the multidomestic strategy, the global strategy, the transnational strategy and the collective strategy.

The macroeconomic analysis of Japanese FDI by Nakagane is supplemented by **Tomoo Marukawa**'s investigation into the microeconomic behaviour and performance of Japanese companies active in China. Thus the contraction of Japanese FDI in China in the mid-1990s is explained by the limit of internal resources and the low evaluation of market conditions. Marukawa goes on by examining in detail the three most important industries: the automotive industry, the electronics and household appliance industry, and the textile and apparel industry. Together they account for almost half of Japan's FDI in China in the 1990s. His three main findings are: First, Japanese firms are risk averse, but once they have invested, they will not change their minds easily and will build up supplier networks. Second, the core competence of Japanese firms is the production of sophisticated key components. Third, China, endowed with abundant and cheap labour, is increasingly used as a production base to supply products to Japan.

China's most important economic partner abroad is neither Japan nor the US but the overseas Chinese, which comprise 'the people of Chinese descent who live in countries or regions other than mainland China', such as Hong Kong, Macao, Taiwan and South-East Asia. **Yan Zhu** examines their important and dominant role in Sino–Japanese trade and investment relations. Thus he looks at the role of Hong Kong as an entrepôt and a transhipment centre, and the function of overseas Chinese firms as middlemen between Japan and mainland China. The overseas Chinese firms appear to be even more important partners in Japan's investment and business activities on the mainland, since they have privileged access to the information, human networks as well as to the government authorities. Moreover, they have mastered the local business practices and styles.

1

The Rise of China as an Economic Power: Implications for Asia and Japan*

C. H. Kwan

Introduction

The emergence of China as an economic power is having a strong influence on other Asian economies. China is seen as a promising market and destination for foreign direct investment (FDI), on the one hand, and as a competitor in export markets, on the other. As a general rule, higher income countries with trade structures complementary to that of China are likely to benefit, while lower income countries that compete with China are likely to be hurt.

Economic relations between China and Japan can be characterized as complementary rather than competitive, reflecting the prevailing gap in the level of development. The potential complementarity between the two countries, however, has not been fully exploited, as indicated by the low level of Japanese investment in China. Both countries can benefit by promoting a division of labour according to comparative advantage, with China specializing in labour-intensive products and Japan specializing in high-tech products. To this end, Japan needs to facilitate the relocation of declining industries to China instead of imposing import barriers to protect them, while China should improve its investment environment.

The rise of China

China has firmly established itself as the fastest growing country in the world, and has strengthened its links with the global economy through trade and direct investment since the late 1970s when it adopted a reform-driven, open-door policy. At the same time, China has transformed itself into a newly-industrializing country, with comparative advantage in labour-intensive products. These trends are likely to accelerate after its entry into the WTO.

---

* This chapter extends Kwan (1995) to take into consideration the latest developments.

China's integration into the world economy

China has achieved an annual rate of economic growth averaging almost 10 per cent over the last 20 years. This rate of growth is considerably higher than that of the pre-reform period and compares well with that of Japan and the NIEs during their high growth eras. China's economic record also offers a pleasing contrast to the stagnation and confusion that have beset Russia and most other states of the former Soviet Union, which are also trying to replace their planned economies with market-based systems. The onset of the Asian crisis notwithstanding, China has maintained an annual growth rate of over 7 per cent since 1997. Although China's GDP was only US$ 980 billion in 1999 (compared with the United States' US$ 8351 billion and Japan's US$ 4079 billion), it reached US$ 4112 billion on a purchasing power parity (PPP) basis to surpass Japan (US$ 3043 billion by the same measure) as the world's second largest economy (World Bank, 2000).[1]

Rapid growth in China has been accompanied by a fast expansion of overseas trade. Exports expanded from US$ 9.8 billion in 1978 to US$ 195.2 billion in 1999, while imports rose from US$ 10.9 billion to US$ 165.8 billion. China now ranks as one of the top-ten trading nations of the world (Table 1.1).

Table 1.1   Leading exporters and importers in world merchandise trade, 1999

	Exports				Imports		
		US$ bn	*Share, %*			*US$ bn*	*Share, %*
1	United States	695.2	12.4	1	United States	1059.1	18.0
2	Germany	541.5	9.6	2	Germany	472.5	8.0
3	Japan	419.4	7.5	3	United Kingdom	320.3	5.4
4	France	300.4	5.3	4	Japan	311.3	5.3
5	United Kingdom	269.0	4.8	5	France	290.1	4.9
6	Canada	238.4	4.2	6	Canada	220.2	3.7
7	Italy	230.6	4.1	7	Italy	216.9	3.7
8	Netherlands	200.4	3.6	8	Netherlands	187.6	3.2
9	China	195.2	3.5	9	Hong Kong	180.7	3.1
10	Belgium	176.3	3.1	10	China	165.8	2.8
11	Hong Kong	174.4	3.1	11	Belgium	160.9	2.7
12	Korea	144.7	2.6	12	Mexico	148.7	2.5
13	Mexico	136.7	2.4	13	Spain	144.8	2.5
14	Taiwan	121.6	2.2	14	Korea	119.8	2.0
15	Singapore	114.7	2.0	15	Singapore	111.1	1.9
16	Spain	110.1	2.0	16	Taiwan	110.7	1.9
17	Sweden	84.9	1.5	17	Switzerland	79.9	1.4
18	Malaysia	84.5	1.5	18	Australia	69.1	1.2
19	Switzerland	80.4	1.4	19	Austria	68.8	1.2
20	Russian Fed.	74.3	1.3	20	Sweden	68.5	1.2
	World	5625.0	100.0		World	5881.0	100.0

Source: WTO.

Preliminary data show that it overtook the Netherlands and Italy to become the seventh in 2000, with exports reaching US$ 249 billion. China is already a very open economy, with total trade amounting to 36.7 per cent of GDP in 1999 (far higher than Japan's 16.7 per cent).

China now receives the largest amount of FDI among developing nations. Annual inflow, which exceeded US$ 10 billion for the first time in 1992, has stayed above US$ 40 billion since 1996. On a cumulative basis, total inflow of FDI has exceeded US$ 340 billion. Foreign companies heavily dependent on imported capital goods and intermediate goods on the one hand, and overseas markets on the other, account for about half of China's international trade (47.9 per cent of exports and 52.1 per cent of imports in 2000).

China's trade and investment ties have been particularly strong with Hong Kong and Taiwan. The three areas together, more and more often referred to as Greater China, have emerged as a major force in the global economy, as indicated by the rapid expansion of their combined trade and foreign exchange reserves. Indeed, the US now imports more from Greater China than from Japan, while Japan also imports more from the region than from the USA (Figure 1.1). The combined foreign exchange reserves of China, Taiwan and Hong Kong reached US$ 380 billion at the end of 2000 to surpass Japan's US$ 362 billion.

China's entry into the WTO will represent a further step in its long march towards integration into the global economy. While Chinese products will have more secure access to international markets, foreign goods and services will have much greater access to the Chinese market than before. China's import barriers will be sharply reduced following WTO entry (see Chapter 5): average import tariffs on industrial products will be lowered to 9.4 per cent by 2005, while those on agricultural products will be reduced to 17 per cent. Import quotas on industrial products will be eliminated within five years. China will also participate in the 'Information Technology Agreement' (ITA), which will eliminate tariffs on a wide range of information technology and telecommunications products. In addition, foreign companies will also be given trading and distribution rights.

At the same time, restrictions on foreign investment in China will be relaxed. Foreign companies will be granted the rights to participate in major services sectors such as distribution, telecommunications, financial services, professional services and tourism. China also agrees to implement the 'Agreement on Trade-Related Investment Measures' (TRIMs) and to eliminate and cease enforcing trade and foreign exchange balancing requirements as well as local content requirements imposed on foreign companies.

China as a newly industrializing country

Rising trade and investment have been accompanied by drastic changes in China's trade structure, with manufactured goods now accounting for 90 per cent of total exports, up from 50 per cent in 1980. Here we take a

Japanese Imports by Region

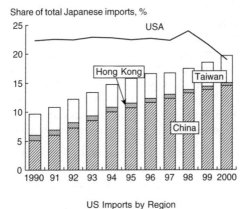

US Imports by Region

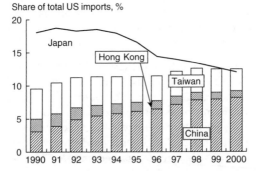

Figure 1.1   Growing importance of Greater China in the Japanese and US markets
Source: Compiled by the author based on Japanese and US trade statistics.

closer look at the evolution in China's comparative advantage in international trade, also taking into consideration its heavy reliance on imported machinery and intermediate goods.

In line with the 'flying-geese pattern of economic development', a country's comparative advantage usually shifts from the production of primary commodities to labour-intensive manufactured goods and, later on, to capital- and technology-intensive products.[2] These shifts are reflected in a country's trade structure, which progresses from that of a developing country to that of a newly-industrializing country and finally to that of an industrial country.

The revealed comparative advantage of a country can be shown by calculating the specialization indices for its major industries. For a particular industry, the specialization index is defined as its trade balance divided by the volume of two-way trade (that is [exports − imports]/[exports + imports]).

By definition, the value of the specialization index ranges from minus 1 to plus 1, with a higher value implying stronger international competitiveness for the industry concerned.

Following Kwan (1994), a country's comparative advantage structure (as revealed by its trade structure) can be classified into one of four categories based on the relative magnitude of the specialization indices of the country's primary commodities (SITC sections 0–4), machinery (SITC section 7, a proxy for capital- and technology-intensive products), and other manufactures (SITC sections 5, 6, 8, 9, a proxy for labour-intensive products). A country typically passes from one category to another in the following sequence:

1. the developing country stage, with primary commodities more competitive than other manufactures and machinery;
2. the young NIE stage, with other manufactures becoming more competitive than primary commodities, which maintains its lead over machinery;
3. the mature NIE stage, with machinery overtaking primary commodities while other manufactures maintain their overall lead; and
4. the industrial country stage, with machinery overtaking other manufactures, which maintain their lead over primary commodities.

Most Asian countries have followed these stages in the course of economic development, with some moving faster than others. Applying the present framework to China confirms that the country's comparative advantage structure has undergone a process of rapid transformation (Figure 1.2). Starting as a typical developing country, China became a young NIE in 1992 when the specialization index of other manufactures surpassed that of primary commodities. Subsequently, it attained mature NIE status in 1999 when the specialization index of machinery also overtook that of primary commodities. The current comparative advantage structure of China corresponds to that of Taiwan in the early 1970s. Based on the same classification, Taiwan became a young NIE in 1967 and a mature NIE in 1972 (Kwan, 1994).

Winners and losers

The rise of China as an industrial power will be a major force shaping the economic landscape in Asia in the twenty-first century. While higher-income countries are likely to benefit by exploiting their complementarity with China, lower-income countries will face keener competition with China in both trade and FDI.

Repercussions through trade

The development of the Chinese economy can be characterized by export-led growth based on its vast labour resources. China's industrialization increases the supply of labour-intensive goods to international markets while increasing demand for capital-intensive goods, leading to a decline in

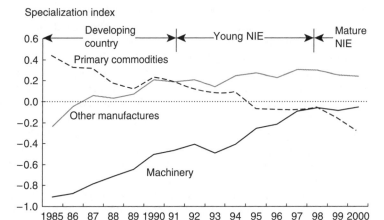

Figure 1.2 Stages of China's trade structure

Note: Four Stages of Trade Structure

	Specialization index
Developing country stage	Primary commodities > Other manufactures > Machinery
Young NIE stage	Other manufactures > Primary commodities > Machinery
Mature NIE stage	Other manufactures > Machinery > Primary commodities
Industrial country stage	Machinery > Other manufactures > Primary commodities

$$\text{Specialization index} = \frac{\text{Exports} - \text{Imports}}{\text{Exports} + \text{Imports}}$$

Source: Compiled by the author based on Chinese trade statistics.

the prices of labour-intensive goods relative to capital-intensive goods. This implies a worsening of its terms of trade (the ratio of export prices to import prices), and an improvement in the terms of trade for the rest of the world. Through this deterioration in China's terms of trade, other economies are also able to benefit from the growth of the Chinese economy. For China itself, however, the deterioration in the terms of trade implies a decline in real income, partly offsetting the benefit of higher economic growth.[3]

Among countries in the rest of the world, however, a distinction should be made between winners and losers. On one hand, countries with trade structures complementary to that of China should gain because their import prices should fall relative to their export prices as China's terms of trade deteriorate. On the other hand, the reverse is true for countries with trade structures similar to that of China (for a theoretical analysis of the impact of China's export-led growth on the rest of the world, see Appendix A.1).

China's entry into the WTO, which is expected to promote the integration of China into the global economy according to comparative advantage, should have similar effects on relative prices. The reduction in import tariffs should induce a shift of resources from the importable goods (capital-intensive goods) sector to the exportable goods (labour-intensive goods) sector. The resulting increases in the supply of labour-intensive goods and in the demand for capital-intensive goods should lead to a deterioration in China's terms of trade. As in the case of export-led growth, countries with trade structures complementary to that of China, therefore, are more likely to benefit than countries with trade structures competing with China.

In order to identify which Asian economies are competing with China in the area of trade, and which have complementary relations with it, we propose a simple way to compare their trade structures involving the following two steps.[4]

First, calculate the specialization indices of major categories of manufactured goods for China and other Asian countries (Table 1.2). To focus on the manufacturing sector, we limit ourselves to the following four categories of goods: chemicals and related products (SITC section 5), manufactured goods classified chiefly by material (SITC section 6), machinery and transport equipment (SITC section 7), and miscellaneous manufactured articles (SITC section 8). The trade structure of each country can then be represented by a vector consisting of these specialization indices. In the case of China, the vector of specialization indices shows that the country is competitive in miscellaneous manufactured articles but not in chemicals and related products, with manufactured goods classified chiefly by material and machinery and transport equipment lying somewhere in between.

Second, compare the trade structure of each Asian country with that of China by calculating the correlation coefficient between their respective vectors. The correlation coefficient so derived should be high (close to plus one) for countries competing with China and low (close to minus one) for

Table 1.2 Specialization indices for major categories of manufactured goods, 1999

	Chemicals and related products	*Manufactured goods chiefly classified by material*	*Machinery and transportation equipment*	*Miscellaneous manufactured articles*
China	−0.40	−0.02	−0.08	0.76
Korea	−0.03	0.30	0.28	0.23
Taiwan	−0.28	0.31	0.11	0.22
Hong Kong	−0.11	−0.10	−0.07	0.17
Singapore	0.15	−0.28	0.06	−0.09
Indonesia	−0.31	0.52	−0.04	0.84
Thailand	−0.36	−0.08	0.05	0.69
Malaysia	−0.29	−0.09	0.13	0.34
Philippines	−0.80	−0.54	−0.06	0.33
Japan	0.15	0.19	0.54	−0.13

Source: Compiled by the author based on ADB (2000).

countries with trade structures complementary to that of China.[5] Since the trade structure of a country is broadly in line with its level of economic development, our results confirm that China tends to have competitive relations with the ASEAN countries and complementary relations with the Asian NIEs and Japan (Figure 1.3). For example, the correlation coefficient between Thailand and China is very high (0.98) while that between Japan and China is actually negative (−0.63).

Most Asian countries have increased their dependence on China as an export market (Figure 1.4). This is particularly true for Japan and the Asian NIEs, which have trade structures complementary to that of China. Hong Kong, in particular, has taken advantage of its geographic and cultural proximity to serve as an entrepôt for China's fast-growing international trade. Reflecting these developments, Hong Kong has become the busiest container port in the world, and re-exports have risen from around 25 per cent of total exports in the late 1970s to nearly 90 per cent now. Most of Hong Kong's re-exports involve China either as a source or a destination.

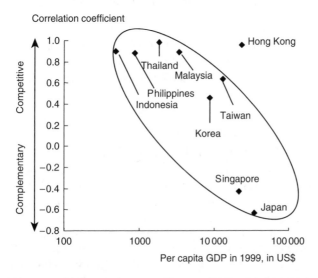

Figure 1.3   Competitive relations between China and other Asian countries, 1999

Notes: 1. The degree of competition between an Asian country and China is calculated as the correlation coefficient between their respective vectors showing the specialization indices ([exports−imports]/[exports+imports]) of major categories of manufactured goods. To focus on competition in the manufacturing sector, a four-category classification comprising chemicals and related products (SITC section 5), manufactured goods classified chiefly by material (SITC section 6), machinery and transport equipment (SITC section 7), and miscellaneous manufactured articles (SITC section 8) is used.
2. The specialization indices for Hong Kong, and thus its degree of competition with China, have been distorted by the presence of re-export trade.

Sources: Compiled by the author based on Table 1.2.

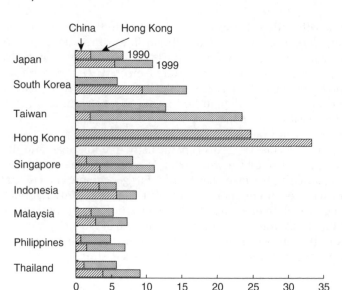

Figure 1.4   Asian countries' dependence on China and Hong Kong as export markets

Note: A large portion of exports to Hong Kong is re-exported to China.

Sources: IMF, *Direction of Trade Statistics Yearbook* and *Monthly Statistics of Exports and Imports*, Taiwan.

Repercussions through foreign direct investment

The emergence of China as an attractive destination for investment has altered the flow of FDI in Asia. Higher-income countries rich in funds and technology are likely to benefit, while lower-income countries that compete with China for foreign capital are likely to suffer (Appendix A.2). Thus Japan and the Asian NIEs can get high returns by investing in China, while the ASEAN countries may suffer a diversion of investment funds to China.

Companies from Hong Kong and Taiwan account for about 50 per cent of the annual inflow of FDI into China. By taking advantage of much lower costs of labour and land in the mainland, they have strengthened their competitiveness in international markets.

Investment by Hong Kong in the mainland has surpassed US$ 150 billion on a cumulative basis (according to Chinese statistics). Assuming that it earns a rate of return of 10 per cent a year (a somewhat conservative guess given a prime rate almost as high), the income on this investment should amount to US$ 15 billion, equivalent to 10 per cent of Hong Kong's GDP.[6] Hong Kong's strengthening ties with China have brought major changes to its economic structure. The number of workers in Hong Kong's manufacturing sector has contracted from a peak level of about 900 000 in the mid-1980s to 230 000 in 2000, at the same time that the manufacturing sector's share of GDP has dropped from 25 per cent to less than 6 per cent.

Following in Hong Kong's footsteps, Taiwanese manufacturers have also been expanding their investment in China. Reflecting rising indirect exports to China, Taiwan's trade surplus with Hong Kong has exceeded its trade surplus with the USA since 1991. As in the case of Hong Kong, the manufacturing sector's share of the Taiwan economy (in terms of GDP) has been shrinking since 1988, reflecting the relocation of manufacturing facilities to the mainland (and to other countries).

Until now, Taiwan has maintained tight controls on trade and investment across the Straits, including the requirement that trade needs to go through third countries. Investment in the high-tech sector, infrastructure and projects exceeding US$ 50 million are prohibited, while imports are restricted to intermediate goods essential for enhancing the competitiveness of Taiwanese products. These regulations will have to be relaxed after Taiwan's own entry into the WTO, as they are inconsistent with the provision of most-favoured-nation treatment. This will give Taiwanese companies new business opportunities in trade and investment.

In contrast to higher-income countries that benefit from investing in China, lower-income Asian countries that are highly dependent on foreign investment to support economic development may be affected adversely as investment funds from third countries are diverted to China. Indeed, China has received more FDI than the ASEAN countries together since 1993, and the gap has widened further since the 1997–98 Asian crisis (Figure 1.5). The

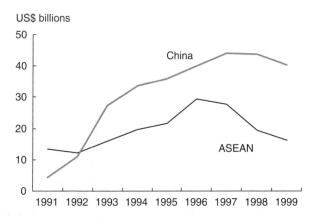

Figure 1.5   Shift of foreign direct investment from ASEAN to China
Source: UNCTAD, *World Investment Report.*

expected further shift of investment to China following its entry into the WTO has caused anxiety within ASEAN over the adverse effects on regional economic development. To enhance their attractiveness to foreign investors, the ASEAN countries are taking steps to deregulate industries and redress domestic structural problems. At the same time, they have decided to establish an ASEAN Free Trade Area (AFTA) by 2002. By liberalizing trade in the region, AFTA should make it more attractive for multinationals to build production networks across national borders within ASEAN.

A closer look at Japan's relations with China

Japan's economic relations with China have deepened in recent years mainly through the increase in trade. Japanese companies have taken a very cautious stance towards investing in China because the risks involved are judged to be high. China's investment environment should improve with its entry into the WTO, and Japanese companies should take this opportunity to seek a division of labour with China according to comparative advantage.

Diverging performance between trade and investment

China has emerged as Japan's second largest trading partner after the USA. According to official Japanese statistics, Japan's imports from China reached US\$ 55.1 billion in 2000 (accounting for 14.5 per cent of total Japanese imports), while exports to China amounted to US\$ 30.3 billion or 6.3 per cent of total exports. For China, Japan has replaced the USA as its largest trading partner.[7]

A larger and larger proportion of Japan's imports from China is now composed of manufactured goods, reflecting progress in industrialization in China (Figure 1.6). Led by textile products and machinery, manufactured goods rose from 22.6 per cent of Japanese imports from China in 1980, to 82.1 per cent in 2000. Over the same period, the share of mineral fuels (mainly crude oil) in Japanese imports from China dropped from 54.9 per cent to 3.9 per cent. On the other hand, Japanese exports to China have been dominated by machinery and equipment, which accounted for 54.9 per cent of the total in 2000.

Reflecting a very large gap in the level of economic development, trade relations between Japan and China have been dominated by complementarity rather than competition. This can be confirmed by calculating the bilateral specialization indices (as defined above) for major categories of products (based on SITC classification at the two-digit level) traded between the two countries. As expected, there is a clear division of labour between the two countries, with Japan specializing in capital- and technology-intensive products and China specializing in labour-intensive products (Figure 1.7).

The analysis so far has been based on the assumption that comparative advantage reflecting factor endowment forms the basis of trade, but in the

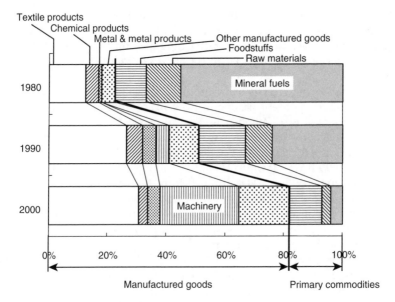

Figure 1.6 Breakdown of Japanese imports from China by product category

Source: Compiled by the author based on Japanese trade statistics.

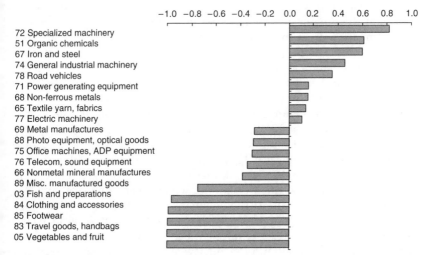

Figure 1.7 Japan–China bilateral specialization indices by major product category, 1999

Source: Compiled by the author based on OECD *Foreign Trade by Commodities, 1994–99*.

future when the income gap between China and Japan shrinks, bilateral intra-industry trade in manufactured goods should increase. This is already apparent in the machinery sector, with China specializing in office machines and consumer products while Japan specializes in industrial machinery and motor vehicles.

In contrast to the growth in trade, the performance of Japanese investment in China has been disappointing (for an analysis of Sino–Japanese investment relations see Chapter 4). According to the Japanese Ministry of Finance (MOF), investment by Japanese companies in China has fallen sharply since the fiscal year 1995 when it peaked at US\$ 4.48 billion, and by fiscal year 1999 it was down to US\$ 751 million.[8] As a result, China's share of total Japanese outward FDI dropped from 8.7 per cent to 1.1 per cent. Although Japanese investment in China rebounded in fiscal year 2000, this share remained at a low level of 2.0 per cent. The stagnation of Japanese investment in China contrasts sharply with the continued increase of American and European investment.

Foreign companies investing in China have to deal with an immature market environment. First, complicated procedures and ambiguous rules allow the authorities great discretion, resulting in frequent intervention in corporate management through licensing and administrative guidance. Typical examples include various taxes and miscellaneous fees imposed on day-to-day operations of foreign companies without legal grounds, as well as discriminatory prices applicable only to foreigners. Second, policies are changed frequently and differ widely from one locality to another, making long-term planning and nationwide operation difficult. Third, trade protectionism at the provincial level and poor infrastructure have prevented foreign companies from building nationwide production and marketing networks. Fourth, protection of intellectual property rights and disclosure of corporate information are insufficient. Finally, the scope of business allowed for foreign companies has been limited while tax preferences and other regulations favour exports over selling in the Chinese market.

While these problems are common to all foreign investors, Japanese companies face additional hurdles specific to them. First, because of the memory of Japan's invasion of China during the Second World War, most Chinese people have a negative image of Japan, making it difficult to build up mutual trust between the two sides. Second, the traditional Japanese remuneration system based on lifetime employment (for white-collar employees) and seniority rules has failed to attract the brightest talents. This in turn has made it difficult for Japanese companies to delegate authority to local managers who know China's business environment better than expatriates sent from their headquarters. Localization of management is particularly urgent for Japanese companies that target the Chinese market. Finally, Japanese companies are criticized for their reluctance to transfer technology to China for fear of the 'boomerang effect'.

It is still uncertain to what extent China's entry into the WTO will revive investment from Japan. On the positive side, the opening up of new sectors (particularly in services) to foreign investors and the transition to a more stable and transparent legal framework should make China a more attractive place to invest. Indeed, the latest annual survey of Japanese foreign investment conducted by the Japan Bank for International Cooperation (JBIC, 2000) ranks China as the most promising place to invest over the medium term, citing the potential of the Chinese market as the major incentive (for Japanese investment strategies in China, see Chapters 8, 9 and 10). On the negative side, Japanese companies may have difficulty competing with their US and European counterparts in the newly-opened services sectors. Even in manufacturing, the sharp reduction in the import tariffs imposed on some 'key industries' (automobiles, for example) should favour accessing the Chinese market by importing from headquarters (or third countries) instead of producing in China.

The rise of China and Japan's hollowing-out problem

The rise of China is posing both challenges and opportunities for Japan. On the one hand, many Japanese companies look at China as a potential market and destination for investment. On the other hand, increasing imports from China have given rise to the need for industrial restructuring at home. In sectors that compete with China, this may take the form of more bankruptcies and higher unemployment. This situation has led to growing fears of a 'hollowing out' of domestic industries and escalating trade friction between China and Japan.

The analytic framework laid down earlier in this chapter can be used to examine the impact of the rise of China on Japan, taking into consideration the complementarity between the two countries in terms of both trade and investment. The improvement in Japan's terms of trade accompanying the rise of China provides an incentive for a relocation of resources (capital and labour) from the importable sector to the exportable sector and may help upgrade Japan's industrial structure. Theoretically, the change in the terms of trade also alters domestic income distribution. According to the Stolper–Samuelson theorem, an improvement in the terms of trade raises the return to the factor used intensively in the exportable sector relative to the return to the factor used intensively in the importable sector. Given Japan's comparative advantage in capital-intensive products and disadvantage in labour-intensive products, an improvement in the terms of trade should benefit capital at the expense of labour. This outcome reflects the fact that higher imports of labour-intensive products are equivalent to an increase in labour supply (imports of labour), while higher exports of capital-intensive products are equivalent to a decrease in capital stock (exports of capital).

The outflow of FDI to China would have a similar effect on income distribution in Japan. The reduction in the capital–labour ratio reduces the marginal productivity of labour and thus the real wage rate on one hand, and raises the marginal productivity of, and thus return on, capital on the other. In the short term, the adjustment may impose deflationary pressure on the Japanese economy. Given downward wage rigidity and the immobility of factors of production, it may also lead to higher unemployment and an increase of excess capacity in some sectors.

Japan should respond to these challenges not through the use of protectionist policies to safeguard domestic industries that have lost export competitiveness but rather through positive industrial adjustments. The latter involves promoting new growth areas at home through deregulation and investment in research and development while at the same time relocating declining industries overseas. The establishment of barriers to limit imports and prevent declining industries from being transferred is like treating the symptoms instead of the disease. Declining industries in Japan are unlikely to recover their competitiveness as a result of government protection. Such policies merely delay the improvement of industrial structure in both Japan and China. In contrast, the relocation of declining industries to China should not only help promote the country's economic development but also free up resources for emerging industries at home.

Following the successful 'catching-up' of Japan in the 1960s, the USA and European countries imposed trade barriers in the form of tariffs and quantitative restrictions on Japanese products. The same measures were applied later to the Asian NIEs and other developing countries. It would be truly regrettable and ironic if Japan, which has firmly opposed such measures, adopted a similar policy towards China now that its position has been reversed.

Japan should abandon the mercantilist view that production and exports are good, while consumption and imports are bad. Instead, it should adopt policies that promote an international division of labour according to comparative advantage. By relocating labour-intensive industries to and increasing imports from China, Japanese producers and consumers should realize gains in real income by lowering the nation's costs of production and imports. Equally important, the resulting growing prosperity in China will promote stability in the Asia-Pacific region, and thus Japan's national security. Indeed, the latest financial crisis in Asia vividly illustrated that it is in Japan's own national interest to be surrounded by affluent and peaceful countries rather than by poor and unstable ones.

Appendix A1   Repercussions through the terms of trade

The relations between economic growth and the terms of trade can be explained using standard trade theory (Johnson, 1955). Consider a two-country (China and the rest of the world), two-good (one labour-intensive and one capital-intensive) model. China is an exporter of the labour-intensive good and an importer of the capital-intensive good. The supply side and the demand side of the world economy (including China) can be summarized, respectively, by a production possibility curve and a set of social indifference curves (Figure A1.1). The initial equilibrium is reached at E_0 where

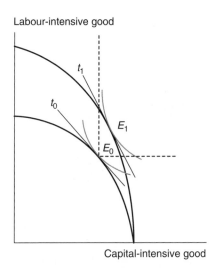

Figure A1.1 China's economic development and terms of trade

the production possibility curve is tangent to the highest social indifference curve. The emergence of China can be represented by an outward shift of the global production possibility curve, with bias towards the labour-intensive product (China's exportable sector). The new equilibrium is reached at E_1 where the new production possibility curve touches a higher social indifference curve. So long as neither goods are inferior (that is, so long as an increase in income does not lead to lower demand for either goods), E_1 lies to the northeast of E_0. The slope common to the production possibility curve and social indifferent curve is steeper at E_1 than at E_0, implying that China's terms of trade deteriorate, while those of the rest of the world improve (the analysis here does not apply to small countries whose influence on the level of global production and international prices is negligible).

While the terms of trade should improve for the rest of the world as a whole, some countries are more likely to benefit than others; some may even suffer a decline in their terms of trade. On the one hand, economies that have a complementary relationship with China will enjoy an improvement in their terms of trade and real incomes. On the other hand, economies that are in competition with China will suffer declines in their terms of trade and real incomes.

First, consider a country whose trade structure is competitive with that of China (Figure A1.2a). At the original terms of trade t_0, production and consumption take place at P_0 and C_0, respectively. The country exports an amount of the labour-intensive good equal to AP_0, and imports an amount of the capital-intensive good equal to AC_0. Suppose the terms of trade deteriorate to t_1 as a result of economic development in China. In response, production shifts to P_1 (with a reduction in the labour-intensive good and an expansion in the capital-intensive good), while consumption shifts to C_1. At the new equilibrium, exports and imports amount to BP_1 and BC_1, respectively. As a result, social welfare (or real national income), as represented by the level of the social indifference curve, declines from I_0 to I_1.

(a) Country competing with China

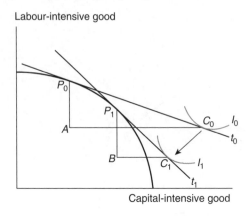

(b) Country complementary to China

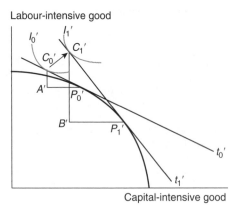

Figure A1.2   The welfare effect of changes in the terms of trade

Next, consider a country whose trade structure is complementary to that of China (Figure A1.2b). At the original terms of trade t_0, production and consumption take place at P_0' and C_0', respectively. The country exports an amount of the capital-intensive good equal to $A'P_0'$, and imports an amount of labour-intensive good equal to $A'C_0'$. Suppose the terms of trade improve to t_1' as a result of economic development in China. In response, production shifts to P_1' (with a reduction in the labour-intensive good and an expansion in the capital-intensive good), while consumption shifts to C_1'. At the new equilibrium, exports and imports amount to $B'P_1'$ and $B'C_1'$, respectively. As a result, the level of social welfare improves from I_0' to I_1'.

Appendix A2   The potential gain from foreign direct investment

The interaction between China and investing countries can be illustrated by the text-book version of the theory of FDI (MacDougall, 1958). As a first approximation, FDI can be treated conceptually as the relocation of capital stock from a capital-abundant country where the rate of return (which reflects the marginal productivity of capital) is low to one where the marginal productivity of capital is high. The investing country usually has a higher level of economic development than that of the receiving country.

Consider two countries, Japan (the investing country) and China (the receiving country), producing an identical output, using labour and capital. The labour force is assumed to be fixed in each country and fully employed. Assuming that perfect competition prevails in both countries, the returns on capital and labour are equal to their marginal products, both measured in terms of the output. In Figure A2.1, the vertical axis measures the marginal product of capital. The horizontal axis measures the capital stock in each country, measured from O for Japan and from O' for China, so that OO' measures the total capital stock of the two countries. AB and $A'B'$ show the marginal product of capital for Japan and China, respectively. Both schedules decline as the capital stock increases, reflecting diminishing marginal productivity, given fixed labour input.

In the absence of international factor mobility, Japan holds OC of capital and China holds CO'. The marginal products of capital (which is equal to the return on capital) for Japan and China are given by r_0 and r_0', respectively, with capital earning a higher return in China than in Japan. The income or output for Japan (China) is given by $OAFC$ ($O'CGA'$), with $OIFC$ ($O'CGH$) accruing to capital owners and IAF (HGA') accruing to labour. In the absence of factor mobility across national borders, the concept of output (or GDP) coincides with income (or GNP).

Assume that restrictions on capital flows between the two countries are removed (but labour mobility remains restricted). Investors in Japan will move capital to China where the return is higher until the returns in both countries become equal. This would require moving DC of capital from Japan to China. At equilibrium, Japan holds OD of capital while China holds $O'D$, both earning a return equal to r_1. Output declines

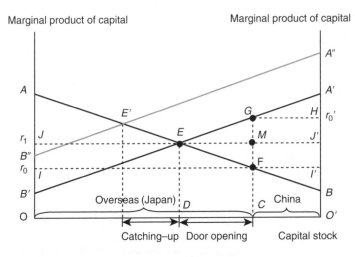

Figure A2.1   The gain from foreign direct investment

Source: Based on MacDougall (1958), with adaptations.

in Japan but rises in China, but income rises in both countries. Japan's GDP falls by *DEFC*, reflecting the decline in capital stock. However, this does not mean a decline in Japan's GNP as return to investment in China as measured by *DEMC* more than offsets the decline in domestic output. The net gain to Japan is given by *EMF*. On the other hand, China's GDP rises by *DEGC*, reflecting the rise in capital stock, but GNP increases only by *EGM*, as *DEMC* accrues to investors in Japan. GNP exceeds GDP by *DEMC* in Japan and the reverse is true for China. The increase in combined GDP (or GNP) of Japan and China, which results from the improvement in the allocative efficiency of the capital stock, equals *EGF*. The gain from capital movement is proportional to the difference between the returns to capital in the two countries (when there is no capital movement), which in turn reflects the complementarity (interpreted here as the difference in factor endowment) between them.

The relocation of capital stock across national borders also alters the distribution of income between labour and capital in both countries. Although the income to be shared by labour and capital increases in both the investing country and the receiving country, labour income falls in absolute terms in the former and capital income drops in the latter. In Japan, where the capital/labour ratio declines, labour income falls by *IJEF*; capital income rises by *IJMF*, *IJEF* at the expense of labour income, and *EMF* gain from improved efficiency. In China, where the capital/labour ratio rises, labour income rises by *EGHJ'*, *MGHJ'* at the expense of capital income and *EGM* gain from improved efficiency. In this way, free flow of capital leads to factor-price equalization across national borders. The emergence of China as a major destination for foreign investment thus implies that the wage level in the investing countries should converge to that of China (adjusted for the difference in productivity). This is analogous to the factor-price equalization theorem that applies to free international trade.

The above analysis has focused on the effect of capital flows accompanying the 'opening' of the Chinese economy to FDI, but the same framework can be applied to study the effect of the 'reform', interpreted here as an increase in the marginal productivity of capital in China. This can be represented by an upward shift of the *A'B'* schedule to *A"B"*. The resulting gap in the rate of return prompts a shift of capital stock from Japan to China. At the new equilibrium *E'*, the divergence between GDP and GNP increases further. As in the case of 'opening', capital flow accompanying 'reform' in China leads to declines in GDP and labour income but to increases in GNP and capital income in the investing country. On the other hand, the receiving country enjoys increases in labour income and capital income, as well as in GNP and GDP.

Notes

1. The same PPP measure raises China's per capita GDP in 1999 from US$ 780 to US$ 3291. This, however, does not change the fact that China is still a very poor country, with its global ranking in terms of per capita GDP improving only marginally from 140 to 128 by shifting to the PPP measure.
2. The flying-geese pattern has been widely used to describe the expansion of the dynamism of the East Asian economies from Japan to the Asian NIEs, and then further to ASEAN and China. Countries specialize in the exports of products in which they enjoy comparative advantage commensurate with their levels of development, and at the same time they seek to upgrade their industrial structures through augmenting their capital stock and technology. FDI from the more

advanced countries to the less developed ones, through relocating industries from the former to the latter, plays a dominant role in sustaining this process (for a detailed analysis, see Kwan, 1994, pp. 81–99).

3. China does not publish statistics on unit prices for exports and imports, making it impossible to calculate its terms of trade. The secular depreciation of the Chinese currency in real terms, however, suggests that the country's terms of trade also have followed a downward trend.

4. In a world with only two goods, a country's trade structure is competitive to that of China if it exports the labour-intensive good and imports the capital-intensive good, and complementary to that of China if it exports the capital-intensive good and imports the labour-intensive good. In the real world, where there are thousands of goods, the degree of similarity in the trade structure between the countries concerned serves as an indicator of the degree of competition and complementarity. As a general rule, the more similar two economies are in terms of their trade structures, the more likely they are to be in competition with each other. Conversely, the less similar their trade structures are, the more likely they are to form a complementary trade relationship.

5. At a more general level, the correlation coefficient so derived should be high for two countries with competitive (similar) trade structures, and low for countries with complementary (different) trade structures.

6. Conceptually, as factor income earned abroad, profit earned in China should be counted as part of Hong Kong's GNP (but not GDP). In reality, however, official national income statistics fail to capture a large part of this income.

7. According to Chinese statistics, China's exports to Japan amounted to US$ 41.7 billion while imports from Japan reached US$ 41.5 billion in 2000. The large discrepancy between the trade figures published by Japan and China largely reflects the different ways of treating re-exports through Hong Kong. For the statistical discrepancies in Sino–Japanese trade, see Chapter 2.

8. According to Chinese statistics, Japanese investment in China dropped less sharply from a peak level of US$ 4.3 billion in 1997 to US$ 3.0 billion in 1999. The large discrepancy between the two sets of figures largely reflects the fact that reinvestment by Japanese companies in China using retained earnings and projects under yen 100 million are not covered in Japan's statistics. For the statistical discrepancies in Japanese FDI in China, see Chapter 3.

References

ADB (Asian Development Bank) (2000) *Key Indicators of Asian and Pacific Developing Countries*, Oxford: Oxford University Press.

JBIC (The Japan Bank for International Cooperation) (2000) *The Outlook of Japanese Foreign Direct Investment*, Tokyo: JBIC.

Johnson, H. G. (1955) 'Economic Expansion and International Trade,' *Manchester School of Economic and Social Studies*, vol. 23 (1), pp. 95–112.

Kwan, C. H. (1994) *Economic Interdependence in the Asia-Pacific Region*, London: Routledge.

— (1995) 'The Emergence of China and its Implications for the Asian Economies', *Asia Club Papers*, Tokyo: Tokyo Club Foundation for Global Studies.

MacDougall, G. A. D. (1958) 'The Benefits and Costs of Private Investment from Abroad – A Theoretical Analysis', *Economic Record*, vol. 36, pp. 13–35.

World Bank (2000) *World Development Report 2000/2001*, Oxford: Oxford University Press.

2
China and Japan: Conflict or Cooperation? What does Trade Data Say?

Hanns Günther Hilpert

Introduction

The relationship between Japan and China goes back some 2000 years. Both countries are closely connected in a web of mutual political, cultural and economical interactions. The nodes of economic contacts range from bilateral trade in goods and services to Japan's foreign direct investment (FDI) in China, its transfer of technical and management know-how, its official development aid (ODA), and the migration of labour from China to Japan. Since the opening up of China in the late 1970s, the bilateral relations have become ever more close, intense and complex. Apparently the recent bilateral economic relations have proved to be mutually beneficial. Nevertheless the unresolved legacy of the Second World War, the political rivalry as well as various contentious economic issues gave birth to bitter conflicts between these two politically and economically leading nations of East Asia (comprising Japan, China, Taiwan, Korea and Southeast Asia). The simultaneous occurrence of benefits and conflicts raises some basic questions: Is the Sino–Japanese relationship inherently conflictive or cooperative? Which aspect of the relationship prevails? Can the conflicts be resolved? How are the benefits distributed?

To answer these questions one could analyse the many different contentious issues and try to identify the key factors shaping the relationship. The following procedure, however, is more focused, as the analysis concentrates specifically on quantitative trade data. By looking at this single important factor, the analysis aims to clarify at least the economic side of the relationship. What does quantitative trade data say about the issue? Why did Sino–Japanese trade grow so quickly in the 1990s? Will the data support the conflictive or the cooperative view? How will (trade) relations evolve in the future?

What is the nature of Sino–Japanese relations?

Theoretically there are two contrasting views on the Sino–Japanese relationship. A political scientist looking at international relations with the rationale of the balance of power approach would probably conclude that the differences between China's and Japan's national interests were irreconcilable, and adjustment issues arising from bilateral economic closeness were just minor issues before a major, brewing storm. China distrusts a Japan unable to resolve the legacy of its war atrocities. China feels uneasy about an Asia dominated by an economically and technologically strong Japan, which is allied by a security treaty to the USA and has close links to Taiwan. Japan, on the other hand, is challenged by a rapidly growing and advancing China striving to reassume its central, dominant position in Asia. Moreover, Japan is wary of China's increasing military capacities. Looking at these contrasting views it is easy to conclude that the Sino–Japanese relationship will be shaped by economic and strategic rivalry (for an example of this view, see Hasegawa and Nakajima, 1996; Segal, 1993, pp. 27–32).

An economist looking at international trade under the assumptions of the neo-classical trade theory would see economic relations between Japan and China as basically complementary. China has abundant natural resources and cheap labour as well as a fast-growing market. These are all factors that Japan needs for its economic security. Japan, on the other hand, possesses all the capital, technology and human skills China needs for its modernization and industrialization. Japan can also utilize Chinese resources for the manufacture of low-cost products for the world market. Furthermore, the increasing supply of low-cost Chinese products improves Japan's international terms of trade. Hence, by virtue of complementary economic patterns, both Japan and China can enhance their welfare if they increase bilateral trade and intensify their economic integration. (For an example of the neo-classical view, see Chapter 1.)

The juxtaposition above contrasts a political scientist's view of an inherent conflictive Sino–Japanese relationship shaped by antagonistic national interests with an economist's view of a bilateral cooperative relationship shaped by mutual profitable interaction. A comparison of these theoretical views is indeed useful for the further investigation, but a few positive and normative qualifications should be added at the outset.

The positivist position

Both political science and economics are social sciences that consist of more than one well-established approach to explain reality and to investigate causes. Therefore, it should be of no surprise that alternative theories exist and that they may result in different propositions about the nature of the Sino–Japanese relationship.

In the field of political science the neo-liberal institutionalist school would argue that a much higher level of Sino–Japanese cooperation can be achieved than neo-realists (or balance of power theorists) believe possible. Followers of this school would assume that more and better information, or the existence of binding (bilateral and multilateral) agreements, could play a positive role in the relationship and enhance mutual cooperation (Jin, 2002, pp. 106–10). More specifically, regime theorists would look at domestic business or policy interests that have a stake in a smooth cooperative relationship and influence the state's attitude towards cooperation (Kojima, 2000, pp. 33–47; Whiting, 2000, pp. 15–31). Furthermore, it can be argued that the bilateral relationship does not exist in splendid isolation. Japan's and China's relations with the USA and with its Asian neighbours have to be taken into account as well (Austin and Harris, 2001; Funabashi, 1999, pp. 79–83).

On the other hand there are spatial economic arguments that challenge the unreserved cooperative view of the neo-classicists: Japan with its full-set industrial structure and its sophisticated consumer and corporate demand is traditionally the centre of economic gravity in East Asia. However, China may develop an economic core of its own along with the continuous formation of new industrial clusters and the rapidly increasing volume of domestic production and demand. From spatial economics it is known that there are specific locational rents for the industrial and economic cores. Thus, it is important where a core locates, and the likely emergence of a new economic core in China will be an effective challenge to the established Japanese position. Japan, facing displacement competition by China, will be compelled to carry out its industrial restructuring; in order to sustain its industrial and economic lead Japan will also need to increase its attractiveness for high-productivity investment, innovate its industries and advance into service sectors (Hilpert, 1998, pp. 234–43, 261–5).

The normative view

On the normative side, neither a completely conflictive nor an entirely cooperative bilateral relationship are the kind of scenarios that a sensible political and economic leadership should be striving for, neither in Japan nor in China, because the conflict scenario may manifest itself in an escalating bilateral confrontation. Both sides would certainly be negatively affected by the economic, political and perhaps even military damages that might be incurred. On the other hand, a close Sino–Japanese economic and political cooperation may lead to a rather insecure and fragile geopolitical environment in East Asia. If a Japan–China axis really materialized, Japan and China could dominate the region at the expense of the smaller countries. Such a situation, however, would result in deep concern among the other great powers of East Asia, notably the USA, but also Russia, Korea and the ASEAN countries. As both Japan and China are assumed to be sensible political actors who rationally pursue their self-interests, and as both countries depend economically on the USA and on the rest of East Asia and are sensitive to the concerns of their political and trading partners, it can be expected that wise political leaders would refrain both from confrontation and from closer cooperation. Thus, they may be inclined to steer a middle course, as they did during the past two decades.

To be sure, neither the recognition that there are many different (positive) views on the nature of the Sino–Japanese relationship nor the assumption that a sensible political leadership would refrain from destabilizing established behavioural patterns invalidate the conflict or the cooperation scenario. Both scenarios are supported by weighty theoretical arguments and cannot be easily dismissed.

Sino–Japanese trade: the statistical evidence

The objective of the following analysis of quantitative trade data is to show whether the empirical facts on trade support either the conflict or the cooperation scenario. The analysis will be based on the simple assumption that a high or an increasing volume of trade shows a tendency for bilateral cooperation, while a low or a decreasing volume of trade shows a tendency for bilateral conflict.[1] Only after having determined these simple facts can we ask in later sections why the bilateral trade volume is specifically high or low, increasing or decreasing, and what conclusions can be drawn from these findings.

Trade volumes in absolute values

Table 2.1 shows the development of Sino–Japanese trade from 1980, the year after China opened its doors, until 2000 in absolute volume values. It can be seen that over the last 20 years Sino–Japanese trade has surged in both directions. However, the rise was not smooth. After 1985, China restricted imports from Japan in order to cut down its trade deficit and to reduce its unilateral import dependency on Japan, most notably with respect to cars and consumer durables. Only after 1990 did Japanese exports to China start to increase again. On the other hand, Chinese exports to Japan took off only after 1986. As a result, Japan's bilateral trade balance with China fell into deficit in 1988 and it has remained there ever since. The appreciation of the yen preceding the Asian crisis in 1997 as well as the economic downturn in the aftermath of the crisis resulted in stagnating Japanese (1995–98) and Chinese (1997–98) exports. But in 1999 and in 2000 a strong rebound occurred in both directions.

Statistical issues

With a closer look at Table 2.1 one can easily recognize fairly large discrepancies between the Japanese and the Chinese statistical records. In both statistics, imports show considerably larger volumes than the respective exports of the trading partner. What are these differences based on? In trade statistics, exports are classified by country of destination and registered on a fob basis (free on board), whereas imports are classified by country of origin

Table 2.1   Japan's and China's bilateral trade, 1980–2000 (US$ millions)

Year	Japan's trade with China[1]			China's trade with Japan[1]		
	Exports	Imports	Balance	Exports	Imports	Balance
1980	5 109	4 346	763	4 032	5 169	−1 137
1981	5 076	5 283	−207	4 747	6 183	−1 436
1982	3 500	5 338	−1 838	4 806	3 902	904
1983	4 918	5 089	−171	4 517	5 495	−978
1984	7 199	5 943	1 256	5 155	8 057	−2 902
1985	12 590	6 534	6 056	6 091	15 178	−9 087
1986	9 936	5 727	4 209	5 079	12 463	−7 384
1987	8 337	7 478	859	6 392	10 087	−3 695
1988	9 486	9 861	−375	8 046	11 062	−3 016
1989	8 477	11 083	−2 606	8 395	10 534	−2 139
1990	6 145	12 057	−5 912	9 210	7 656	1 554
1991	8 605	14 248	−5 643	10 252	10 032	220
1992	11 967	16 972	−5 005	11 699	13 686	−1 987
1993	17 353	20 651	−3 298	15 782	23 303	−7 521
1994	18 687	27 569	−8 882	21 490	26 319	−4 829
1995	21 934	35 922	−13 988	28 466	29 007	−541
1996	21 827	40 405	−18 578	30 888	29 190	1 698
1997	21 692	41 827	−20 135	31 820	28 990	2 830
1998	20 182	37 079	−16 897	29 718	28 307	1 411
1999	23 450	43 070	−19 620	32 399	33 768	−1 369
2000	29 886	53 944	−24 058	44 571	38 311	6 260

Note: [1] Exports are registered on a fob basis (free on board), imports on a cif basis (cost, insurance, freight). Both Japanese and Chinese imports include imports via Hong Kong, but Japanese and Chinese exports via Hong Kong are not included. The latter are recorded as exports to Hong Kong.

Source: IMF, *Direction of Trade Statistics*, Japan and China Tables.

and registered on a cif basis (cost, insurance and freight). Thus some part of the discrepancy can be explained by the differing methods of export and import registration. Quite simply, the transport share of the traded goods' value is recorded only in the import but not in the export statistics. In addition to the fob–cif differences, Chinese import values are inflated because the Chinese import statistics are distorted by over-invoicing, which is a convenient way to evade foreign exchange control.

Another major cause for the distortion of the Chinese trade statistics is the uneven registration of entrepôt trade through Hong Kong. A large volume of the bilateral Sino–Japanese trade is transshipped and marketed through Hong Kong. Unfortunately this trade appears only in the respective import statistics. Whereas both Japan and China regard their bilateral imports through Hong Kong correctly as imports, their bilateral exports through Hong Kong are considered exports to Hong Kong. Thus both Japan and China understate their bilateral exports (and overstate their exports to Hong Kong), but correctly record their bilateral imports. Consequently, the statistics for both

Japan and China overstate their bilateral trade deficits and understate their bilateral trade surpluses.

The distortion in Sino–Japanese trade can be corrected if both countries' indirect exports (through Hong Kong) are included in the bilateral trade recordings. Fortunately the Hong Kong Census and Statistics Department provides fairly detailed data of the territory's re-exports.[2] The adding of the estimated values of Japan's and China's indirect bilateral exports to the officially recorded bilateral direct exports leads to the values of Japan's and China's total bilateral exports (see Table 2.2). The adjusted bilateral export figures in the Sino–Japanese trade are higher and are much closer to the respective import figures, yet they still do not match.

From the analysis of Hong Kong's trade figures it can be recognized that the (Hong Kong) entrepôt assumes an unsymmetrical role in the Sino–Japanese trading relationship. Hong Kong is significantly more important

Table 2.2 Japan's and China's bilateral trade (including indirect exports through Hong Kong), 1980–2000 (US$ millions)

Year	Japan's trade with China[1]			China's trade with Japan[1]		
	Exports[2]	Imports	Balance	Exports[2]	Imports	Balance
1980	5 292	4 346	946	4 155	5 169	−1 014
1981	5 365	5 283	82	4 901	6 183	−1 282
1982	3 770	5 338	−1 568	4 946	3 902	1 044
1983	5 264	5 089	175	4 670	5 495	−825
1984	8 003	5 943	2 060	5 354	8 057	−2 703
1985	13 853	6 534	7 319	6 323	15 178	−8 855
1986	10 731	5 727	5 004	5 439	12 463	−7 024
1987	9 375	7 478	1 897	6 970	10 087	−3 117
1988	11 151	9 861	1 290	9 122	11 062	−1 940
1989	9 971	11 083	−1 112	9 947	10 534	−587
1990	7 599	12 057	−4 458	11 027	7 656	3 371
1991	10 715	14 248	−3 533	12 498	10 032	2 466
1992	15 337	16 972	−1 635	14 528	13 686	842
1993	27 450	20 651	6 799	20 393	23 303	−2 910
1994	30 410	27 569	2 841	27 336	26 319	1 017
1995	33 960	35 922	−1 962	36 108	29 007	7 101
1996	34 072	40 405	−6 333	39 928	29 190	10 738
1997	34 446	41 827	−7 381	40 667	28 990	11 677
1998	32 342	37 079	−4 737	37 022	28 307	8 715
1999	35 247	43 070	−7 823	39 903	33 768	6 135
2000	43 314	53 944	−10 630	53 850	38 311	15 539

Notes: [1] Exports registered on a fob basis (free on board), imports on a cif basis (cost, insurance, freight).

[2] Exports include indirect exports via Hong Kong.

Source: IMF, Direction of Trade Statistics, Japan and China Tables; Hong Kong External Trade (monthly).

for Japanese exports to China than for Chinese exports to Japan. In this respect Sino–Japanese trade is markedly different from Sino-US trade, in which the Hong Kong entrepôt trade assumes an non-symmetrical role in the opposite direction, being more important for Chinese exports to the USA than for US exports to China.

Relative trade shares

What is the relative importance of China in Japan's external trade? What is the relative importance of Japan in China's external trade? First, from the

Table 2.3   Japan's trade by export destinations and import sources, 1980–2000 (%)

	1980	1985	1990	1995	2000
EXPORTS (*Trade partner*)					
USA/Canada	26.3	40.2	34.0	28.9	31.4
EU-15	15.2	13.1	20.4	15.9	16.3
East Asia[1]	25.8	24.1	29.6	42.2	39.6
China	3.9	7.1	2.1	5.0	6.2
China (adjusted)[2]	4.1	7.8	2.6	7.7	9.0
Hong Kong	3.7	3.7	4.6	6.3	5.7
NIEs-3[3]	11.2	9.1	15.2	18.8	18.1
ASEAN-4[4]	7.0	4.2	7.7	12.1	9.5
Rest of world	32.7	22.6	16.0	13.0	12.7
IMPORTS (*Trade partner*)					
USA/Canada	20.8	23.7	26.1	25.8	21.5
EU-15	7.1	7.8	16.2	14.5	11.6
East Asia[1]	22.3	25.6	23.2	31.8	39.9
China	3.1	5.0	5.1	8.1	14.4
Hong Kong	0.5	0.6	0.9	0.8	0.7
NIEs-3[3]	4.7	7.1	10.1	11.5	12.0
ASEAN-4[4]	14	12.9	7.1	11.4	12.8
Rest of world	49.8	42.9	34.5	27.9	27.0
TOTAL TRADE (*Trade partner*)					
USA/Canada	23.4	33.2	30.5	27.6	27.0
EU-15	11	10.9	18.5	15.3	14.2
East Asia[1]	24	24.7	28.7	38.7	39.7
China	3.5	6.2	3.5	7.4	9.8
China (adjusted)[2]	3.6	6.6	3.8	9.0	11.4
Hong Kong	2.0	2.4	2.9	3.9	3.5
NIEs-3[3]	7.9	8.2	12.9	15.6	15.5
ASEAN-4[4]	10.6	7.9	8.9	11.8	11.0
Rest of world	41.6	31.2	22.3	18.4	19.1

Notes: [1] East Asia: China, Hong Kong, Macao, NIEs-3, ASEAN-4.
  [2] Exports include indirect exports via Hong Kong.
  [3] NIEs-3: Korea, Singapore, Taiwan (Taiwan 2000: estimate).
  [4] ASEAN-4: Indonesia, Malaysia, Philippines, Thailand.

Source: IMF, *Direction of Trade Statistics; Hong Kong External Trade* (monthly).

Japanese perspective, trade with China has grown increasingly important in the last two decades, being surpassed in the latest year under review only by its bilateral trade with the USA. In the year 2000, China was Japan's second most important import source. As a destination for Japanese exports, China is the number four location – after the USA and closely behind Korea and Taiwan (Table 2.3). Second, from the Chinese perspective, apart from the 'internal' Sino-Hong Kong trade, Japan is now the most important import

Table 2.4 China's trade by export destinations and import sources, 1980–2000 (%)

	1980	1985	1990	1995	2000
EXPORTS (Trade Partner)					
USA/Canada	6.2	9.4	9.2	17.6	28.5
USA/Canada (adjusted)[1]	7.1	11.7	19.6	37.4	41.2
EU-15	13.7	8.6	10.0	12.9	14.5
East Asia[2]	52.8	58.8	64.8	55.9	45.4
Japan	22.2	22.3	14.6	19.1	14.3
Japan (adjusted)[1]	22.9	23.1	17.6	24.2	17.3
Hong Kong	24.0	26.2	43.2	24.2	21.4
NIEs-3[3]	2.3	7.5	4.4	8.9	6.8
ASEAN-4[4]	4.3	2.7	2.9	3.7	2.6
Rest of world	27.3	23.2	16.0	13.6	11.6
IMPORTS (Trade Partner)					
USA/Canada	23.8	14.9	15.0	14.2	9.7
EU-15	15.7	15.6	17.0	16.1	11.9
East Asia[2]	32.8	49.6	51.4	54.6	61.7
Japan	26.5	35.7	14.2	22.0	16.3
Hong Kong	2.9	11.2	27.0	6.5	19.1
NIEs-3[3]	1.0	0.6	6.2	21.5	19.8
ASEAN-4[4]	2.4	2.1	4.0	4.5	6.4
Rest of world	27.7	19.9	16.6	15.1	16.7
TOTAL TRADE (Trade Partner)					
USA/Canada	15.3	12.8	11.8	16.0	20.4
USA/Canada (adjusted)[1]	16.1	13.7	17.4	26.5	27.5
EU-15	14.7	12.9	13.2	14.4	13.4
East Asia[2]	42.4	53.0	58.8	55.4	54.1
Japan	24.4	30.4	14.4	20.4	15.1
Japan (adjusted)[1]	24.8	30.8	16	23.2	16.8
Hong Kong	13.1	17.0	35.7	15.9	20.4
NIEs-3[3]	1.6	3.3	5.2	14.9	12.4
ASEAN-4[4]	3.3	2.3	3.4	4.1	4.3
Rest of world	27.6	21.3	16.2	14.2	12.1

Notes: [1] Exports include indirect exports via Hong Kong.
[2] East Asia: China, Hong Kong, Macao, NIEs-3, ASEAN-4.
[3] NIEs-3: Korea, Singapore, Taiwan (Taiwan 2000: estimate).
[4] ASEAN-4: Indonesia, Malaysia, Philippines, Thailand.

Source: IMF, *Direction of Trade Statistics; Hong Kong External Trade* (monthly).

source and, following the USA, the second largest export market. However, the relative importance of Japan for China's exports and imports decreased by three to four percentage points in the course of China's foreign trade expansion in the 1980s and 1990s, the temporary relative increase in the mid-1990s notwithstanding (Table 2.4).

Bilateral trade interdependence

For an assessment of the trade interdependence between two countries, both trade volumes in absolute values and relative trade shares are poor indicators; they are always dependent on the world market share of the respective trading partner. To put it in more concrete terms: as Japan is the third largest trading nation worldwide, one should expect that it assumes a prominent role in the Chinese export trade. Nevertheless, China may still fail to assume its reasonable share in Japan's share of world imports. On the other hand, along with the dynamic growth of the Chinese import market, Japanese exports to China could have grown rapidly compared to Japan's exports or to world trade. However, Japanese exports may have failed to keep pace with China's rapidly increasing share of world imports.

Therefore, the more adequate indicator of the trade interdependence between two countries are so-called trade intensity indices, which quantitatively measure the relationship between a trading share and the world market share of the trading partner.[3] Trade intensity indices give a measurable assessment of the extent of trade biases towards a particular trading partner – for example, the export bias of Japan towards China or the export bias of China towards Japan – relative to the neutral assignment of trade across all partners. The value of the index is unity if the trade relationship is just average. That is, the trade intensity index of any country with the world is unity. When the value of the index exceeds unity, it indicates the existence of a positive trade bias between the countries considered. In the examples at issue, the value of the index would exceed unity if Japan trades with China more intensively than China trades with the rest of the world, or if China trades with Japan more intensively than Japan trades with the rest of the world.[4]

Figure 2.1 shows the development of the index of trade intensity for Japan's export trade with China, East Asia and the USA from 1980 until 2000. In 2000 the intensity index of Japanese exports to China reached the high value of 1.76. If Japan's indirect exports to China via Hong Kong are included, the index value at 2.46 is even higher. By the latter measure, Japan exports about two and a half as much to China as she does on average to the world. In the course of the last two decades the Japan–China export intensity index first fell (from 1980 till 1990), then rose (from 1990 to 1998), and since then has fallen again. When China was a closed economy there were apparently special links between Japan and China. These special relations were recognized and enforced by the bilateral Long-Term Trade Agreement of 1978 (Zhang, 1998, pp. 66–9). Thus the very little trade China had at this

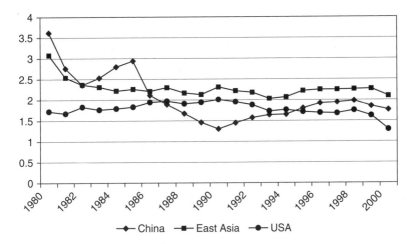

Figure 2.1   Japanese export intensity index, 1980–2000: China, East Asia and the USA compared

Notes: 1.   The Japanese export trade intensity index is the ratio of the share of Japanese exports to a specific trading partner (i.e. Japan, East Asia, USA) in the total of Japanese exports to the share of the trading partner's imports in the world import market.
2.   Japanese exports to China including indirect exports via Hong Kong.
3.   East Asia = China, NIEs-4, ASEAN-4, Macao.

Source: IMF, *Direction of Trade Statistics*; *Hong Kong External Trade* (monthly); own calculations.

period was extremely biased towards Japan. When China opened up to the world, her trade became more diversified, and consequently the bias towards Japan had to come down. Moreover, in 1985 China restricted its imports from Japan, resulting in an abrupt fall of the index. But in 1990 a turnaround occurred, and since then the index has been converging to the East Asian average (which also includes China). If Japan's indirect exports to China via Hong Kong are included, the resulting index movements in the 1990s are even more pronounced, because the adjusted index intersects the East Asian average in the year 1993 and has become higher ever since. Furthermore, it is important to note that the adjusted Japanese export bias to China became higher in the 1990s than the Japanese export bias to the USA.

Figure 2.2 shows the development of the index of trade intensity of China's export trade with Japan, East Asia and the USA from 1980 until 2000. In 2000 the intensity index of Chinese exports to Japan amounted to the high value of 2.50. Thus China exported two and a half times as much to Japan as she did, on average, to the world. The index was even higher in 1980 with a value of 3.03. But when her formerly closed economy opened up in the 1980s, China diversified trade and the former Japan bias declined substantially. Again in 1990 a turning point can be observed. From 1990 until 1998 the China–Japan export intensity index rose. However, in 1999

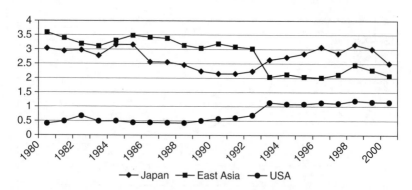

Figure 2.2   Chinese export intensity index, 1980–2000: Japan, East Asia and the USA compared

Notes: 1. The Chinese export trade intensity index is the ratio of the share of Chinese exports to a specific trading partner (that is Japan, East Asia, USA) in the total of Chinese exports to the share of the trading partner's imports in the world import market.
2. Chinese exports to Japan exclude indirect exports via Hong Kong.
3. Chinese exports to the US exclude indirect exports via Hong Kong.
4. East Asia = Japan, NIEs-4, ASEAN-4, Macao. Chinese exports to East Asia exclude indirect exports via Hong Kong (estimates).

Source: IMF, *Direction of Trade Statistics; Hong Kong External Trade* (monthly); own calculations.

and 2000 it fell again. In 1993 it intersected the China–East Asian export intensity index, which was on a continuous declining trend since 1980. The development of the intensity index of Chinese exports to the USA is a mirror image of the China–Japan export intensity index. From a low value in 1980 (0.41) it first rose quickly (1993: 1.13) and since then has been moving sideways. The bias of Chinese exports to the USA has never been as high as the respective bias towards Japan.

Figure 2.3 shows the development of the index of trade intensity of China's export trade with Japan, East Asia and the USA from 1980 until 2000, with China's indirect exports via Hong Kong included in the index composition. The structure in Figure 2.3 is quite similar to the structure of the preceding Figure 2.2. However, the index values for Japan and East Asia are now smaller and thus closer to the international norm. On the other hand, the index values for the USA have risen to account for the large amount of indirect exports from China to the USA.

In summary, following the opening up of China, the trade interdependence between Japan and China initially fell considerably due to the diversification of China's trade. However, since 1990 the mutual bias has been rising again and has already attained a level that is higher than both partners' trading relations to the rest of East Asia and to the USA, but also – not shown here – to the EU and Canada, trading partners with whom China's trade relationship has traditionally been less intensive.

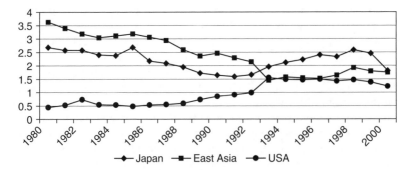

Figure 2.3 Chinese export intensity index 1980–2000: Japan, East Asia and the USA compared (adjusted)

Notes: 1. The Chinese export trade intensity index is the ratio of the share of Chinese exports to a specific trading partner (that is Japan, East Asia, USA) in the total of Chinese exports to the share of the trading partner's imports in the world import market.

2. Chinese exports to Japan include indirect exports via Hong Kong.

3. Chinese exports to the US include indirect exports via Hong Kong.

4. East Asia = Japan, NIEs-4, ASEAN-4, Macao. Chinese exports to East Asia include indirect exports via Hong Kong (estimates).

Source: IMF, *Direction of Trade Statistics; Hong Kong External Trade* (monthly); own calculations.

Why the rapid growth of Sino–Japanese trade?

The statistical analysis brings up the question as to the driving forces of the Sino–Japanese trade intensification: Why did the Sino–Japanese trade interdependence grow so quickly in the 1990s? Why were the growth rates of Sino–Japanese trade in the same period even higher than the growth rates of both countries' trade with the rest of East Asia? The answer to these questions will not only provide an understanding of the historical trade flows of the 1980s and 1990s but may also allow conclusions to be drawn regarding the further development of the future bilateral trade relations.

The dynamic development of Sino–Japanese trade can, of course, be put down to the two obvious facts that (1) China's total foreign trade has grown quickly in the aftermath of the opening-up and liberalization of China, and that (2) Japan and China are geographically close to each other. But since Sino–Japanese trade is more dynamic than other trade in East Asia, it is worth inquiring into the economic causes of this dynamism. Since Ricardo it has generally been acknowledged that trading volumes and trading structures are defined by the comparative advantage of nations. Hence the specific competitive advantages of Japan and China in each other's markets determine the bilateral trade between China and Japan. As will be shown below, Sino–Japanese trade is mainly Heckscher–Ohlin trade, based on the distinctly differing factor endowments of the two countries. Thus the dynamic development of Sino–Japanese trade in the 1990s stems from the simple fact that suppliers from both countries were very competitive in the import market of their respective trading partner. They were able to offer (at a competitive price) exactly the kind of goods and services the customers in the other country wanted. It stands to reason that a comparative advantage has to be acquired by the continuous (investment) efforts of the private firms involved, which in the case of Sino–Japanese trade are often backed by politics. However, foreign direct investments in trade, service and manufacturing are not only complementing but also substituting the bilateral trade. Other factors influencing the volume and the structure of Sino–Japanese trade, apart from comparative advantage (and acquired comparative advantage), are the valid tariff rates, other trade barriers and the general trading climate.

Japanese exports to China

Japan's trade statistics show that the comparative advantage of Japan clearly lies in the production and the supply of capital-intensive and R&D-intensive goods. Japan's exports are highly concentrated in the SITC category 7, machinery and transport goods, which embodies considerably more capital and technological know-how than other categories and amounted in 1999 to a share of 68.7 per cent of its total exports. In principle, Japan's exports to China are no exception to this general pattern. However, in 1999 Japan's share of SITC category 7 exports amounted in the case of China to only 49.8 per cent, somewhat lower than Japan's SITC 7 share in its total exports. On the other hand, the Japanese exports of other manufactured goods (SITC category 8), such as textile yarns, pulp and paper, and steel products, to China are disproportionately high, accounting for a share of 30.7 per cent in Japan's total exports to China in 1999 (author's own calculations from OECD, 2000, pp. 392–465).

Japan's trade with China stands out because of two particular structural characteristics. First, China with its generally low wages and the promise of a large and growing market is a highly attractive location for manufacturing investment in Japan's immediate geographic vicinity. Second, China's import market is protected by high tariffs and other trade barriers which can only be overcome by manufacturing and service investment. The still high entry barriers to China's distribution system and service economy notwithstanding, both features act as prominent pull factors for Japanese FDI towards China. Of course there is an important investment push factor, too: Japan's labour-intensive industries are losing competitiveness due to the high manufacturing costs in Japan, and a rising yen has compelled companies to shift manufacturing capacities to low-cost locations.

What effects has Japanese FDI had on Sino–Japanese trade? Japanese investment in China attracts additional imports from Japan, such as industrial plant and machinery, industrial components and other intermediate products, but also promotes re-exports back to Japan. On the other hand, Japanese FDI substitutes Chinese imports from Japan in accordance with China's national industrialization plan. Following the examinations by MITI (since 2001: METI) on the trade effects of Japanese FDI in Asia at the aggregate level, it may be congruently assumed for the case of China that in the short term FDI stimulates Japanese exports rather than substituting them or promoting imports (from China). After three to four years, however, the net trade effect becomes negative (Legewie, 1999, pp. 34–5). Certainly, these volume effects are particularly strong in the case of export-processed-based investment, which is a widespread pattern among Japanese investment in China. Moreover, Japanese FDI in China has also had a structural effect on Sino–Japanese trade. Since Japan exported to China fewer finished goods and more components and materials for processing in the latter half of the 1990s (Mino, 2001, pp. 114–5), the share of SITC category 7 goods declined, and the share of SITC category 8 goods increased (as already mentioned above).

The great number of bilateral political conflicts in the 1990s, and the recent trade frictions of 2001 notwithstanding, domestic politics both in Japan and in China seem to have a long-term interest in the promotion of bilateral economic cooperation, which advances the industrial modernization of China and raises the bilateral trade flow (Kojima, 2000, pp. 45–7; Whiting, 2000, pp. 23–30). There are various examples for such promotional activities, most notably the (1) generous loans and grants of Japanese ODA to China, which function as a catalyst for Japanese exports and investment towards China; (2) the Japanese investment in China's energy and environmental protection infrastructure; (3) the active promotion of Japanese FDI into China by the Chinese and the Japanese government; and (4) a proactive role for Sino-Chinese institutions, such as the Japan–China Trade Expansion Council (1986), the Japan–China Investment Promotion Organization (1990) and an estimated 100 semi-public or private Sino–Japanese associations. Moreover, the Chinese domestic political support for increasing Sino–Japanese trade ties would not be conceivable had China not, since 1978, been gradually changing its economic system. The systemic transformation process has not only reoriented China's development focus towards export promotion and FDI attraction; it has also profoundly changed its foreign trade relationship with Japan. The reform process made it increasingly costly for China (and Japan as well) to resist the expansion of bilateral economic links (Zhang, 1998, pp. 71–167, 175–8, 182–5).

Chinese exports to Japan

In the course of the opening and liberalization of its foreign trade, China's export trade pattern and international comparative advantage has changed fundamentally from formerly agricultural and natural resource-intensive goods to presently labour-intensive goods (Zhang, 2000, pp. 53–7, 216–22). The commodity structure of China's exports to Japan altered accordingly. Whereas in the early 1980s Japan imported mainly raw materials such as oil, coal, food staples, cotton, silk and the like from China, in the late

1980s and in the 1990s Chinese exports to Japan became increasingly labour-intensive. Now they predominantly consist of manufactured goods; manufactured goods from China are cheap and their quality has markedly improved in recent years. They dominate the Japanese import market in an increasing product range, most notably in foodstuff, textiles and apparel, footwear, sporting goods, toys and games. Furthermore, suppliers from China are also gaining a foothold in Japan's import market of additional capital-intensive products, such as inorganic chemicals, electrical motors and generators, video and sound equipment and cameras (JETRO, 2000). It is even expected that machinery and equipment will be the main Chinese export items to Japan by 2006 (Mino, 2001, p. 115). Apparently China is capable of supplying the kind of labour-intensive (industrial and agricultural) products that are in high demand in Japan's industrial and consumer markets but cannot be produced in Japan at such low costs. Since most Chinese exports to Japan are channelled through Japanese production and distribution networks, they do not seem to be affected by Japan's structural import impediments, most notably the Japanese distribution system, in the same way as for various industrial products from other sources.

A major driving factor of Chinese exports to Japan seems to be the Japanese manufacturing investment in eastern and north-eastern China. Since the beginning of the 1990s, China-based, Japanese-owned companies and their local joint venture partners have been increasingly producing consumer and industrial goods for the Japanese market. Since small and medium-sized companies shifting manufacturing capacities from Japan to China occupy a fairly large part of Japan's total investment in China (JBIC, 2001), it may be reasonably assumed that Japanese investment to China is, to a larger extent, cost-driven and probably more export-oriented than the foreign investments of other industrialized countries. As a great many Japanese investors intend to supply their (Japanese) home market from the Chinese manufacturing base, it seems certain that Japanese investment in China contributed considerably to the dynamic growth of Chinese exports to Japan in the 1990s (Chan, Tracy and Wenhui, 1999, pp. 136–9; Kreinin, Plummer and Abe, 2001, pp. 54–62).

Chinese exports to Japan receive a similar political backing as the Japanese exports to China by the various governmental and private institutions mentioned above, and they are, of course, a consequence of the systemic transformation of China's foreign trade (Kojima, 2000, pp. 45–7; Zhang, 1998, pp. 71–167, 175–8). However, as manufacturing imports from China are increasingly driving out industrial and agricultural products 'made in Japan', protectionist sentiments are rising. Whereas in the 1990s Japan retreated repeatedly from requested protectionist measures to curb surging Chinese manufactured imports, most notably in the field of textiles and apparel (Zhang, 1998, pp. 121–38), a change of policy seems to have occurred in April 2001. Pressured by the agricultural lobby, import safeguards against three agricultural products from China, namely scallions, shiitake mushrooms and rushes, were introduced and the monitoring of other sensitive products was taken up. China retaliated with penal import duties on Japanese-made automobiles, cellular phones and air conditioners. It seems unlikely, but cannot be precluded, that these events mark the turn from a co-operative to an adverse bilateral trade policy.

Summary

Recapitulating, Japan's and China competitive advantage in each other's import markets is a convincing explanation for the fast increase in bilateral trade. Furthermore, Japan's and China's differing factor endowments and supply structures imply a complementary nature of the bilateral economic relationship. The complementary factor endowments remain the essential cause for the Ricardian inter-industry trade between these two countries. Considering China's huge population and its generally low level of education, it will take decades rather than years of high economic growth until China's comparative advantage lies within the sphere of capital-intensive or skill-intensive products. However, China already possesses a large pool of skilled labour and is capable of providing the capital needed for industrial development. Taking into account China's links to the technological and organizational know-how as well as to the financial resources of the overseas Chinese, and considering the accommodating role of industrial policy, it can be easily foreseen that China may increasingly gain competitive strength in various manufacturing industries (Abe and Lee, 2001, pp. 310, 316–9). Subsequently, China's export trade structure may change accordingly. As a matter of fact, the structural analysis of China's export trade structure shows that until 1996 China has not only improved its international competitive position in unskilled labour-intensive industries, but also in products and sectors that are human capital-intensive such as household appliances, electronics, power generating equipment, railway equipment or agricultural machinery, or which are physical capital-intensive such as cement, pig-iron, ships, plastic articles or inorganic chemicals (Zhang, 2000, pp. 53–7, 216–22).

Thus it can even be argued that China is on the threshold of the investment-driven stage of economic development within Porter's dynamic perspective on competitive advantage (Raupach-Sumiya, 2000, pp. 17). In light of these empirical facts, it may be assumed that along with the upgrading of China's exports, the bilateral inter-industry trade structure will be increasingly enriched by bilateral intra-industry trade. According to the empirical research of Hu and Ma, there is already substantial evidence for intra-industrial trade between Japan and China in the year 1995, albeit significantly less than between China and Hong Kong or Macao (Hu and Ma, 1999, p. 87). Thus Japan's and China's competitive advantages in each other's import markets are not merely derived from the differing factor endowments, but also from economies of scale and product differentiation as well as from the increasing human capital-intensity in China's export products. It can be concluded that the trade interdependence between Japan and China will intensify in future, provided that political problems do not derail the bilateral relationship.

Conclusions

The analysis of Sino–Japanese trade interdependence clearly shows a cooperation pattern in the bilateral economic relationship. From the Chinese viewpoint, the Japanese market is the second most important export market after the USA in absolute volume and by relative shares. The export intensity indices show that Chinese exports are more biased towards the Japanese market than towards any other major import market (USA, East Asia). On the other hand, China is presently the fourth most important market (behind the USA, Korea and Taiwan) for Japanese exporters, and the export bias towards the Chinese market is exactly as high as towards the rest of East Asia and higher than towards the US market. The differences in factor endowments and the existing potential for intra-industry trade are plausible causes for continued expansion of bilateral trade and the increase of the mutual trade bias. Thus, the empirical analysis of the Sino–Japanese trade clearly confirms the neo-classical conception of international economic relations.

Although Japanese FDI flows are less impressive than trade, it seems justifiable to generalize the results of trade investigation to the whole domain of the economy, because the other bilateral economic transactions such as FDI, ODA and technology transfer are complements rather than substitutes for trade. Of course the existence of economic (and political) conflicts between Japan and China cannot and should not be denied. But the empirical trade analysis makes an assessment of the Sino–Japanese economic conflicts possible. Economic conflicts are not part of the substance of the Sino–Japanese relationship. They are rather the consequence of a very fruitful and beneficial relationship that generates large cooperation gains for both sides. Conflict may arise from time to time, however, with respect to the distribution of these gains. The outcome of market processes and the results of negotiations on the micro level may not be acceptable to politics and/or the parties involved under some circumstances. Or politics may interfere so as to change the market results in favour of their constituencies. There are many examples at hand: market access concerns, anti-dumping charges, the grant of investment licenses, the employment of ODA and so on. The plain issue is who is getting what.

Although it is certainly permissible to generalize from trade to economics, a further generalization from economics to politics is not conclusive. In international political relations the driving forces are different. Although you may have a win–win situation in bilateral trade, in politics it may be a zero-sum game. There is, in fact, a long and still unresolved debate in political science on the (positive versus negative) nature of the relationship between international trade and bilateral conflict/cooperation (Pollachek, 1980). Although empirical studies tend to show that trade positively influences the political relationship between actual or potential foes (Reuveny and Kang, 1996), a stringent relationship between (booming) trade and political cooperation cannot generally be ascertained. This principal caveat notwithstanding, it can be reasonably assumed that cooperative economic relations will most likely have a positive effect on the overall Sino–Japanese relationship. A flourishing bilateral trade and mutual economic benefits may not be the crucial factors, but the positive economic effects will not go unnoticed by politics and the politicians concerned. For rational political actors who are interested in the well-being of their country, it makes sense to continue to promote trade and to increase economic interdependence and cooperation. Thus, the more intense the trade relationship is, the less likely the conflict scenario and the more likely the cooperation scenario between China and Japan.

Notes

1. To be sure, trade and economic interdependence do not necessarily preclude political conflict or confrontation, as historical examples clearly show. In the extreme, trade can even cause conflict when traders compete for scarce resources (Choucri and North, 1975). Although such a pattern cannot be excluded, the opposite view seems to be more convincing. A nation trying to maximize its economic welfare will be averse to conflict with trade partners. With increasing trade interdependence, a growing number of domestic interest groups will argue in favour of the foreign entity. Thus, increasing economic interdependence makes political conflict more and more costly (Pollachek, 1980).
2. For the estimation method see Sung, 1993, pp. 113–5. Since 1993 the Hong Kong Census and Statistics Department has provided exact accounts of the major destinations of the (Hong Kong) re-exports originating from China and Japan. The author is grateful to Yan Zhu for informing him on the source of these accounts, namely the *Hong Kong External Trade* (monthly).
3. For a detailed discussion of the use of the trade intensity index in bilateral trade analysis, see Anderson and Norheim, 1993, pp. 23–4, 47–8; Drysdale and Garnaut, 1982, pp. 62–84.
4. In general terms the export trade intensity index (I_{ab}) is defined as $I_{ab} = EX_a/IM_b$, in which EX_a = the share of country B in country A's exports, and IM_b = the share of country B in the world import market excluding imports from country A, because a country cannot export goods to itself.

References

Abe, S. and C. H. Lee (2001) 'Economic Development in China and its Implications for Japan', in M. Blomström, B. Gangnes and S. La Croix (eds), *Japan's New Economy. Continuity and Change in the Twenty-First Century*, Oxford: Oxford University Press, pp. 307–22.

Anderson, K. and H. Norheim (1993) 'History, Geography and Regional Economic Integration', in K. Anderson and R. Blackhurst (eds), *Regional Integration and the Global Trading System*, New York and London: Harvester-Wheatsheaf, pp. 19–51.

Austin, G. and S. Harris (2001) *Japan and Greater China: Political Economy and Military Power in the Asian Century*, Honolulu: University of Hawaii Press.

Chan, T., N. Tracy and Z. Wenhui (1999) *China's Export Miracle. Origins, Results and Prospects*, Houndmills Basingstoke: Macmillan – now Palgrave.

Choucri, N. and R. North (1975) *Nations in Conflict: National Growth and International Violence*, San Francisco: Freeman.

Drysdale, P. and R. Garnaut (1982) 'Trade Intensities and the Analysis of Bilateral Trade Flows in a Many-Country World', *Hitotsubashi Journal of Economics*, vol. 22 (2), pp. 62–84.

Funabashi, Y. (1999) 'Where Does Japan Fit in the China–Japan–U.S. Relationship?' in Japan Centre for International Exchange (ed.), *New Dimensions of China–Japan–U.S. Relations*, Tokyo and New York: JCIE, pp. 79–83.

Government of Hong Kong, Census and Statistics Department (various years) *Hong Kong External Trade* (monthly), Hong Kong: Census and Statistics Department.

Hasegawa, K. and M. Nakajima (1996) *Chûgoku kiki to Nihon. Honkon henken o yomu* [Japan and the China Crisis. How to Interpret the Return of Hong Kong?], Tokyo: Kobunsha.

Hilpert, H. G. (1998) *Wirtschaftliche Integration in Ostasien in raumwirtschaftlicher Analyse*, Berlin und Munich: Duncker & Humblot.

—(1999) 'Japan und China im ostasiatischen Wirtschaftsraum: Komplementaritäten und Konflikte', in M. Taube and A. Gälli (eds), *China's Wirtschaft im Wandel. Aktuelle Aspekte und Probleme*, Munich: Weltforum Verlag, pp. 29–66.

Hilpert, H. G. and K. Nakagane (2002) 'Economic Relations. What Can we Learn from Trade and FDI? in M. Söderberg (ed.), *Chinese–Japanese Relations in the 21st Century, Complementarity and Conflict*, London and New York: Routledge, pp. 224–46.

Hu, X. and Y. Ma (1999) 'International Intra-Industry Trade of China', *Weltwirtschaftliches Archiv*, vol. 135 (1), pp. 82–101.

IMF (International Monetary Fund) (various years) *Direction of Trade Statistics*, Washington, DC: IMF.

JBIC (Japan Bank for International Cooperation) (2000) *Kaihatsu Kinyû Kenkyûsho Hô* [Institute of Development Finance, Report] (January), Tokyo: JBIC.

JETRO (Japan External Trade Organization) (2000) *White Paper on International Trade*, Tokyo: JETRO.

Jin, X. (2002) 'The Background and Trend of China–Japan Partnership' in M. Söderberg (ed.), *Chinese–Japanese Relations in the 21st Century: Complementarity and Conflict*, London and New York: Routledge.

Kojima, T. (2000) 'Japan's China policy', in P. Drysdale and D. D. Zhang (eds), *Japan and China, Rivalry or Cooperation in East Asia?* Canberra: Asia Pacific Press, pp. 33–47.

Kreinin, M., M. G. Plummer and S. Abe (2001) 'Export and Direct Foreign Investment Links: A Three Country Comparison', in M. Blomström, B. Gangnes and S. La Croix (eds), *Japan's New Economy. Continuity and Change in the Twenty-First Century*, Oxford: Oxford University Press, pp. 47–64.

Legewie, J. (1999) 'Beschäftigungswirkungen von Auslandsinvestitionen: Das Beispiel Japan', *Zeitschrift für Wirtschaftspolitik*, vol. 48 (1), pp. 27–44.

Mino, H. (2001) 'China's Accession to the WTO and Japan–China Economic Relations: A New Stage of Bilateral Division of Labour', in I. Yamazawa and K. Imai (eds), *China Enters WTO: Pursuing Symbiosis with the Global Economy*, Tokyo: Institute of Developing Economies, pp. 83–109.

OECD (Organization for Economic Cooperation and Development) (2000) *International Trade by Commodities Statistics 1994/99*, Paris: OECD.

Pollachek, S. (1980) 'Conflict and Trade', *Journal of Conflict Resolution*, vol. 24, pp. 55–78.

Raupach-Sumiya, J. (2000) *Chinese Firms as Emerging Competitors – Challenges for Japan's Industry*, DIJ Working Papers 00/4, Tokyo: German Institute for Japanese Studies.

Reuveny, R. and H. Kang (1996) 'International Trade, Political Conflict/Cooperation, and Granger Causality', *American Journal of Political Science*, vol. 40 (3), pp. 943–70.

Segal, G. (1993) 'The Coming Confrontation between China and Japan?' *World Policy Journal*, vol. 10 (2), pp. 27–32.

Sung, Y.-W. (1993) 'China's Impact on the Asia-Pacific Regional Economy', *Business and the Contemporary World*, vol. 6 (1), pp. 105–28.

Whiting, A.S. (2000) 'China's Japan Policy and Domestic Politics', in P. Drysdale and D. D. Zhang (eds), *Japan and China, Rivalry or Cooperation in East Asia?* Canberra: Asia Pacific Press, pp. 15–31.

Zhang, D. D. (1998) *China's Relations with Japan in an Era of Economic Liberalisation*, Commack, NY: Nova Science Publishers Inc.

Zhang, X.-G. (2000) *China's Trade Patterns and International Comparative Advantage*, Houndmills Basingstoke: Macmillan – now Palgrave.

3
Japanese Direct Investment in China: Its Effects on China's Economic Development*

Katsuji Nakagane

Introduction

Since the opening of China's economy in the early 1980s, anything conducive to economic development has been allowed and foreign input has been encouraged. Japan has provided China with a tremendous amount of official development assistance (ODA), massive private loans, and numerous grassroots technical aids, but what has stimulated China's economic development most seems to be trade and foreign direct investment (FDI). This chapter focuses on the relationship between Japanese investment in China and China's economic development, as well as prospects for future Sino–Japanese FDI relations. The chapter is organized as follows: in the next section I briefly describe the recent trends of Japan's direct investment in China. The relationship between FDI and economic growth in China is then analysed, making own estimates of its FDI functions. The focus is then turned on Japan's direct investment in China, its nature, and its effects on growth of the Chinese economy. The final section forecasts possible Sino–Japanese FDI relations in the years to come.

An overview of Japanese investment in China

Sino–Japanese economic relations are multifaceted and include trade, tourism, loans and ODA and FDI, but, with regard to future prospects for the economic relationship between the two countries, trade and FDI are most important factors.

* This work has been financially supported by the Murata Science Foundation. An earlier version of the chapter was presented at the 'Workshop on the Chinese–Japanese Relationship' in Stockholm, August 2000, organized by the Swedish Institute of International Affairs and the European Institute of Japanese Studies.

Japan's direct capital flows to China

China's FDI inflows from the world are displayed in Table 3.1. Foreign direct capital inflows to China peaked in 1993 on a contract basis, and in 1998 on an actually implemented basis. In 2000, FDI in China began to rebound after it had sharply decreased due to the Asian financial crisis in the late 1990s. Since 1993 the relative shares of Hong Kong and other major Asian investor countries have been decreasing, which implies that China's FDI has been dispersed to attract capital more widely in recent years. The United States and European countries are now expanding their volumes of FDI in China. On the other hand, Japan's share in China's foreign capital inflows was considerably smaller in the late 1990s than it had been in the 1980s. Its share has been declining to almost the same level as Taiwan's, and it has been surpassed by the USA. However, Japanese FDI, which held a share of more than 7 per cent in 1999, is still an indispensable part of China's capital inflow as a whole.

Table 3.2 shows Japanese FDI flows to China in absolute figures (both value and items) and in percentage shares of Japan's FDI to Asia and of

Table 3.1 FDI flows to China by major source countries

Year	Total flows (US$ billions)		Flows by major source country (%)			
	Contract	Actual	Hong Kong	Japan	Taiwan	USA
1983	1 723	636	–	–	–	–
1985	5 932	1 661	48.9	16.1	–	18.3
1990	6 596	3 487	54.9	14.4	6.4	13.1
1993	11 144	2 752	62.8	4.9	11.3	7.5
1995	91 282	37 521	53.4	8.5	8.4	8.2
1998	50 102	45 463	40.7	7.5	6.4	8.6
1999	41 223	40 319	40.6	7.5	6.5	10.5

Source: *Statistical Yearbook of China*, various issues.

Table 3.2 Japanese FDI flows to China, 1980–2000

Year	Japanese FDI flows to China		Shares in Japanese FDI to Asia (%)		Shares in total Japanese FDI (%)	
	Items (no.)	Value (US$ mn)	Items	Value	Items	Value
1980	6	14	0.9	1.0	0.3	0.3
1985	118	100	17.2	7.0	4.5	0.8
1990	165	355	11.0	4.9	2.8	0.6
1995	770	4 615	47.3	36.2	26.9	8.7
1999	76	838	14.4	10.5	4.4	1.1
2000	102	1 099	22.8	16.8	6.1	2.0

Note: Figures as reported by Japanese firms and individuals to the Ministry of Finance.

Source: Ministry of Finance, *Zaisei Kinyû Tôkei Geppô* (Fiscal and Financial Statistics Monthly), various issues.

Japan's total FDI. It is evident that Japanese FDI in China is marked by a high degree of fluctuation. It suddenly rose in the middle of the 1980s, then stagnated for a few years and reached a peak in the middle of the 1990s. Since 1995, Japanese FDI in China has been in relative decline, both in terms of Japan's FDI in Asia or in the world total. This seems to suggest that Japanese investors' interest gradually shifted away from China in the late 1990s. Moreover, it may imply that Japan's investment in China declined quite suddenly after the end of the 'China boom' in the early 1990s, when many Japanese small and medium-sized firms rushed to China eager for large profits but without careful preparation. Nevertheless, as will be discussed below, the interest in investing in China resumed around 1999 with China's impending membership in the WTO. A new investment boom arrived in 2001 with China's entry into the WTO.

It should be noted here, however, that host and source countries' FDI statistics sometimes show considerable discrepancies. There are significant differences between the figures for Japanese FDI in China as reported by the statistics of the Japanese Ministry of Finance (MOF) and by the official data from China. The differences are particularly large for the period after 1994, when Japanese FDI to China declined after having reached its peak (see Figure 3.1). The discrepancies are due in particular to the differing methods

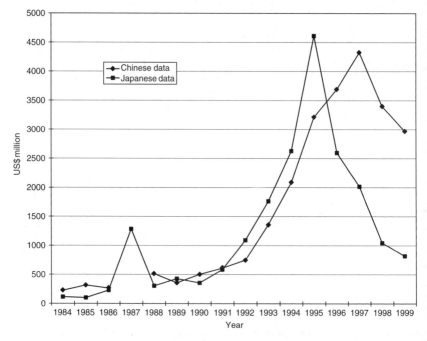

Figure 3.1 Japan's investment in China: Japanese and Chinese statistics compared

of FDI registration in Japan and in China. The Japanese figures are based on notifications by domestic investors to the MOF, while the Chinese data of 'realized foreign investment' originate from those compiled by the investment authorities of the regions where the projects are located. Therefore, a range of statistical leakages or errors is likely to take place. For example, investing Japanese firms may not make accurate reports of their foreign investment to the MOF, while the regional governments in China may exaggerate the Japanese FDI inflow to the central statistical bureau for political purposes.

Furthermore, different statistical bases result from the different methods of registration. For instance, some projects that have been reported to the MOF may have proved abortive in China; and, most important, China's FDI statistics include reinvestments of profits earned by foreign invested enterprises (FIEs) in China, while the Japanese statistics do not. Moreover, some statistical discrepancies can be derived from other sources. For example, the Japanese FDI statistics cover only large-scale investment of more than yen 30 million before 1993, and of more than yen 100 million after 1994, while the Chinese statistics cover all types of investment. Moreover, part of the statistical gaps can be explained by the exchange rate; the Japanese figures in Figure 3.1 are converted from yen to US$ on the basis of Chinese statistics of exchange rates on yearly averages.

Characteristics of Japan's FDI in China

Contrasting Japanese FDI in China with that of other major source countries, the following characteristics emerge.

Industry

Most of the Japanese FDI in China is drawn to the manufacturing sector. This feature is also the case for other source countries, such as the United States, but it is especially pronounced in the case of Japanese investment (see Table 3.3). In addition, Japanese FDI in China is biased towards light, labour-intensive industries like food processing and textiles and apparel. Moreover, in contrast to Hong Kong and other overseas Chinese capitals, relatively few Japanese firms have ever tried to enter the Chinese service and real estate markets. This pattern is closely related with the fact that Japan's FDI in China is more or less export related, as discussed below. The sectors and industries that received Japanese capital are highly likely to export their products to Japan or to third countries. In general, the contribution of FDI to exports is high in China. In 1996, 40.8 per cent of China's total exports were made by foreign enterprises (Naughton 1996). The respective share for Japanese FIEs in China is probably even higher.

Firm size

A majority of Asian investors in China are small and medium-sized, and Japanese investors are no exception. This feature is reflected in the relatively

Table 3.3 US and Japanese FDI in China by industry (total stocks at the end of 1998, %)

	USA	Japan
Petroleum	14.4	–
Manufacturing	58.7	63.5
of which: Food	1.9	4.2
Textiles	–	8.7
Chemicals	5.1	4.0
Metals	2.6	5.4
Machinery	7.3	8.1
Electric and electronic	23.2	16.6
Vehicles	2.8	6.1
Services and trade	20.5	17.6
Total	100.0	100.0

Source: KKJS (2000).

low average amount of capital invested, which is in clear contrast to European investment in China. In 1997, for example, the average amounts of FDI in China (on a contract basis) by companies from Germany, the United Kingdom and France were US$ 2.8, 4.8 and 7.5 million respectively, whereas Japanese companies invested only US$ 2.4 million, on average. Only a few Japanese large-sized corporations have ever been involved in big projects in China. For example, it is well-known that Toyota Motors refused to invest in China in the 1980s, despite strong urging from the Chinese side, while Volkswagen AG actively responded to it later. Other famous Western multinational corporations (MNCs) such as Royal Dutch Shell, British Petroleum, the Dow Chemical Company, and Royal Philips Electronics N.V. are now planning to carry out huge projects in China. In contrast, Japanese MNCs have been criticized for their lack of a global strategy, at least regarding their China investments.

Implementation

A higher percentage of investment contracts is actually implemented by Japanese firms. The implementation ratio of Japanese FDI in China, that is the ratio of investment contracts which are actually realized, is significantly higher than in the case of other countries. As reported in an expert interview with a Japanese representative of the Hitachi television plant in Fuzhou, a Japanese company places a greater emphasis on 'marriage' rather than 'engagement'.

Geographical location

Like most other FDI in China, Japanese capital is concentrated in the coastal areas – as much as 82.6 per cent of Japanese FDI in China from 1979 to 1996 was in those areas (Zhu, 1999). But Japanese FDI is also concentrated to some extent in the northern and central parts of China, while the focus of investment by the overseas Chinese is more on Guangdong and Fujian, both regions to which strong cultural ties exist. Many Japanese enterprises invest in Dalian in the province of Liaoning, which is a city in China with a pre-war Japanese legacy. It is often pointed out that investment decisions by the Japanese are not necessarily made for only economic reasons.

How FDI has contributed to Chinese economic development

By bringing in advanced technology, capital and management know-how from the developed world, FDI contributes to economic growth and development in the host countries in the developing world. The four major contributions by FDI to economic growth in developing countries according to Bende-Nabende (1999, pp. 80–91) are:

1. FDI helps to improve human resource capacities, whether entrepreneurial, technological or managerial, by way of education, training and the creation of new employment opportunities (educational effect).
2. FDI brings new technology to host countries (technology effect).
3. FDI also brings capital from abroad, which adds to domestic capital formation in host countries (capital effect). Whether FDI is a substitute for or a complement of domestic savings is a matter of empirical verification.
4. FDI can contribute to economic growth in developing countries by promoting their international trade (trade effect).

How these four types of FDI effects are realized depends, in essence, on host countries' economies, but also on political, social and institutional factors. Many empirical studies verify, for example, FDI's trade effects, supporting a hypothesis that it generates more exports than it replaces, at least in the initial stages (Bende-Nabende, 1999, p. 90).

Statistical tests show that FDI has facilitated China's economic growth. Since China opened its doors and started reforming its economy, it achieved rapid growth concomitant with its foreign capital inflows. Several authors have estimated China's economic growth functions including FDI as one of the explanatory variables and illustrate how it has helped economic development in China. Chen, Chang and Zhang (1995), for instance, explain China's economic growth for the period 1968–90 by one-year lagged savings and FDI, thus ascertaining that these two factors are significantly related to GNP growth in China. Their analysis can be extended to cover the post-reform period as a whole (1980–99) and the same conclusion applies. Wang and Swain (1995), on the other hand, make a simple regression to determine China's FDI with many variables: market size (specified as GDP level plus growth rate), relative wage (China's wage level relative to America's), exchange rate, imports, average growth rate of OECD countries, domestic productivity, tariff rates and political stability.

In order to capture a linkage between economic growth and FDI in China, we hypothesize, first, that its economic development is associated with investment, both foreign and domestic, as well as trade; and second that its FDI is a function of accumulated foreign capital inflows, growth rate and economic openness. Thus we regress economic development on FDI, along with FDI on growth. As a result the following regressions can be derived:

$$\text{GDP} = -16.656 + 0.0552FDIa + 0.278DI + 0.553Trade \tag{3.1}$$
$$(-0.554) \quad (2.52)^{**} \quad (2.45)^{**} \quad (3.28)^{***}$$
$$\text{Adjusted } R^2 = 0.986, \ DW = 0.709$$

$$\text{FDI} = -201.552 + 0.033AFDI + 9.180Growth + 10.527Open \tag{3.2}$$
$$(-2.91)^{**} \quad (7.13)^{***} \quad (2.17)^* \quad (2.65)^{**}$$
$$\text{Adjusted } R^2 = 0.917, \ DW = 1.55$$

where *FDIa* is foreign investment in total social assets; *DI* is investment in such assets constructed by domestic funds alone; *Trade* is total trade; *AFDI* is accumulated FDI; *Growth* is the rate of GDP growth; and *Open* is the degree of openness measured by the ratio of export to GDP.

Figures in parentheses show *t*-values. Asterisks ***, **, * indicate the significance level of 1 per cent, 5 per cent, and 10 per cent respectively. *DW* is the Durbin–Watson ratio. The period covered is 1981–98 for regression (3.1) and 1983–98 for regression (3.2). The regressions are all made by the OLS method. *DI, Trade*, and *FDI* data are all deflated by the GDP deflator. All data are derived from the Chinese official statistics. The value of *DW* in equation (3.1) is too low, implying that there can be a positive serial correlation in the error term of the model. To some extent, however, this problem can be solved by introducing the fourth variable like a dummy, say 1981–91 = 0 and 1992–98 = 1, which identifies the period of 'socialist market economy' since 1992.

What the above two regressions indicate is quite obvious:

- First and foremost, FDI has definitely served China's economic development, as many previous estimates of a similar sort have proved.
- Second, FDI does not necessarily substitute for domestic investment in China. Inflows of foreign capital are usually accompanied by an increase in domestic investment.
- Third, economic growth, in turn, accelerates FDI, probably because the growth rate represents future prospects of China as an expanding market. The developing Chinese market as well as its sheer size attracts many foreign investors, as shown below.
- Fourth, openness is also highly associated with FDI inflows. That is to say, the more widely the Chinese economy is opened, the more foreign capital flows in the mainland. But the latter result must be interpreted with

caution, since the high statistical significance of the *Open* coefficient may result just from the fact that export trade and FDI are closely interrelated in the Chinese context. As we have observed above, many foreign firms, from Asia in particular, invest their capital in China for the sake of exporting the products they manufacture to the world market, and their processing exports naturally lead to expanding imports to China.

- Fifth, accumulated foreign capital seems to have been more conducive to China's FDI than domestic growth and the degree of openness, which are the other two variables in equation (3.2). In other words, there is a sort of self-reinforcing effect that is an agglomeration effect of FDI. So far we have used the FDI statistics of investment in total social assets, but even if we change the data into the total figure of 'realized foreign direct investment', our conclusions are basically unchanged.

Next we look at FDI regressed by *Trade* and *Growth*, both of which are one-year lagged:

$$LogFDI(t) = -15.959 + 4.211LogTrade(t-1) + 0.073Growth(t-1) \qquad (3.3)$$
$$(-9.59) \qquad (13.13) \qquad (3.49)$$
$$\text{Adjusted } R^2 = 0.925, DW = 1.409$$

The period covered is 1984–99, and data are all from Chinese official statistics. The Durbin–Watson value indicates no serial correlation in the error terms of this model at the 2.5 per cent significance level.

The above regression appears to simply imply that foreign trade and economic growth – the latter being a proxy for the potential of an expanding domestic market – attract foreign capital to China. Then, a causality issue arises. Has foreign capital accelerated economic growth, which in turn facilitates more capital inflows from abroad to China? Or, has economic development attracted more foreign capital? Shan, Tian and Sun (1999) tested three hypotheses regarding the causality relation between economic growth and FDI. They conclude that the two-way causality hypothesis is supported in the case of China, rather than the FDI-led growth or the growth-driven FDI hypothesis. Their conclusion seems to be applicable to our model, too.

How is FDI linked to the domestic economic development in China in terms of the four FDI effects described above? In our view, FDI has contributed to China's economic development, directly or indirectly, via five transmission channels, namely capital formation, technology transfer, transfer of management know-how, export promotion and structural transformation.

Capital formation

The share of FDI in China's total domestic investment has been rising since 1985, though it remains clearly lower than domestic financing (see Table 3.4). Thus we may conclude that foreign capital has not played a dominant role

Table 3.4   China's total domestic investment in fixed assets by financing sources, %

Year	State budget	Domestic loans	Foreign investment	Fundraising	Others
1985	16.0	20.1	3.6	60.3	–
1990	8.7	19.6	6.3	52.4	13.1
1995	3.1	21.0	11.5	53.2	13.8
1998	4.2	19.5	9.2	52.3	15.8

Note: Foreign investment includes not only FDI but also all other increases of fixed assets initially constructed by foreign funds.

Source: *Statistical Yearbook of China*, various issues.

in China's capital formation. It must be noted, however, that foreign capital often triggers domestic investment. Domestic investment, in turn, stimulates foreign direct capital inflows, since developed infrastructure is one of the important requirements for FDI. FDI is usually drawn to regions where infrastructure is relatively developed. Local government authorities in China set up economic development zones to attract foreign capital. Once foreign capital arrives at these zones, local capital has an incentive to start a new business, for instance as a supplier to the FIEs. In other words, domestic and foreign investment are complementary rather than substitutional.

Technology transfer

China has imported technology from abroad through various channels, first by setting up complete plants, by acquiring technical licenses, by introducing technical services, by technical consulting, or by engaging in Sino-foreign joint production ventures. These different forms of technology imports are connected to FDI in one way or other. The relation is particularly strong in the case of plant imports. Second, China has introduced new foreign technology, either through governmental agencies and other official routes or through private foreign investors. As Xu (1997) points out, since 1992 private enterprises, not the government, have become the major player of importing foreign technology to China. Third, with the end of the Mao regime, China gradually began to understand the concept of patents and know-how and the importance of the 'invisible' parts of technology, even paying the costs for the know-how involved in technological imports. Undeniably, foreign capital has brought in relatively advanced technology to China. According to a questionnaire survey conducted by Jiang and Feng (2000), 42.1 per cent of foreign high-tech firms in Beijing employ 'relatively advanced' technology viewed even from their parent companies' standard, and 26.2 per cent of them utilize 'the most advanced' one, even if only partially in products and manufacturing processes.

Transfer of management know-how

FDI is often said to be a form of transfer of managerial resources from one country to another. Along with capital flows, more advanced management methods are also transferred. When they are introduced to a firm in China, they can be easily assimilated and transmitted to other Chinese firms, usually at no cost. For example, the concept of the 'Japanese system of management' – comprising elements such as total quality control (TQC) and *kaizen* – has been transferred to China. Hao (1999) analyses how Chinese television companies, both state-owned and joint ventures, have tried to import the Japanese style of management together with hard technology and have adapted the concept to the local Chinese environment.

Export promotion

As implied by the above growth and FDI regressions, inward FDI is closely linked to China's exports. Therefore, under the export-oriented strategy, other things being equal, the more outward looking a country is, the more rapidly it grows. China has followed such an outward looking policy as was previously employed by other Asian economies. Balasubramanyam, Salisu and Sapsford (1996) have tested Bhagwati's hypothesis that FDI's growth-enhancing effects are more significant for nations under the export promotion strategy rather than under an import substitution regime. Their finding is that this hypothesis is corroborated by cross-country data from 46 nations. Nakagane takes up a well-known theme in development economics, asking whether trade is an 'engine' or a 'handmaiden' of growth, applying Shims' causality test to the Chinese experiences of economic development during the period of 1978–95. Export volume data supports the handmaiden hypothesis; but when one looks at the growth rate of exports, both hypotheses cannot be denied – a two-way causality can be identified (Nakagane 1999, pp. 295–7).

Structural transformation

FDI affects China's economic development not only in terms of the four effects mentioned above, but also in a more indirect way. We can call it the reform effect of foreign capital inflows. No doubt, China's open-door policy has prompted its economic reform as well as its industrial transformation. Therefore, FDI has changed both the industrial and the systemic structure in China. Guo (2000) insists that FDI in China has been concentrated too much in the manufacturing sector, therefore it should be induced more to the relatively underdeveloped service industries, grading up China's industrial structure. In the same vein, the more widely and deeply opened areas have made their industries more efficient. Perkins (1996) found that the TFP (total factor productivity) of FIEs, particularly if they are export-oriented, is remarkably higher than the TFP of other types of firms in China. At the same time, the more FDI is attracted, the more successfully the benefited industries grow out of the planned into the market economy. It goes without saying that the further China succeeds in transforming its structure, the more highly it will be able to raise the growth rate.

Other effects of FDI on China's development

Although FDI has had very positive effects on China's economic growth, there are two sides of the coin. FDI has also contributed to the widening of regional disparity and income distribution, and the experience of China's economic development shows that the regional disparity has been worsening along with foreign capital inflows. Sun and Chai (1998) applied a simple regression analysis for provincial data for the period 1986–93 and found that the growth enhancing effect of FDI was significantly different among provinces; effects were remarkably larger in coastal regions than in the interior. FDI is also known for its agglomeration effects; the more FDI is accumulated in specific regions – the coastal provinces and cities in the case of China – the more investment is agglomerated in the same regions.

And what attracts foreign capital is not only confined to the existing accumulated capital; major investment motivates low wages, tax incentives or other inducements to foreign investors such as import duty reductions, and relaxed rules on labour management. Head and Ries (1996) analysed 54 Chinese cities and 931 foreign-funded equity joint ventures and determined that not only existing capital – domestic or foreign – but also incentive zones and transportation development are effective in attracting foreign investment. Furthermore, they discovered that low wages are not necessarily associated with FDI locations within China. Cheng and Kwan (2000), on the other hand, found that wage costs have quite a negative effect on FDI. They insist that labour productivity is more important for foreign capital's regional distribution.

Japan's FDI and China's growth

What motivates Japanese enterprises to invest in China? What is the major objective of their FDI to China? Are their motives in China the same as in other countries? These questions can be answered by either a direct or an indirect approach. On the one hand, the actual or the potential investors from Japan can be queried. On the other hand, motives can be ascertained indirectly by estimating macroeconomic FDI functions for Japan's investment in China.

Subjective motives of direct investment by Japanese firms in China

There are two systematic surveys at the firm level on Japanese investment in China. One is conducted by the Japan China Investment Promotion Organization, a private organization established under the Nitchû Keizai Kyôkai

(Japan-China Economic Association), which promotes Japanese investment in China and tries to settle investment conflicts. This association has carried out interview surveys (hereafter JCIPC surveys) on the management situation of Japanese firms operating in China almost every two years since 1990. The other type of survey is carried out by the Japan Bank for International Cooperation (formerly Japan Bank for Export and Import) which has conducted regularly systematic surveys on foreign investment and its prospects by Japanese manufacturing enterprises every year since 1989 (hereafter JBIC surveys). The JBIC survey of 1999 is summarized in Table 3.5.

The table indicates that Japanese FDI is generally market-related, be it safeguarding existing markets, opening up new markets in host countries or exporting to third countries. Investment in China is no exception. However, when it comes to Japanese FDI in developing countries such as China and Southeast Asia, utilizing cheap labour and exporting their products to Japan are the most important investment purposes next to market-related ones. In other words, Japanese companies decide to invest in China, not only to open and expand their product markets, but also to enjoy the comparative advantage derived from the local factor endowment. This finding is supported by the JCIPC survey as well. However, there is a different result from a survey on about 100 FIEs in China by Du Pont. According to his survey, investors from Japan, the USA, Sweden and Germany are more motivated by demand-side factors such as China's domestic market size and market potential. On the other hand, firms from Taiwan, Hong Kong, South Korea and Singapore are more export-oriented, and are more motivated by production-related considerations such as reducing production costs and the supply of cheap labour (Du Pont, 2000, p. 187). The latter result is partly due to the focus on four specific industries, namely agriculture and food processing, motor vehicles,

Table 3.5 Motives of Japanese FDI in 1999 by host region, %

Motives	China	ASEAN-4	USA/Canada	EU	Average
Maintenance and expansion of existing markets	68.8	64.4	74.5	70.6	67.1
Opening up a new market	48.4	42.4	45.5	45.1	44.3
Export to third countries	20.3	35.6	9.1	5.9	18.0
Development of goods suited to host countries	14.1	16.9	21.8	19.6	15.8
Utilization of cheap labour	29.7	33.9	0	0	15.5
Supply of parts to assembly makers	14.1	23.7	18.2	15.7	15.5
Overseas dispersion of production sites	14.1	27.1	10.9	9.8	14.9
Export to Japan	23.4	25.4	5.5	2.0	13.6

Note: Figures indicate percentage of investment purposes based on multiple answering methods.
Source: JBIC (2000).

cement and paper. If more labour-intensive industries such as electric appliances had been included in the survey, Japanese investors might have responded more actively to cheap labour considerations.

Estimated functions of Japanese FDI in China

On the basis of earlier studies on Japanese outward FDI, for example Akyüz (1998) and Inaba (1999), and building on the estimates of China's inward FDI derived above, we construct our own estimates of macroeconomic functions of Japan's FDI in China, though in a very simplified form. The following variables can be explanatory variables for Japanese FDI in China:

- the wage differential between Japan and China;
- market size and future prospects of the Chinese economy;
- openness or restrictions on trade and FDI; and
- other Japan and/or China-specific factors.

We employ a trial-and-error approach and estimate relatively simple functions of Japan's investment in China for the period 1983–98. Two types of FDI variables are regressed on several explanatory variables, namely the number of projects invested and the total investment value, both in figures as reported to the Japanese MOF. One of the best results is as follows:

$$FDIno = -678.108 + 24.104Growth + 11.423WDr \qquad (3.4)$$
$$(-3.23)*** \qquad (1.95)* \qquad (4.51)***$$
$$\text{Adjusted } R^2 = 0.588, \ DW = 1.353$$

where *FDIno* is the number of Japanese investment projects reported; *Growth* is China's GDP growth rate, which not only indicates the expanding size of the Chinese market but also represents the degree of attractiveness of its future prospects for Japanese investors; and *WDr* is the relative wage of the Japanese manufacturing sector *vis-à-vis* the Chinese one, which implies the improved cost structure or comparative advantage of FDI in China. (Better results can be obtained, however, if a variable of nominal and absolute wage gaps is employed instead.)

If we add another variable, that is openness as measured by the ratio of export to GDP (*Open*) to the above regression, the result changes somewhat as follows:

$$FDIno = -763.065 + 28.242Growth + 6.724WDr + 22.225Open \qquad (3.5)$$
$$(-4.01)*** \qquad (2.54)** \qquad (2.14)* \qquad (2.13)*$$
$$\text{Adjusted } R^2 = 0.676, \ DW = 2.108$$

Several important implications can be derived from the above results. First, regressions (3.4) and (3.5) seem to indicate that Japanese investors have always had at least two motives for their investment in China. Contrary to Du Pont's observation, they have been strongly attracted by lower wages in

China, particularly after the drastic appreciation of the yen in the late 1980s. But China's expanding market as well as seemingly bright future prospects have been major motivations, too. In this sense, Japan's investment in China follows the same popular motives as FDI from other source countries. There is, however a difference in the agglomeration effects caused by inward FDI. Ding (1998) found that Japanese FDI in China, in general, and in the textile and apparel industry in particular, demonstrates stronger agglomeration effects than does US FDI in China. In the case of the electronics and electric machinery industry, he concludes that the American presence in a region increases the possibility that Japanese investors select the same region for their investment site. Ding, for example, looked at agglomeration effects of Japanese and US investment in China, based on the conditional logit analysis following Head and Ries (1996).

Second, the openness of the Chinese economy has also been conducive to Japanese capital inflows. This conclusion, too, is consistent with almost all China FDI functions that have been tested so far. China's open-door policy, that is reducing trade restrictions and giving preferential incentives for foreign investors, has definitely promoted FDI inflows.

Third, if, however, the value of capital investment (*FDIvalue*) is chosen as a dependent variable in the equation instead of the number of investment projects (*FDIno*), the result changes:

$$FDIvalue = -1968.73 + 44.014 Growth + 46.816 WDR \qquad (3.6)$$
$$(-1.43) \qquad (0.54) \qquad (2.82)^{**}$$
$$\text{Adjusted } R^2 = 0.289,\ DW = 0.742$$

Compared to regression (3.4), both the significance levels of the regression coefficients and the fitness of the model (R^2) decline. Moreover, the *DW* ratio is so low that a positive serial correlation may exist in the model as in regression (3.1). In addition, the growth rate does not significantly affect *FDIvalue*. This fact seems to imply that the principal decisions taken by Japanese investors as to whether or not to invest in China are basically determined by the above factors, that is China's growth rate, the wage differentials and China's openness, but the amount of Japanese investment is probably determined by other considerations. This result may be interpreted with respect to the fact that the majority of Japanese investors in China are small enterprises. When China's economy was booming, these small investors crowded in.

Fourth, if the value of Japan's investment is regressed on the same three explanatory variables as in regression (3.2), that is growth rate, wage differential and openness, then the result would differ again:

$$FDIvalue = -2696.42 + 79.461 Growth + 6.562 WDr + 190.368 Open \qquad (3.7)$$
$$(-2.52)^{**} \qquad (1.27) \qquad (0.37) \qquad (3.25)^{**}$$
$$\text{Adjusted } R^2 = 0.590,\ DW = 1.649$$

Obviously, the model's fitness is improved, while the wage differential variable loses statistical significance. We can say that the relative wage cannot explain the variation of Japanese investment in China in its value. *FDIvalue* is mostly explained by China's openness, which is a proxy for exports. Thus we may infer that the total value of Japanese FDI in China is largely affected by China's exportability, which is in keeping with Japanese investors' motives, as we have noted above.

The results derived above reveal the robustness of certain explanatory variables. Whether Japanese FDI is measured by its quantity or its value, it is strongly influenced by China's openness. Neither growth nor wage differentials alone can fully explain the direction of the Japanese capital outflows to China.

Last but not least, it must be acknowledged that the above analyses are of quite limited and tentative nature. It is true that there are many variables that should be added to our equations. For example, we have not considered the Japanese economic growth rates as one of the key factors that determine foreign capital outflows from the supply side. No attention has been paid to the exchange rate effects involved in Japanese FDI abroad, either. Certain policies by China such as regulations or incentives for foreign capital, and factors affecting capital supply by Japan such as hardening of environmental restrictions, are to be considered. In addition, industry and area-specific FDI functions are in need of future research.

Future Sino–Japanese FDI relationships

Thus far we have reviewed and analysed how FDI has affected China's economic development. Based on our tentative models as well as on other studies, a rough picture that portrays the structural relationship between economic growth, exports and FDI for the Chinese economy (see Figure 3.2) can be drafted.

As the figure illustrates, a dynamic relationship exists among these three factors within the Chinese economy. Given the huge disparities in wages between China and Japan, the expanding market in China would attract more and more Japanese (and other foreign) capital. The foreign capital contributes to China's increasing exports and economic growth, which in turn stimulates even more capital inflows to China. Yet this process is not endless and eternal. Consider the following case. If China's economic growth came to a halt, for example because of a failure in its systemic transformation process or because of a WTO supply shock, the virtuous cycle could be weakened or even vanish. If Japanese (and other foreign) investors thought that the Chinese market was unfair and distorted by frequent government intervention, they would cease to bring further capital to China, so that China's economic growth could be affected seriously. Thus a vicious cycle could arise centring on growth, FDI and exports.

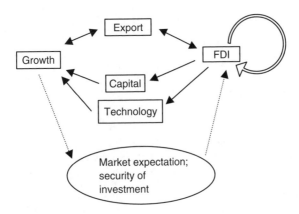

Figure 3.2 Dynamic relations among growth, export and self-reinforcing effects

The model depicted in Figure 3.2 is subject to an important premise that Chinese development strategy is basically export-oriented. Under an export-oriented strategy, quite a number of foreign investors, particularly from Hong Kong, Taiwan and Japan, have set up factories in coastal regions, and manufacture exportable labour-intensive commodities. Such export-processing trade has been vigorously promoted in China, particularly in incentive areas like the Special Economic Zones. But the Chinese government is now revising its development strategy and is turning its focus more inward in order to build up a more domestic, demand-oriented economy. Foreign capital is being more carefully selected in order to build up a more ideal economic structure; thus high-tech and other key industries are strongly welcomed, and investors from the USA and from Europe have followed this line of FDI policy change. This is one of the reasons why their China investments increased in the late 1990s, while Asian countries decreased their investment flows to China.

MNCs are restructuring their industries and enterprises, relocating industrial sites, and rearranging global relations with their trade and production partners. Many companies around the world now consider China a promising market for their products, an indispensable supplier of their parts, and still an important manufacturing base for the world market. China's entry into the WTO, of course, will promote the globalization of the Chinese economy even further. The increasing importance of China within the current globalization trends seems to have taught Japanese investors a lesson in selecting host countries. According to the JBIC survey, almost two-thirds to three-quarters of the enterprises surveyed consider China the most promising country for their FDI long- and medium-term points of view (see Table 3.6). The China share had temporarily declined in the late 1990s, but it rose again in 1999. It is questionable, however, whether Japanese

Table 3.6   The most promising country for Japanese FDI: positive responses in numbers

	1995 survey			1999 survey		
Ranking	Country	Enterprises	Share	Country	Enterprises	Share
1	China	215	78	China	170	66
2	Vietnam	113	41	US	77	30
3	India	98	36	India	71	27
4	US	83	30	Thailand	61	24
5	Indonesia	66	24	Vietnam	47	18
6	Thailand	66	24	Indonesia	46	18
7	Myanmar	40	15	Brazil	36	14
8	Malaysia	35	13	Malaysia	20	8
9	Philippines	31	11	Philippines	20	8
10	UK	16	6	Mexico	17	7
	Total	274	100	Total	259	100

Note: Based upon multiple answering method.

Source: JBIC Questionnaire Survey: JBIC (2000).

companies are gaining profits from their existing projects in China, and whether they will gain profits from their future investment.

Although the recent JCIPC survey reports that about 70 per cent of the surveyed enterprises are running profits from their China investment, their profitability is declining even though their sales are rising (see NTSK, 2000). Although their FDI in China is not necessarily profitable, they continue to invest there. It is not difficult to see the Japanese companies' ambivalent attitude towards future investment in China. The figures of profitability from China investment, however, have to be dealt with carefully. Kakei (2000, pp. 14–15) points out that the term 'profit' is quite misleading. If the salaries of Japanese managers were deleted from such profits, he says, the profitability of those firms would be significantly deteriorated.

With regard to FDI in China, Japanese investors have repeatedly asserted that numerous problems remain to be solved, in spite of the supposedly 'rosy' investment environment. According to the JCIPC survey report, many Japanese firms have, in particular, strong complaints about the unequal and arbitrary adaptation of the Chinese government's regulations and policies, about too many regulations, such as the government control of foreign exchange and of Chinese currency (RMB) borrowing, and about weak and immature laws and institutions in China. Other complaints are the frequent and sudden institutional changes, the opaque adaptation of institutions and the insufficient infrastructure.

On the other hand, the Chinese government and enterprises are dissatisfied with Japanese FDI in China. Japanese firms are criticized for their transfer of only low-level technology. Japan, they assumed, is afraid of 'boomerang' effects. Tang (1997), for instance, reported on his interview survey with

35 Chinese enterprises, which have imported technology from Japan, the USA and Germany:

> 60 per cent of the Chinese enterprises found that Japanese technology was easy to apply but less advanced; 40 per cent believed that it was relatively expensive; and 30 per cent believed that the terms for the transfer were harsh. (Tang, 1997, p. 197)

His conclusion is that 'Japanese enterprises are usually reluctant to transfer their advanced technology'.

Such criticism may be challenged. Japanese firms have also gradually, though more slowly than US and European firms, transferred their relatively advanced technology to China through FDI. More important, however, China still has a comparative advantage in labour-intensive products. As Kojima stresses, the transfer of technology suitable for the host country's factor endowment is most conducive to its economic and industrial development (Kojima, 1985, chapter 2). Furthermore, if more attractive measures were employed and a more favourable investment environment for the absorption of higher technology were provided, much more Japanese FDI embodying advanced technology would arrive in China.

As the complaints of the Japanese firms cited above illustrate, China is still lacking a sufficient infrastructure for foreign capital inflows. Subsequently, Japanese enterprises do not transfer their advanced technology to China because they are friendly, generous and cooperative to the Chinese, but because they expect a profit at least in the long run. Why did the NEC Corp. decide to set up its high-tech video tape recorder production in China? Why did Hitachi Ltd. decide to transplant its Digital Video Disk technology to China? These two companies probably reckoned that under the present leadership, the 'Chinese market card' will effectively stimulate the import of advanced technology to China. As the survey results cited above show, most Japanese firms do indeed expect profits from an expanding Chinese market. They believe that the opening Chinese markets will invite more and more foreign capital and generate increasingly hard competition with both global and domestic Chinese companies.

As trade and FDI generally contribute heavily to the development and the growth of the Chinese economy, so does Sino–Japanese trade and Japanese FDI in China. It can be expected that the Japanese economy will be linked increasingly closely with China, as Figure 3.2 implies. Thus the present picture of FDI relations between Japan and China is likely to change; China will continue to absorb more foreign capital, albeit selectively, and the country will become an economic giant next to Japan by 2025 latest. In view of these perspectives, the larger-sized Japanese firms will increase their investment in China, even though they suffer short-term losses in their China business. They will widen and deepen the horizontal division of labour between the two countries and create a more neatly interwoven network of global production involving all the Asian economies. At the same time, they will gradually adapt their main investment motives and attitudes. The importance of low wages and export benefits will shrink and the importance of the Chinese domestic market will increase. Thus more technology transfer will be involved. Put another way, the larger Japanese companies seem to have realized that they have to be more strategic in their investment in China, rather than seeking merely short-run profits. This situation will probably lead to a very delicate relationship between the two nations, which in turn will generate a new economic order within Asia and the entire world as well.

References

Akyüz, Y. (1998) 'New Trends in Japanese Trade and FDI: Post-Industrial Transformation and Policy Changes', in R. Kozul-Wright and R. Rowthorn (eds), *Transnational Corporations and the Global Economy*, Houndmills, Basingstoke: Macmillan – now Palgrave, pp. 279–317.

Balasubramanyam, V. N., M. Salisu and D. Sapsford (1996) 'Foreign Direct Investment and Growth in EP and IS Countries', *Economic Journal*, vol. 106 (January), pp. 92–105.

Bende-Nabende, A. (1999) *FDI, Regionalism, Government Policy and Endogenous Growth. A Comparative Study of the ASEAN-5 Economies, with Development Policy Implications for the Least Developed Countries*, Aldershot: Ashgate.

Chen, C., L. Chang and Y. Zhang (1995) 'The Role of Foreign Direct Investment in China's Post-1978 Economic Development', *World Development*, vol. 23 (4), pp. 691–703.

Cheng, L. and Y. Kwan (2000) 'The Location of Foreign Direct Investment in Chinese Regions – Further Analysis of Labour Quality', in T. Ito and A. Krueger (eds), *The Role of Foreign Direct Investment in East Asian Economic Development*, Chicago: University of Chicago Press, pp. 13–235.

Ding, J. (1999) 'Agglomeration Effects in Manufacturing Location – are there any Country's Preferences?' *Economia Internazionale*, vol. 52 (2), pp. 59–78.

Du Pont, M. (2000) *Foreign Direct Investment in Transitional Economies: A Case Study of China and Poland*, Houndmills, Basingstoke: Macmillan – now Palgrave.

Guo, K. (2000) 'Waishang zhijie touzi dui woguo chanye jiegou-de yingxiang yanjiu' [A Study of the Effect of Foreign Direct Investment upon China's Industrial Structure], *Guanli Shijie* [Management World] no. 2, pp. 34–45.

Hao, Y. (1999) *Chûgoku no keizai hatten to nihonteki seisan shisutemu* [China's Economic Development and Japanese Production System], Tokyo: Minerva.

Head, K. and J. Ries (1996) 'Inter-City Competition for Foreign Investment: Static and Dynamic Effects of China's Incentive Areas', *Journal of Urban Economics*, vol. 40 (1), pp. 38–60.

Hilpert, H. G. and K. Nakagane (2002) 'Economic Relations. What can we Learn from Trade and FDI?' in M. Söderberg (ed.), *Chinese–Japanese Relations in the 21st Century: Complementarity and Conflict*, London and New York: Routledge, pp. 224–46.

Inaba, K. (1999) *Kaigai chokusetsu tôshi no keizaigaku* [Economics of Foreign Direct Investment], Tokyo: Sobunsha.

JBIC (Japan Bank for International Cooperation) (2000) *Kaihatsu kinyû kenkyûsho hô* [Institute of Development Finance, Report] (January), Tokyo: JBIC.

Jiang, X. and Y. Feng (2000) 'Heyixing, yizhixing yu zhengce zuoyong kongjian: wais-hang touzi gaoxinjishu qiyede xingwei fenxi' [Suitableness, Consistency and the Room where Policies Function – An Analysis of Foreign Businessmen's Behaviour to Investment in High-tech Enterprises], *Guanli Shijie* [Management World], no. 3, pp. 46–52.

Kakei, T. (2000) 'Chûgoku tôshi zensen ijô nashi' [All Quiet on the China Investment Front], *Chûgoku Jôhô* [China Information], no. 185 (August), pp. 14–15.

KKJS (Kokusai Kinyû Jôhô Sentâ) [Japan Centre for International Finance] (2000) *ôbeikigyô no Ajia shinshutsujôkyô to honpôkigyô no taiô* [How Western Firms Make Inroads in Asia and How Japanese Firms Cope with it], Tokyo: KKJS.

Kojima, K. (1985) *Nihon no kaigai chokusetsu tôshi* [Japanese Direct Investment Abroad], Tokyo: Bunshindo.

Nakagane, K. (1999) *Chûgoku keizai hattenron* [Economic Development and Transition in China], Tokyo: Yuhikaku.

Naughton, B. (1996) 'China's Emergence and Prospects as a Trading Nation', *Brookings Papers on Economic Activity*, vol. 2, pp. 273–344.

NTSK (Nitchû tôshi sokushin kikô) [Japan–China Investment Promotion Organization] (2000) *Dai rokuji nikkei kigyô anketo chôsa shukei/bunseki kekka* [Results of compilation and analysis of the 6th survey on Japanese enterprises in China] (March), Tokyo: NTSK.

Perkins, F. C. (1996) 'Productivity Performance and Priorities for the Reform of China's State-Owned Enterprises', *Journal of Development Studies*, vol. 32 (3), pp. 414–44.

Shan, J., G. Tian and F. Sun (1999) 'Causality between FDI and Economic Growth', in Y. Wu (ed.), *Foreign Direct Investment and Economic Growth in China*, Cheltenham: Edward Elgar, pp. 141–54.

Sun, H. and J. Chai (1998) 'Direct Foreign Investment and Inter-regional Economic Disparity in China', *International Journal of Social Economics*, vol. 25 (2/3/4), pp. 424–47.

Tang, S. (1997) 'Sino–Japanese Technology Transfer and its Effects', in C. Feinstein and C. Howe (eds), *Chinese Technology Transfer in the 1990s – Current Experience, Historical Problems and International Perspectives*, Cheltenham: Edward Elgar, pp. 152–68.

Wang, Z. and N. Swain (1995) 'The Determinants of Foreign Direct Investment in Transforming Economies: Empirical Evidence from Hungary and China', *Weltwirtschaftliches Archiv*, vol. 131, pp. 359–82.

Xu, J. (1997) 'China's International Technology Transfer: The Current Situation, Problems and Future Prospects', in C. Feinstein and C. Howe (eds), *Chinese Technology Transfer in the 1990s – Current Experience, Historical Problems and International Perspectives*, Cheltenham: Edward Elgar, pp. 82–95.

Zhu, Y. (1999) 'Chûgoku no kokuyûkigyô kaikaku to Nihon no taichûtôshi' [China's SOE Reform and Japan's China Investment], *FRI Kenkyû Report* [FRI Research Report], vol. 45, pp. 1–36.

4
Implications of China's Accession to the World Trade Organization*

Deepak Bhattasali and Masahiro Kawai

Introduction

The ability of China to raise per capita income by over 8 per cent a year over the last two decades places it in a very small group of countries experiencing rapid economic growth. Rising standards of living, including lifting nearly 250 million people out of poverty, have been made possible through a factor-accumulation-based strategy that drew on China's immense labour resources, assisted by massive investments in physical capital and industrial infrastructure. Changes in incentives and organizations buttressed this strategy and resulted in rising total factor productivity (TFP) averaging nearly 3 per cent per year. In the 1990s, growth slowed, reflecting a combination of macroeconomic and external sector policies and intensified structural bottlenecks. The regional economic slowdown since the beginning of the Asian financial crisis has also had an adverse effect. Visible urban unemployment (estimated to be about 9 per cent of the workforce), factory closures, and massive excess capacities in industry, price deflation and a real growth rate that dipped to 7.1 per cent in 1999 are some of these signs.

China's desire to join the World Trade Organization (WTO), despite fears that increased competition from abroad would cause further labour market stress, stems from the belief that the net gains in economic efficiency, employment and welfare will likely be positive in the medium and long term. Its negotiating stance on specific aspects of the accession protocols has reflected its desire to backload many of the projected adverse impacts on

* This is a revised version of the paper presented to the DIJ–FRI International Conference, 'Japan and China – Cooperation, Competition and Conflict, sponsored by the German Institute for Japanese Studies (DIJ) and the Fujitsu Research Institute (FRI) and held in Tokyo on 18–19 January 2001. The authors are thankful to Elena Ianchovichina and Will Martin for discussions and data support, to Hanns G. Hilpert and other conference participants for stimulating comments, and to David Bisbee for editorial assistance. The findings, interpretations and conclusions expressed in this chapter are those of the authors and do not necessarily represent the views of the World Bank, its Executive Directors or the countries they represent.

employment and income. Underlying these positions is a temporal view of how quickly robust and self-sustaining employment creation will follow from the massive structural changes taking place in the economy. In terms of economic management, the key issue is the authorities' ability to maintain the momentum of growth with the fiscal stimulus programme until job creation accelerates, to provide social safety nets to alleviate labour dislocations, and to foster more balanced development in the Western Provinces.

This chapter examines the implications of China's accession to the WTO for its economy, from sectoral, macro and structural perspectives, and for its major trading partners and global competitors.

Four types of structural transformation in China

Four major types of structural transformation have been underway in the Chinese economy, each of which has profound implications for resource allocation, the distribution of income, and the relative emphasis currently given to specific aspects of economic policy. Briefly, these are:

- From a command economy to a market economy, a transformation that, *de jure*, started after the 'opening' of China in 1978. It has been marked by the progressive deregulation of prices and resource allocation decisions. It has also been characterized by a shrinking role for the state in economic activity. The share of retail goods sold at prices fixed by the state fell from 97 per cent in 1978 to 5 per cent in 1999; the share of agricultural goods sold at fixed prices fell from 94 per cent to 23 per cent; and the share of capital and industrial goods sold at fixed prices fell from 100 per cent to 12 per cent. Further, the share of the public sector in total fixed investment fell from 82 per cent in 1980 to 53 per cent in 1999. Similarly, direct funding of investment from the government budget declined from 30 per cent to 6 per cent over the same period.
- From an economy based mainly on agriculture to one based largely on manufacturing and services (see Appendix Table A4.1 for this trend). In 1980, agriculture accounted for 30 per cent of total output. This had declined to 18 per cent by 1999. The share of the workforce in agriculture fell over the same period from 69 per cent to 50 per cent. During the 1990s when the economy as a whole created 67 million new jobs, agriculture shed 31 million jobs, or roughly 3.4 million jobs each year. By contrast, services added 104 million jobs, or nearly 11.5 million jobs per year.
- From an economy with high-fertility and low-longevity, to one with a low-fertility and high-longevity demographic profile. The natural growth rate of the population has slowed from 1.2 per cent per year in 1980 to 0.9 per cent in 1999. Life expectancy rose from 67 years in 1980 to 70 years in 1998. The share of children (aged 14 years or below) in the total population had fallen from 35.5 per cent in 1980 to an estimated 24.9 per cent in 2000, while the share of the aged (aged 65 years or above) had risen from 4.7 per cent to an estimated 6.7 per cent over the same period.[1]

- From a relatively closed to a relatively open economy. While imports and exports used to be controlled by ten to sixteen state trading firms, external trade is now conducted through well over 200 000 direct importers and exporters (Ianchovichina, Martin and Fukase, 2000b). Although non-tariff barriers (NTB) distort China's trade regime, they are now estimated to have fallen to a tariff-equivalent level of 9.3 per cent, covering 33 per cent of China's imports. The average weighted tariff rate for the economy is now estimated to be 18 per cent; nearly three-quarters of imports come in at zero, or close-to-zero, tariffs. As a result, China's trade (exports plus imports) as a share of GDP rose from 13 per cent in 1980 to 44 per cent in 1999. With on-shore foreign currency deposits of US$ 128 billion, the second largest in the world after the United Kingdom, China's economy is more open than generally believed.

Any one of the above types of transformation could be expected to result in significant resource movements in an economy. In China they are occurring simultaneously. Given the nature of these transitions and the size of its economy, it is relatively easy to see that the resource reallocations that may be required as the country adjusts to a post-WTO accession world, while important, can only be small by comparison.[2] Equally, it is difficult to judge the net impact of many impending changes. This refers not just to obtaining parametric estimates of the effects of various factors, but also in judging the direction of change (or, in the language of the economists, the 'signs' attached to the parameter values). With a general caution, therefore, about relying excessively on numerical estimates of the likely effect of WTO accession, we also consider what the likely effects are, striking a balance between the quantitative results from a global trade model and the qualitative assessment of specific sectors.

Effects of WTO accession on the Chinese economy

In this section, we examine the likely effects of WTO accession on the major sectors of the Chinese economy in terms of likely employment, output and trade effects, and their broad implications for the economy as a whole and income distribution. However, to set the discussion in context, the section begins with a brief description of the trade liberalization measures that China is likely to introduce as a result of joining the WTO.

Main features of proposed liberalization measures

Since China applied for membership in the General Agreement on Tariffs and Trade (GATT) in 1984, it has been engaged in negotiations to enter into the multilateral trading arrangements that now characterize the WTO. Eventually WTO membership was granted at the end of 2001. Although the specific details regarding the agreements China has struck with its trading partners are still not fully documented at the time of this writing there is sufficient information in the public domain to construct a broad picture of the liberalization measures that will be adopted (Martin, 1999; United States Government, 2000; Addonizio and Bhattasali, 2000).

Table 4.1 summarizes the major features of the China–USA agreement reached in November 1999, which may be regarded as the core of the likely final agreement.[3] As the table indicates, China has committed itself to a broad menu of market access measures, some of which become effective immediately upon accession. In many areas, the range of liberalization measures agreed surpasses efforts made in many developed and developing countries. Even commitments to the most general of WTO principles, such as unconditional most-favoured-nation (MFN) treatment, national treatment and transparency will result in major changes in economic practices of China. In accordance with these general principles, for example, China will have to promptly publish all trade regulations and tariff rates, and use price-based measures such as tariffs rather than quotas, licenses and designated trading to restrict imports. China's obligations to more specific measures, such as reductions in tariff levels and time-bound phase-outs of trade-distorting practices, such as export subsidies and trading and distribution restrictions, will prompt further reform. Some will revolutionize the organization of business activity in China and the modes and intensity of government regulation. These include the requirements for transparency in the operation of state-owned enterprises (SOE), especially in their purchasing and sales, implementation of intellectual property regimes consistent with the Agreement on Trade-Related Intellectual Property Rights (TRIPS), customs valuation methods that are consistent with the Agreement on Customs Valuation, and judicial review of administrative decisions.

The major liberalization measures include:

- Full market access for foreign firms to distribute their products in China.
- Tariff reductions immediately upon accession, with further phase-ins over an eight-year period. For example, the average tariffs for all agricultural products will be reduced from 20 per cent in 1998 to 17 per cent by 2004, and the average tariffs on all manufactures will fall from 18.5 per cent in 1998 to 9.4 per cent by 2005.
- Bindings of all tariffs and elimination of quantitative restrictions (quotas, licenses and designated trading). A tariff-rate quota (TRQ) system will be established for bulk commodities (including wheat, cotton and rice), with quota quantities rising over time, and subject to tariffs between 1 and 3 per cent. Quotas and non-tariff barriers will be eliminated within five years (and most within two to three) after accession.
- More open services sectors, including finance (banking, non-bank firm financing, securities and insurance), value-added telecommunications, distribution and sales, tourism, construction, professional and business services, and audio-visual services.
- Immediate resolution of outstanding problems with sanitary and phytosanitary standards.

Table 4.1   Summary of important features of the China–USA WTO agreement

Sectors	Agreements
Agriculture	Average tariffs reduced from 20 per cent to 17 per cent by January 2004 A tariff-rate quota (TRQ) system established for bulk commodities, with quota quantities increasing over time, and subject to tariffs between 1 and 3 per cent Export subsidies on cotton and rice eliminated Foreign exporters given the right to sell and distribute their products directly to consumers
Manufacturing	Average tariffs reduced from 18.5 per cent in 1998 to 9.4 per cent by 2005; phased in linearly, with large cuts for automobiles, high tech products, wood, and paper Quotas and non-tariff restrictions eliminated within five years (and most in 2002–03) Foreign firms given full trading and distribution rights for imported goods
Services	*Telecommunications*: All geographic restrictions on services phased out in two to six years. 49 per cent foreign ownership allowed in all services on accession, rising to 50 per cent in some sub-sectors in two years *Banking*: Foreign banks allowed to conduct RMB business with Chinese enterprises after two years of accession, and retail business after five years. Non-bank firms allowed to offer auto financing on accession *Insurance*: Geographic and service restrictions phased out over three to five years. 50 per cent foreign ownership in life insurance and 51 per cent ownership in non-life insurance permitted on accession. Reinsurance made fully open on accession *Securities business*: Foreign firms allowed to hold minority stakes in securities funds, with shares rising from 33 per cent initially to 49 per cent after three years *Distribution and sales*: Foreign firms with existing domestic investments allowed to undertake wholesale business with a Chinese partner on accession. Foreign invested retail business permitted in a limited number of major cities on accession, and all quantitative and geographic restrictions removed by January 2003. Foreign firms allowed full access to import and export rights three years after accession
Textiles and clothing	Import quotas on China's textiles and clothing exports eliminated by end-2005, subject to anti-surge provisions through 2008.

Source: IMF.

Table 4.2 summarizes China's likely weighted average tariff rates with and without WTO accession. Despite considerable difficulty in quantifying the degree of protection in agriculture, rates of pre-WTO protection are assumed to be sustained after accession, because the bindings are estimated to be above the previously applied protection rates. For industrial products, average tariffs on imported manufactures that are subject to tariffs will drop from 24 per cent to 7 per cent. Rates of protection of beverages and tobacco, textiles and apparel products, and automobiles will fall dramatically. Overall, China's WTO offer will lower the average tariff protection on imports from 21 per cent to 8 per cent.[4]

On the export side, China will receive MFN treatment from many WTO members. The most important change will be the elimination of import quotas that fall under the WTO Agreement on Textiles and Clothing (previously known as the Multi-Fibre Agreement, MFA). This means that China will be allowed to expand its export of textiles and clothing without facing the importers' quota restrictions, starting at end 2005. This impact will be significant, given that China was excluded from the Uruguay Round Agreement on Textiles and Clothing. Most quotas for China's exports of textiles and clothing will be phased out over five years, and special textile safeguards

Table 4.2 Weighted average tariffs in China with and without WTO accession

	Without WTO accession (%)[1]	With WTO accession (%)[1]
Foodgrain[2]	0.00	0.00
Feedgrain[2]	6.03	6.03
Oilseeds[2]	4.16	4.16
Meat and livestock[2]	10.14	10.14
Dairy[2]	26.74	26.74
Other agriculture[2]	22.09	22.09
Other food	27.68	27.68
Beverages and tobacco	123.50	20.38
Extractive industries	3.59	1.26
Textiles[3]	57.10	9.39
Wearing apparel[3]	75.99	14.85
Wood and paper[3]	21.57	4.80
Petrochemicals[3]	20.17	6.94
Metals[3]	17.52	6.22
Automobiles[3]	129.07	13.76
Electronics[3]	21.69	3.44
Other manufactures[2]	23.53	6.74
Agriculture total[2]	17.09	16.88
Manufactures total[3]	24.27	6.95
Total	21.41	7.85

Notes: [1]The tariff rates are the stated rates on imports that are subject to tariffs. As many imports enjoy duty exemptions currently and are expected to continue to do so with WTO accession, these stated rates overstate the actual rates. The rates without WTO are for the year 1995. [2]The degree of agricultural protection is assumed to be virtually unchanged with WTO accession. [3]The table highlights the large 'offer' made by China on manufacturing protection.

Source: Ianchovichina, Martin and Fukase (2000b).

introduced under the agreement will be phased out over eight years (Rosen, 1999; United States Senate, 2000).

It is evident that 'preparing' the Chinese economy for WTO accession involves a large number of reforms, not just in the way business is conducted but also in the legal and regulatory frameworks in which they operate. Such preparatory measures will be most important in the services sector, which labours under considerable government restriction at present, and where the most important market segments are dominated by state monopolies. In addition, in sectors such as manufacturing and finance, rapid regulatory development is necessary as liberalization proceeds and competition in the domestic market intensifies.

Effects on the Chinese economy: sectoral analysis

We start with an assessment of the likely trends in the three major sectors – agriculture, manufacturing and services. The discussion below highlights the main expected effects in the short term as well as in the medium to long term.

Table 4.3 provides a summary of quantitative information concerning the medium-term impact of China's WTO accession on the values of output and wage bills in various disaggregated sectors of the economy. It shows the baseline values for 1995 and 2005 without WTO accession as well as pro-jected values for 2005 with WTO accession. The table draws on the results obtained by Ianchovichina and Martin (2001), who applied the GTAP model of global trade to an aggregated version of Version 4 GTAP database.[5] This database combines detailed bilateral trade, transportation and protection data accounting for international linkages between China and other economies and the 1995 input–output data accounting for intersectoral linkages within each economy.

In addition to such quantitative information, some qualitative informa-tion is also provided and assessed in this section.

Agriculture

With half the national workforce and nearly one-fifth of national output cur-rently, the degree to which agriculture will be affected by accession is of great importance. However, it is not an easy task to assess the impact on agricul-ture because of the lack of complete information and clarity concerning agri-cultural protection. In accordance with its schedule of commitments, China will lower tariffs partially on agricultural products upon accession, and phase in further reductions within five years. At the end of this period, it will lower its overall average tariff by more than half, and several non-tariff barriers will be eliminated. However, it will continue to maintain TRQs for several key agricultural products. It will continue to use a state trading system to restrict external trade in grains (wheat, maize and rice), soybean oil and cot-ton. Therefore, the effect on actual protection levels is difficult to estimate.

Table 4.3 China's output values and wage bills as a result of WTO accession: 1995–2005 (US$ millions at 1995 prices)

	Value of output			Wage bills skilled labour			Wage bills unskilled labour		
	1995	2005		1995	2005		1995	2005	
		w/o WTO	w/WTO		w/WTO	w/o WTO		w/o WTO	w/WTO
Foodgrain	63 277	92 575	91 436	0	0	0	18	22	22
Feedgrain	10 878	14 022	13 804	0	0	0	43	46	46
Oilseeds	4 014	5 315	5 311	2	2	2	196	216	216
Meat and livestock	72 163	126 285	130 832	9	14	14	719	1017	1059
Dairy	3 640	6 366	6 712	0	0	0	5	7	7
Other agriculture	74 656	114 373	111 984	7	10	10	920	1182	1157
Other food	34 773	52 334	52 786	26	23	23	122	80	80
Beverages and tobacco	29 370	53 071	33 423	6	6	4	42	32	20
Extractive industries	104 543	169 254	167 477	46	76	74	960	1487	1461
Textiles	83 176	142 729	156 370	107	113	123	654	492	535
Wearing apparel	40 319	63 301	146 560	260	266	609	1887	1368	3130
Wood and paper	45 034	91 689	87 320	64	82	78	384	347	328
Petrochemicals	203 375	418 545	403 902	165	190	182	879	715	684
Metals	128 942	303 917	291 668	108	141	135	607	560	534
Automobiles	25 668	74 335	24 693	4	6	2	22	24	7
Electronics	35 957	87 195	96 760	180	249	274	879	860	946
Other manufactures	243 018	563 073	548 006	977	1417	1369	5310	5452	5267
Utilities	81 236	165 072	163 447	7	7	7	19	13	13
Trade and transport	229 835	484 723	492 767	323	325	327	1422	905	909
Construction	131 809	326 756	328 205	–	–	–	–	–	–
Business and finance	88 115	180 283	180 724	409	517	515	594	531	529
Government services	81 983	151 668	152 406	276	431	431	180	199	199

Note: The expression w/o WTO means the case of no WTO accession and w/WTO means the case of WTO accession.

Source: Background data in Ianchovichina and Martin (2001).

Table 4.3 assumes that the same level of protection is maintained in agriculture in the medium term following WTO accession.

As with the other sectors, WTO-related liberalization will bring both obstacles and opportunities for agriculture. In the short run, the maintenance of a TRQ system will likely mitigate the liberalization pressure, and the persistence of international barriers to China's agriculture will prevent the full exploitation of benefits. In comparison to the case of no WTO accession, Table 4.3 indicates that WTO accession has a positive impact on meat and livestock while it has a negative impact on other agriculture. The net aggregate impact on the agricultural sector as a whole, while varying across provinces, will be slightly positive. Over the longer term, increased liberalization in China will accelerate the shift of agriculture away from areas of comparative disadvantage towards its comparative advantage. There is likely to be a more pronounced decline in the production of land-intensive sectors, such as grains and cotton, and an increase in the production of more labour-intensive agricultural sectors, such as livestock, fruit, flowers and vegetables. Liberalization of global agricultural barriers should augment this trend, as it provides China with increased access to other countries' markets in return for its remarkably large concessions.

Actual trade and output patterns, however, are affected by many more factors than just trade liberalization. Therefore, the degree to which farmers experience a change in income due to WTO entry will depend on many factors. For example, farming in China is increasingly a part-time occupation. To the extent that farmers have access to off-farm employment, which varies by province, they will be able to supplement farm incomes in varying degrees. Further, the international community has committed itself to liberalize textiles and apparel, which will benefit Chinese farmers in these sectors. These additional employment opportunities will increase farmers' income, thereby mitigating the negative impact of WTO entry on some inefficient sub-sectors within agriculture.

All of this points to the need to take a comprehensive view of WTO accession effects. Some quantitative estimation of economy-wide effects has yielded indicative results of the magnitude and direction of change. One caution is that the incomplete information base and sometimes unavoidably crude assumptions on which such modelling exercises were conducted suggest the potential for a wide margin of errors in terms of the quantitative estimates of the WTO accession impact.[6] Nonetheless, the models suggest that the use of TRQ could provide transitional protection to farmers, as the quotas are likely to fill quickly (after which tariffs at high levels come into play).

For specific products, the likely outcomes are as follows:

- Wheat – per capita wheat consumption in China is as high as in many developed countries. It is likely, therefore, that the growth of wheat consumption will be modest. Production levels have fallen in recent years, given a sharp drop in prices. China now sees net import levels of seven to eight million tons per year. Changes in domestic consumption patterns suggest that the substitution of home-grown wheat with imports is likely, so production can be expected to fall and imports expand.

- Maize – domestic prices for maize have also fallen, but are still above international prices. High-cost maize production has been sustained by active government procurement policies, motivated by food security considerations. Lately, domestic production has fallen back from the record levels achieved in 1998, but China is a net exporter of maize. This may not last, however, as large procurements have taken their toll on government finance, and the overhang of government and private stocks continues to depress the price. Further production declines are likely. As four-fifths of maize is used as feed in the livestock industry, which continues to experience strong domestic and regional growth, imports are projected to rise. Again, the TRQ is expected to bind quickly, offering some transitional protection to production of this crop.
- Rice – domestic prices are low relative to those in international markets, and have been falling. The quota under the TRQ established for rice is fairly large, and surpasses by far the historic levels of rice imports in China. As such, it is unlikely that the TRQ for rice will bind. Nevertheless, given China's low prices, WTO accession is unlikely to have a negative effect on farmers. In fact, with increased trade liberalization globally, China could expand its exports of rice, resulting in higher returns for rice producers.
- Soybeans – there is no TRQ for soybeans, and the domestic price is close to border prices. Although there is little direct import competition for soybeans, there will be competitive pressure from the maize sector after accession. Maize, protected by TRQ, is the primary crop that competes with soybeans for resources. As maize imports exceed the TRQ, their prices could soar to about 165 per cent of the import price, while soybeans prices are likely to remain at international levels.

In sum, the short-run effect of WTO entry on agriculture is likely to be small. The observed and projected declines in crop production will not have a visibly adverse effect on agriculture, because farm incomes could well rise once the TRQ bind.[7] Over the long run, as China further liberalizes its market and the quota size increases, trade patterns should increasingly mirror China's comparative advantage. China has a low ratio of capital stock and of arable land relative to labour. As China has liberalized its economy over the past several years, its external trade patterns have increasingly followed its comparative advantage. Even while the share of agriculture in China's total trade has fallen from above 20 per cent two decades ago to below 8 per cent in 1999, traded agricultural products increasingly consist of labour-intensive exports and land-intensive imports. For example, horticultural and animal products, which are labour intensive, have steadily risen in their share of exports from about 45 per cent to 78 per cent over this period. Over time as a member of the WTO, the share of land-intensive commodities in China's imports is likely to rise.

An important, and possibly beneficial, effect over the long run will be the inability of the government to maintain prices higher than international levels through the national procurement system. For example, if China produces more of any grain than is needed to meet domestic demand, it must either export the surplus or add to its stocks. Under the accession protocols, China has committed not to use export subsidies. Maintaining high stocks even at current levels is too costly for the public exchequer, which accounts for a procurement level that is well below the benchmark targets established since 1996. In this way, domestic prices must be reduced and converge to world market levels. If the grain trade is in balance, domestic prices cannot deviate significantly from border prices without an increase in imports, which when added to domestic supply would put downward pressure on prices. Thus, in the long run, an environment is being created whereby China's agriculture will develop along lines of its comparative advantage. This is welfare enhancing, and a significant resource use advantage that China will enjoy over other developed and developing countries that have chosen to protect their increasingly inefficient agricultural sectors.

Concerning the long-run impact on China's post-WTO agriculture, the studies cited in end-note 10 would suggest that after approximately five years following accession, the profitability of grain production, especially wheat and maize, would decline. This decline will likely reduce grain output, the incomes of farmers in grain production, and employment. Over a ten-year projection horizon, there will be a dramatic increase in grain imports, with rice being the exception, given its competitiveness in international markets.

Manufacturing

Several key characteristics of China's manufacturing sector make it apparent that WTO accession will cause greater impact here than in agriculture. Tariff rates on manufacturing imports that are subject to tariffs without duty exemptions will fall sharply from an average of 24 per cent in 1997 to 7 per cent within five years of accession (see Table 4.2). Within this total, tariffs on information and communications technology (ICT) products (for example, computers, semi-conductors) will be eliminated, compared to an average tariff of about 13 per cent today. Auto tariffs will be cut from 80–100 per cent today to 25 per cent by 2006. Auto parts will come down to an average of 10 per cent. Such changes could be expected to have a significant effect on FDI, especially when seen in the light of the proposed liberalization of the services sector.

As pointed out by Naughton (2000), manufacturing trade is characterized by a marked dualistic structure, that is, a liberal export processing regime and a protected trade regime. The incentive-based export-processing regime, which covers goods produced entirely for export and often dominated by foreign invested enterprises (FIEs), accounted for 48 per cent of exports in 1999 and 53 per cent of imports. Imports of intermediate inputs and capital goods are duty free. However, its domestic value added is typically below 20 per cent of export value. The trade regime for other products, which covers products traded mainly by SOEs and collectives, remains quite restrictive with high tariffs and non-tariff barriers, including restrictions on trading rights and distribution. A range of companies with trading rights manages such trade, and it is here that most of China's trade liberalization measures have been concentrated in recent years. Also, it is this segment of the trading regime that will bear the brunt of the post-accession liberalization of tariff and non-tariff barriers. However, the rationale for continuing with the existing export-processing regime will also be eroded with the general reduction of such barriers in China.

There is a distinct difference in ability between medium-sized and large-sized firms, when benchmarked to international standards. The former have typically operated in more competitive domestic markets, are fast-growing, have aggressively entered foreign markets, and, most importantly, have evolved flexible cost structures that permit them to compete.[8] On the other hand, the larger firms are far behind their global competitors, and the gap has been widening (Nolan, 2000; McKinsey & Co., 2000). Thus, despite their size, 'legacy positions', and the WTO transitional rules, they may expect wrenching competition in the medium to long term. Such firms dominate the electrical equipment, oil and petrochemicals, aerospace, metallurgical, chemical and pharmaceutical industries.

Since 1993, Chinese manufacturing has entered a period of severe retrenchment and restructuring, reflecting the effects of a policy-induced slowdown in the macroeconomy, high levels of domestic and foreign competition as trade liberalization accelerated, and the slowdown in the regional and world economy at the time of the Asian financial crisis. Large excess capacity exists in manufacturing but, due to the structure of the labour market, excess labour is still carried on the books of many firms. Profitability is low in most segments, including textiles, automobiles, beverages and tobacco, which are given high levels of protection. Except for a few sectors with solid market leaders, entry into the WTO can be expected to accelerate the process of consolidation in these industries.

In view of the above, further trade liberalization in the context of WTO entry will adversely affect profitability in several manufacturing sub-sectors and firms in the short to medium term, and will affect employment quite severely in others as well over a longer period. At the outset, some of the capital-intensive industrial sector such as automobiles, petrochemicals and metals will suffer, with additional labour unemployment in these industries ranging as high as 12 per cent of their existing workforce. A second tier of adverse effects is expected in the energy, processed food and pharmaceutical sectors, where a surge of competition from well-positioned foreign firms is expected. Foreign firms' market shares would likely increase most rapidly in this segment of the manufacturing sector. In contrast, the electronics sub-sector is expected to gain as a result of China's WTO accession.

A significant boost to the Chinese economy is expected to come from the phase-out of the WTO Agreement on Textiles and Clothing by 2005, which has substituted for the previous Multi-Fibre Agreement. As China is the world's largest textile producer and exporter, the potential gains are enormous. The growth of textiles and apparel exports has been slowed by the fact that, due to its exclusion from the Uruguay Round Agreement on Textiles and Clothing, it could not benefit from quota growth on the importers' side as much as other manufacturing countries. According to Table 4.3, China's wearing apparel output and wage bills will rise by 130 per cent. The textiles sub-sector will also expand.

Services

By far the most dramatic changes in China's employment, consumption and production structure are expected to come from the projected boom in the services sector following WTO accession. Although many services have grown rapidly since the government officially initiated promotional policies in 1992, there is large variability in the quality and cost of services. More significantly, measured services are estimated to be about 33 per cent of GDP, well below China's income comparators, although somewhat to be expected because of the lagged development of consumer services in socialist economies. In addition, there are large gaps in the provision of basic producer services.[9]

A fundamental reason for the underdevelopment of China's services sector is economic: a highly restrictive policy regime for services delivery that does not allow it to respond effectively to the growing demand for services. As most services are tightly managed and controlled by the government, the dominant services providers are able to operate with great monopoly power (for example, banking, insurance, telecommunications, passenger air transport, and railways). In other areas such as housing, health care, urban transport and education there is a strong emphasis on social welfare dimensions. This often results in high policy-induced barriers to entry and price regulation that seldom promote resource-use efficiency, product innovation or quality improvements, and often undermines desirable social welfare outcomes (for example in the areas of banking, insurance or healthcare). In addition, low rates of urbanization, labour market skills and mobility, and the development of Hong Kong as a major provider of services to Mainland China firms (mostly internationally benchmarked for quality) are also factors in the slow growth of services. The result has been inadequate and poor quality services accompanied by ever-rising prices.

China has promised far-reaching liberalization measures in the services sector as has been seen in Table 4.1, and these are expected to have a notable effect. A substantial liberalization of the financial sector is expected, with foreign banks allowed to conduct *renminbi* (RMB) businesses with Chinese firms and, at a later stage, with retail customers. Restrictions on foreign participation in the securities business, auto financing by non-bank firms, and the fast-growing insurance business will also be substantially reduced. With the foreign market shares in these sectors currently extremely small (for example, in mid-1999 foreign banks accounted for 1.6 per cent of bank assets), such developments represent potentially enormous changes. In the initial stages, foreign banks are likely to focus on servicing the RMB needs of foreign firms and a few domestic blue-chip enterprises. The scope of their businesses will be limited, however, due to the lack of a deposit base, retail networks, and the underdeveloped interbank market. The main risk to domestic banks is that their best borrowers can migrate to foreign banks, thus worsening the overall quality of their assets. Foreign institutions' entry into financial services will undoubtedly require major reforms on the part of domestic institutions and regulatory frameworks.

In the telecommunications sector, all segments will be progressively liberalized, including value-added and paging services, mobile voice and data services, domestic and international services, and, to a lesser degree, internet and satellite services. By far the most significant liberalization measures are those that will affect transport, domestic trade and logistics management, as China allows foreign entry into distribution. All restrictions on distribution services for most products will be removed within three years after accession.

The nature of services (for example, intensive customer interface, labour intensity, high domestic content) implies that the growth of this sector has direct and favourable effects on employment creation in the broader domestic economy. With improved labour mobility in the Chinese economy, both the efficiency and welfare gains are expected to be large. This may explain why almost all the credible quantitative models of the post-WTO economy suggest that the wages of unskilled workers in China will grow between 60 and 90 per cent faster than those of skilled workers, despite large-scale retrenchment in manufacturing and a secular decline in agricultural employment. Elements of the coming services revolution not captured in current analyses, however, include the level effect that liberalization and foreign entry can be expected to have on the entire cost structure of manufacturing and consumption activity in China, and the growth effect that the high-quality services content, especially knowledge, embodied in consumer and producer goods (as well as in other services) may bring about in the economy.

The role of foreign direct investment

One additional economy-wide effect is worth highlighting. There is at present a lively and interesting debate on the effect that WTO accession will have on the volume of and environment for FDI in China. Specifically, the question is whether the investment regime becomes rules-based, as opposed to the widely perceived 'relationships-based' regime that exists. Undoubtedly, entry into the WTO will require the amendment of laws, regulations and practices to align them with a number of international investment-related rules – the General Agreement on Trade in Services (GATS), the Agreement on Trade-Related Investment Measures (TRIMS), and the Agreement on Trade-Related Intellectual Property Rights (TRIPS). However, as noted by several observers, there are significant gaps in the WTO investment rules.[10] Therefore, our assessment of the situation would suggest that although FDI can be expected to increase sharply following entry in the WTO, this would be mainly due to increases in market opportunities. It is unlikely, therefore, that there would be a fundamental shift to a rules-based investment policy regime, not because of China's unwillingness, but the limited effect that the WTO has on investment policies anywhere.

Macroeconomic and social impact

Not surprisingly, trade liberalization is initially expected to have a negative, though modest, impact on China's aggregate output, based on IMF projections. GDP growth would be about 0.25 percentage points lower than the baseline a year after WTO accession, but thereafter exceed the baseline forecast by increasing amounts. Initially, the negative impact of trade liberalization on output would be offset partly by the expansionary effect of greater FDI and larger exports. After three years, however, GDP growth would be boosted by higher TFP growth as corporate restructuring and SOE reform begin to bear fruit, and later by an increasing boost from the textile and clothing sector as textiles and apparel exports are expected to rise.

Together with the initial, modest fall in output, labour-market pressures could increase in the short run, especially in the capital-intensive manufacturing sector and, to a lesser extent, in the agricultural sub-sectors. The released workforce needs to be reemployed in other sectors. Rural farmers on marginal land could be seriously affected, resulting in greater poverty. In urban areas, given the already existing labour market pressures, the scope for reemployment could be limited in the manufacturing sector until textiles, apparel and other emerging sectors begin to be active. Most of the manufacturing sector labour force to be released will have to be reemployed in the expanding services sector, which will mitigate the unemployment pressure.

Therefore, to the extent that labour dislocations emerge at least in the initial stage, WTO accession may exacerbate income distribution. The export-intensive coastal provinces will gain, while the inland provinces – which contain the bulk of grain production and capital-intensive SOEs – may not gain much, or they may lose. Rural–urban income disparities may widen. This requires further efforts to strengthen the social safety net and to foster regional development in the inland provinces.

Three broad conclusions that are relevant for policy can be drawn from the macroeconomic and social impact:

- WTO accession is unlikely to lead to significant pressures on GDP growth, aggregate employment, or the external accounts in the short run.
- If developments were markedly unfavourable – for instance, if FDI did not increase much or if labour dislocations were serious – GDP growth would be marginally lower (about 0.5 percentage points lower in one to three years after WTO accession), while the overall balance of payments would still be in significant surplus.
- In the initial period, before the beneficial effects of higher TFP growth and textile and clothing export growth are felt, there is a possibility of rising labour market dislocations, mainly from the capital-intensive manufacturing sector as well as the grain-producing agricultural sector.

Quantitative effects on the global markets

China's WTO accession is expected to have a significant impact on the competitive position of China and the rest of the world in the global markets in certain highly affected sectors and on their incomes. This section provides detailed quantitative estimates from a global market point of view by taking into account the likely effect of China's liberalization measures and the *quid pro quo* changes expected of other countries.

Sectoral impact in China: quantitative assessments

Table 4.4 summarizes the implications of the baseline growth scenario and the WTO liberalization scenario for China's share of world output, export and import markets at sector levels. It draws heavily on the results obtained by Ianchovichina, Martin and Fukase (2000b), who used the GTAP model of global trade (see end-note 5 for explanation of the GTAP model).

The table demonstrates the rapid growth in China's share of world output, exports and imports even in the absence of WTO accession. Changes in consumption patterns and costs in the world drive this result, which is noted by Wang (1997) and People's Republic of China (1998). Without accession, China's total share of world output is projected to rise from 3.4 to 5.3 per cent over the decade, its share of exports from 3.7 to 4.8 per cent, and its share of imports from 3.4 to 5.3 per cent. While the accession offer has almost no impact on China's share of world output, it has a large positive impact on the share of world trade. With implementation of the accession offer, China's share of world export markets rises to 6.8 per cent, and of world import markets, to 6.6 per cent.[11]

At the sectoral level, the overall impact of China's WTO accession on agriculture is limited. China's agricultural exports face a more restrictive international trading environment than do its manufactures. As pointed out by Martin (1999), on average China's agricultural goods face restrictions that approximate a tariff of 32 per cent in regional markets, compared to about 8 per cent for its manufactured exports. Clearly, with reciprocal arrangements

Table 4.4   Global impact of China's WTO accession on major sectors in China

	China's output as a share of world output (%)			China's exports as a share of world exports (%)			China's imports as a share of world imports (%)		
	1995	*2005*		*1995*	*2005*		*1995*	*2005*	
		w/o WTO	*w/ WTO*		*w/o WTO*	*w/ WTO*		*w/o WTO*	*w/ WTO*
Foodgrain	14.3	19.6	19.4	0.3	0.1	0.1	6.5	16.4	16.0
Feedgrain	8.3	10.6	10.4	0.7	0.1	0.1	3.2	9.2	9.1
Oilseeds	5.1	6.2	6.3	4.1	0.8	0.7	1.2	3.9	4.0
Meat and livestock	6.7	11.6	12.1	3.5	0.5	0.5	2.0	8.9	9.6
Dairy	0.8	1.3	1.4	0.1	0.0	0.0	0.2	0.6	0.6
Other agriculture	10.6	15.7	15.4	2.3	0.4	0.4	2.7	9.6	9.8
Other food	2.3	3.2	3.2	2.6	1.2	1.3	3.1	6.4	6.2
Beverages and tobacco	4.9	7.0	4.4	2.4	1.0	1.0	0.9	1.3	16.2
Extractive industries	8.1	12.3	11.9	1.7	0.1	0.1	1.6	9.1	8.5
Textiles	10.8	13.9	14.2	8.4	8.8	10.6	13.4	18.0	25.5
Wearing apparel	7.0	8.8	20.1	19.6	18.5	47.1	1.0	1.1	3.7
Wood and paper	2.4	3.7	3.4	2.2	2.6	3.0	2.6	3.9	4.6
Petrochemicals	5.0	7.6	7.1	2.6	3.1	3.4	4.0	5.8	6.3
Metals	5.5	9.0	8.4	3.4	5.5	6.5	4.2	5.8	6.6
Automobiles	1.9	3.8	1.1	0.1	0.7	2.2	2.0	1.8	4.8
Electronics	2.6	4.5	4.8	5.0	7.8	9.8	3.6	5.3	5.7
Other manufactures	6.4	10.4	9.8	5.5	8.1	9.9	4.2	5.9	7.5
Utilities	2.7	3.9	3.8	5.8	6.7	7.5	1.2	1.7	1.5
Trade and transport	2.6	3.7	3.7	1.7	2.8	3.1	2.0	2.4	2.2
Construction	3.3	6.2	6.1	0.0	0.0	0.0	1.8	2.8	2.7
Business and finance	0.9	1.3	1.3	1.9	2.5	2.7	1.5	2.0	1.8
Government services	1.6	2.4	2.3	1.0	0.6	0.7	0.7	1.3	1.2
Total	3.4	5.3	5.1	3.7	4.8	6.8	3.4	5.3	6.6

Notes: The expression w/o WTO means the case of no WTO accession and w/WTO is the case of WTO accession. The model assumes the presence of concessional imports in the form of duty exemptions.

Source: Ianchovichina, Martin and Fukase (2000b).

and emergence of better rules for world trade in agriculture, such restrictions can be expected to decline in size. In these circumstances, given China's large cost advantage in the production of fruit, flowers and vegetables, its exports may be expected to make major inroads into regional markets. In this connection it is useful to note the behaviour of foreign investors in agro-industrial fields, mainly from the region and chiefly from Japan, who have flooded into the coastal provinces of China since early in 2000.

The most important impact of WTO accession on China's share in world output is observed in beverages and tobacco (negative), wearing apparel (positive), and automobiles (negative). China's share in world output for beverages and tobacco declines sharply due to the fall in protection of these products, with the resulting rise in imports. China's share in world output for apparels rises dramatically because of the lifting of the burdens imposed by the quota restrictions on China's exports and by China's low cost structure in the industry. China's share in world output for automobiles declines sharply, as the current overcapacities will be eliminated by the removal of protection and the resulting increase in the size/scale of automobile firms. Not surprisingly, China's shares of world export markets for apparel, textiles electronics and other manufacturers rise dramatically due to WTO accession. There is scope for high-tech sectors to grow, as reflected in the expansion of the electronics sector.

On the import side, China becomes a much bigger market for its trading partners. Interestingly, China's import shares in the world market for textiles, apparel, automobiles and other manufactures are expected to rise significantly. WTO liberalization clearly expands opportunities for intra-industry trade in many manufacturing sectors, particularly in textiles, automobiles, electronics and other manufactures. In these sectors, even though the output shares may not rise significantly, both export and import shares rise implying that greater import demand may be export-driven. Important is the fact that greater intra-industry trade benefits not only China but also its trading partners.

Sectoral impact on Japan, North America, the EU and developing economies

Attempts are made to quantify the sectoral impacts of China's WTO accession on major developed and developing countries or regions. Tables 4.5a and 4.5b show China's real imports, measured in 1995 prices, resulting from WTO accession over the period 1995–2005, both by source and sector. The estimates suggest that China's entry into the WTO will provide the greatest benefits to exporters in the Asian newly-industrialized economies (NIEs – such as Hong Kong Special Administrative Region, Korea, Singapore, and Taiwan Province of China) as well as Japan and Western Europe. The benefits accruing to ASEAN exporters are not as large as those to Asian NIEs exporters. The imports with the largest increases are other manufactures, textiles, petrochemicals, metals, wearing apparel, and beverages and tobacco from the Asian NIEs, automobiles from Western Europe (members of the EU and the EFTA), other manufactures, electronics, and textiles from Japan, and beverages and tobacco from North America (the US and Canada). Note that the benefits to the US and Western Europe are concentrated in a specific sector in each case, i.e., beverages and tobacco and automobiles, respectively, while the benefits to Japan and other East Asian economies are spread across various sectors.

According to Table 4.5b, the aggregated impact on exporters in other developing countries is negative, though there are variations in impact across source countries. Though not shown in the table, South Asia is a large beneficiary by way of increasing exports of other manufactured products. In

Table 4.5 China's real imports from developed regions due to WTO accession: 1995–2005 (US$ millions at 1995 prices) (a)

Sectors	North America			Western Europe			Japan		
	1995	2005 w/o WTO	2005 w/WTO	1995	2005 w/o WTO	2005 w/WTO	1995	2005 w/o WTO	2005 w/WTO
Foodgrain	1276	3044	2972	310	874	855	0	0	0
Feedgrain	827	2218	2191	225	593	592	0	0	0
Oilseeds	109	353	364	2	5	6	0	0	0
Meat & livestock	238	1260	1436	98	558	636	33	141	158
Dairy	17	53	55	36	135	139	2	6	6
Other agriculture	829	3005	3118	48	178	186	10	26	26
Other food	544	1010	959	379	550	516	128	166	147
Beverages & tobacco	29	58	5202	11	13	1454	4	4	242
Extractive industries	141	1352	1416	156	1445	2159	32	283	754
Textiles	471	390	0	652	461	1060	3223	1265	7766
Wearing apparel	11	14	145	25	25	140	78	13	684
Wood & paper	1009	1194	688	553	555	1477	375	309	787
Petrochemicals	3560	4328	3423	2883	2339	2150	4388	2855	3520
Metals	924	647	1198	1384	1007	1311	4427	3046	2872
Automobiles	290	91	−259	1897	532	23478	1215	181	−1027
Electronics	1871	2186	1350	2614	2828	1195	3715	2956	8644
Other manufactures	5592	5435	3491	12944	13094	10462	15282	11331	24444
Utilities	0	0	0	0	0	0	0	0	0
Trade & transport	357	131	113	1005	359	301	107	31	22
Construction	2	3	3	254	253	233	0	0	0
Business & finance	809	805	712	2669	1738	1461	279	208	164
Government services	111	74	61	428	435	372	3	1	1
Total	19019	27651	28638	28571	27978	50182	33301	22824	49212

Note: The expression w/o WTO means the case of no WTO accession and w/WTO is the case of WTO accession.

Source: Background data in Ianchovichina and Martin (2001).

(b)

Sectors	Import source								
	Asian NIEs			South-East Asia			Other developing regions		
	1995	*2005*		*1995*	*2005*		*1995*	*2005*	
		w/o WTO	*w/WTO*		*w/o WTO*	*w/WTO*		*w/o WTO*	*w/WTO*
Foodgrain	13	48	41	368	828	794	33	83	85
Feedgrain	0	0	0	0	1	1	42	103	102
Oilseeds	1	3	2	0	1	1	34	104	108
Meat & livestock	88	498	498	138	717	804	223	1116	1298
Dairy	4	12	11	2	7	8	2	6	6
Other agriculture	115	482	439	832	2638	2695	833	3200	3376
Other food	244	389	322	1175	1708	1588	1432	2240	2168
Beverages & tobacco	151	213	6056	4	3	22	1	2	11
Extractive industries	107	476	737	1198	7942	6805	2990	22019	20647
Textiles	11181	11282	35735	489	368	1304	846	940	626
Wearing apparel	895	485	7010	6	7	34	21	49	377
Wood & paper	1831	1750	4668	1400	1595	2254	259	294	225
Petrochemicals	10445	11314	24889	695	621	786	3118	2749	975
Metals	4335	5254	12812	244	226	318	3050	2467	1493
Automobiles	265	86	−224	8	3	−8	295	94	−54
Electronics	3316	3685	5575	133	149	348	38	40	42
Other manufactures	15979	16930	52247	572	648	2140	1105	1530	3573
Utilities	95	92	62	0	0	0	3	1	1
Trade & transport	8897	6109	4401	88	44	38	323	180	169
Construction	40	40	32	10	15	14	99	98	93
Business & finance	351	222	139	135	113	98	347	349	318
Government services	79	61	38	12	32	29	294	840	793
Total	58433	59433	155491	7510	17667	20074	15386	38505	36432

Note: The expression w/o WTO means the case of no WTO accession and w/WTO is the case of WTO accession.

Source: Background data in Ianchovichina and Martin (2001).

essence, while the industrialized countries benefit from China's WTO accession by expanding exports to China, not all developing economies gain. Those that gain are the neighbouring economies capable of exploiting the trade opportunities with China through intra-industry trade in manufacturing including textiles and wearing apparel.

The impacts of China's WTO entry on the global shares of output and trade of developed countries (Japan, North America and the EU) at sectoral levels are summarized in Appendix Tables A4.2–A4.4. It turns out that China's WTO accession has a negligible impact on the total output and trade shares of Japan and North America in the global market, while it has a small negative impact on the EU's total trade share.

Japan's shares in the global output and export markets for textiles and electronics rise modestly relative to the baseline scenario of no WTO accession, while its output and export shares of automobiles decline. There is very little impact on Japan's import share at sectoral levels, except for agriculture which is expected to see some modest increase. The reason for the negligible impact is that China's WTO accession is unlikely to generate large-scale intra-industry trade in manufacturing for Japan, thus limiting its imports of manufactured products.

China's WTO accession has differential impacts on several sectors in North America. It has a direct positive impact on beverages and tobacco by expanding the output and export shares and reducing the import share. It has a negative impact on textiles and apparel by reducing the output and export shares and raising the import shares (for apparel).

It turns out that China's WTO accession leads to a contraction in Western Europe's textiles and apparel sector and other manufactures as their shares in the global output, export and import markets are reduced. Hence, Western Europe will not enjoy trade expansion in these sectors. There will be some boost to the automobile sector, however, by stimulating the output and export shares and cutting the import share.

The impact on other developing countries, particularly China's neighbours in Asia, is mixed (the estimation results are not reported). Taiwan Province of China is one of the economies that will benefit most from China's WTO accession. It will see a rise in the shares in the global output, export and import markets for textiles and petrochemicals, with the consequent expansion of intra-industry trade in these sectors.[12] Similarly, other Asian NIEs also see an expansion of its intra-industry trade in manufacturing with China. On the other hand, countries in Southeast Asia and South Asia will see a relatively large decline in the output and export shares in apparel. These sectors are the ones most adversely affected by China's WTO accession.

Impact on incomes of China and the rest of the world

Table 4.6 demonstrates income changes that are expected to take place between 1995 and 2005 following China's WTO accession.[13] The table demonstrates that the baseline changes in China's income over the decade are substantial (about 39 per cent) and that China will gain an additional 2 per cent, beyond the baseline changes due to WTO accession because the fall in its protection and the removal of the trade partners' barriers on its textile and apparel products improve the country's competitiveness and efficiency in resource utilization. Naturally, the largest percentage gain accrues to China among the economies in the world in terms of the net impact of WTO accession.

North America, Western Europe and Japan also benefit from China's WTO accession as they can increase the efficiency of resource use due to more liberal trade with China. The Asian NIEs, including Taiwan Province of China, benefit significantly because of their expanded exports of textiles and other manufacturing products to China and their engagement in intra-industry trade in manufacturing with China.

Interesting is the observation that the income gain for Japan is much smaller than for North America, Western Europe and the Asian NIEs. The reason is that the impact on Japanese income, including consumer benefits due to greater imports, is limited as Japan is not expected to deepen intra-industry trade in key manufacturing products with China, or with the neighbouring Asian NIEs, as a result of China's entry into the WTO. If Japan wishes to realize greater gains in income, it needs to invest more in China and expand the basis for intra-firm trade.

Other developing economies, mostly those in South and Southeast Asia such as India and Indonesia, that compete with China in third markets lose primarily due to the removal of quotas on Chinese textile and apparel products. Essentially these economies will experience a substantial reduction in the textiles or apparel sector, leading to a net income loss at least in the short to medium term.

Concluding remarks

This chapter has examined some of the issues associated with China's impending accession to the WTO. It has focused on likely developments in agriculture, manufacturing and services, as well as those in the aggregate economy. In the short to medium term, the changes that will take place from WTO accession are significant in themselves, but modest in comparison to the long-term resource reallocations that are taking place as a result of the ongoing socio-economic transformation in China.

On the trade side, the impact of China's WTO accession will depend on the phasing of the agreement, the interaction between tariff reductions and the elimination of quantitative barriers, the extent of other remaining trade barriers including local protection, and the magnitude of FDI. WTO accession will also have important implications for structural reforms underway in China. In broad terms, accession will add urgency to the further acceleration

Table 4.6 Net impact of China's WTO accession on income levels of China and other countries/regions, 1995–2005

Countries/regions	Income (US$ mn, 1995) (baseline), 1995 A	Income w/o WTO (baseline), 2005 B	Income w/WTO (accession) 2005 C	Net income changes W/WTO C−B	Impact of baseline (%) (B−A)/A	Net impact of WTO: from 1995 (%) (C−B)/A
China	713 567	1 290 265	1 318 887	28 622	80.8	4.01
Developed countries	22 141 335	27 381 493	27 401 201	19 708	23.7	0.09
North America	7 976 177	10 537 421	10 546 877	9 456	32.1	0.12
Western Europe	8 649 828	10 477 846	10 484 961	7 115	21.1	0.08
Japan	5 095 149	5 819 510	5 822 431	2 921	14.2	0.06
Australia & New Zealand	420 182	546 717	546 933	216	30.1	0.05
Developing economies	5 464 721	7 399 992	7 407 744	7 752	35.4	0.14
East Asia	1 447 568	2 029 513	2 041 975	12 462	40.2	0.86
Taiwan Province of China	280 853	457 624	462 815	5 191	62.9	1.85
Other Asian NIEs	624 308	861 972	869 791	7 819	38.1	1.25
Indonesia	199 799	249 702	249 531	−171	25.0	−0.09
Other Southeast Asia	342 609	460 216	459 839	−377	34.3	−0.11
South Asia	440 769	689 394	685 431	−3 963	56.4	−0.90
India	331 447	519 507	516 317	−3 190	56.7	−0.96
Other South Asia	109 322	169 887	169 114	−773	55.4	−0.71
Latin America	1 360 294	1 766 251	1 766 308	57	29.8	0.00
Brazil	700 697	891 545	891 514	−31	27.2	−0.00
Other Latin America	659 597	847 706	874 794	88	32.6	0.01
Middle East & N. Africa	848 233	1 126 061	1 125 701	−360	32.8	−0.04
Sub-Saharan Africa	319 542	429 908	429 985	77	34.5	−0.02
Eastern Europe and FSU	792 466	971 226	970 981	−245	22.6	−0.03
Rest of the world	255 850	387 640	387 364	−276	51.5	−0.11
Total	28 319 264	36 071 751	36 127 833	56 082	27.4	0.20

Note: The expression w/o WTO means the case of no WTO accession and w/WTO is the case of WTO accession.

Source: Background data in Ianchovichina, Martin and Fukase (2000b).

of reforms in the state-owned enterprise (SOE) and state-owned commercial bank (SOCB) sectors, spurring the development of the legal and regulatory framework necessary for a market economy.

There are several expected effects. First, at the initial stage, trade liberalization is likely to increase competitive pressures in some agricultural sub-sectors and major capital-intensive manufacturing sectors. Since these sectors account for relatively small proportions of exports and imports, the negative impact on economic growth will be limited. Though agriculture employs half of the labour force, the impact on the sector's employment will be small. As Chinese farmers begin to produce along lines of their comparative advantage, agriculture will become more efficient. Unlike most other developed and developing countries, the Chinese economy will derive major gains from avoiding the resource misallocation involved in subsidizing increasingly inefficient agricultural sub-sectors. In addition, diversification into high value-added agricultural products can also help labour-intensive exports.

Second, while manufacturing is also likely to develop along lines of comparative advantage, this process is likely to be slower due to the coexistence of a variety of adverse factors – sluggish giant SOEs, monopolies, and excessive and inappropriate industrial capacities – and more disruptive with regard to employment. In the short run, automobiles, machinery, petrochemicals and certain other capital-intensive sectors will be forced to adjust, with a large negative impact on employment. On the other hand, the elimination of the textiles and clothing quotas overseas, beginning in 2005, will result in a substantial increase in textiles and apparel exports. With textiles and clothing already accounting for 4.25 per cent of GDP, and 22 per cent of exports, the impact on growth and exports would be non-negligible.

Third, the employment and income gains in services will be significant, partly in response to rising demands for consumer services from the increasingly affluent urban populations, and partly from the reduction of the state's role in core sectors such as housing, health, education and personal services. But the main thrust of growth in the economy is expected to come from the expansion and deepening of producer services, chiefly distribution, logistics and financial services. There will be a considerable increase in FDI, which would be concentrated in finance (banking, insurance and securities), telecommunications and retailing. Once FDI in the distribution sector has been completed, there would likely be a further surge in imports, since the requirement that foreign firms use Chinese distributors has been a major constraint on imports.

Finally, as the effects of increased competition feed through into efficiency gains, higher total factor productivity (TFP) growth is expected. How fast TFP rises will depend on the speed with which supporting reforms in the SOE and SOCB sectors are undertaken and private sector activity develops.

WTO accession is clearly a net gain to the Chinese economy in the medium to the long run, with China's share of world trade expected to double. In the short run, however, the net macroeconomic effect on employment and output would be mildly adverse, which will be broadly manageable. It seems unlikely that GDP growth will fall sharply, or that there will be a major deterioration in the balance of payments. There could be some labour dislocations in certain sectors and a widening of income disparities that will require further efforts to strengthen the social safety net and to foster more balanced regional development. In the medium term, China's growth rates are expected to be higher due to greater efficiency in resource use and higher TFP growth.

Appendix

Table A4.1   Gross domestic product and labour force and employment by sector, 1980–99

	1980		1990		1999	
GDP (in billions of yuan, at current prices)	451.8	(100.0)	1 854.8	(100.0)	8 191.9	(100.0)
Agriculture [1]	*135.9*	*(30.1)*	*501.7*	*(27.0)*	*1 445.7*	*(17.7)*
Manufacturing [2]	*199.7*	*(44.2)*	*685.8*	*(37.0)*	*3 497.5*	*(42.7)*
Other	*116.2*	*(25.7)*	*667.3*	*(36.0)*	*3 247.9*	*(39.6)*
Construction	19.6	(4.3)	85.9	(4.6)	544.3	(6.6)
Trade	21.4	(4.7)	142.0	(7.7)	684.2	(8.4)
Transport and communications	20.5	(4.5)	114.8	(6.2)	446.0	(5.4)
Finance, public administration & others	54.7	(12.1)	324.6	(17.5)	1 573.4	(19.2)
Labour Force (end-year; in millions)[3]	429.0	–	644.8	–	719.8	–
Employed labour force[4]	423.6	(100.0)	639.1	(100.0)	705.9	(100.0)
Agriculture[1]	*291.2*	*(68.7)*	*384.3*	*(60.1)*	*353.6*	*(50.1)*
Manufacturing[2]	*67.1*	*(15.8)*	*97.1*	*(15.2)*	*90.6*	*(12.8)*
Other	*65.3*	*(15.4)*	*157.7*	*(24.7)*	*261.7*	*(37.1)*
Construction	9.9	(2.3)	24.2	(3.8)	34.1	(4.8)
Trade	13.6	(3.2)	28.4	(4.4)	47.5	(6.7)
Transport and communications	8.1	(1.9)	15.7	(2.5)	20.2	(2.9)
Finance, public administration & others	33.6	(7.9)	89.4	(14.0)	159.8	(22.6)
Unemployed[5]	5.4	–	5.7	–	14.0	–

Notes: [1]Agriculture includes farming, forestry, husbandry, sideline production, and fishing. Labour force employed in agriculture refers to those in the primary industry. [2]Manufacturing includes mining, manufacturing, electricity, gas and water. [3]Labour force refers to people within the working age range 16–50 years for men and 16–45 years for women, excluding military personnel, prisoners, and the disabled, and excludes unemployed rural labourers. [4]Employed labour force refers to social labour force that generates income including total staff and workers, employees in urban private enterprises, urban individual labourers, rural labourers and other social labourers. [5]Unemployed refers to unemployed labour force in urban areas only.

Source: National Bureau of Statistics, *China Statistical Yearbook*.

Table A4.2 Impact of China's WTO accession on major sectors in Japan

	Japan's output as a share of world output (%)			Japan's exports as a share of world exports (%)			Japan's imports as a share of world imports (%)		
	1995	2005		1995	2005		1995	2005	
		w/o WTO	w/ WTO		w/o WTO	w/ WTO		w/o WTO	w/ WTO
Foodgrain	22.9	19.3	19.4	0.1	0.1	0.1	19.6	16.0	16.2
Feedgrain	0.9	0.8	0.8	0.0	0.0	0.0	45.3	39.5	39.6
Oilseeds	0.3	0.3	0.3	0.0	0.0	0.0	16.6	15.1	15.1
Meat & livestock	8.4	7.5	7.5	0.3	0.3	0.4	17.6	16.9	16.7
Dairy	8.5	8.1	8.1	0.0	0.0	0.0	9.7	10.1	10.2
Other agriculture	11.7	9.8	9.9	0.3	0.3	0.3	8.4	7.5	7.6
Other food	23.7	22.0	22.0	0.8	0.9	0.9	12.8	11.8	11.9
Beverages & tobacco	22.2	20.3	20.6	0.9	4.3	4.0	7.0	6.0	5.2
Extractive industries	7.7	6.4	6.4	0.4	0.5	0.6	17.8	14.3	14.4
Textiles	12.8	10.9	11.5	5.6	5.2	7.2	3.7	3.2	3.1
Wearing apparel	16.7	14.7	14.5	0.4	0.2	0.4	11.3	11.1	11.2
Wood & paper	19.2	17.4	17.5	1.5	1.5	1.7	7.1	6.7	6.7
Petrochemicals	19.1	17.0	17.1	6.4	6.1	6.1	4.6	4.3	4.3
Metals	20.2	18.0	18.0	7.8	7.7	7.5	5.3	5.0	5.0
Automobiles	14.9	13.3	13.1	17.7	16.4	14.2	2.8	2.9	2.9
Electronics	31.4	28.5	28.8	14.2	12.8	13.4	5.7	5.7	5.9
Other manufactures	19.0	17.1	17.2	15.3	14.6	14.3	4.5	4.3	4.3
Utilities	12.8	11.5	11.5	0.0	0.0	0.0	0.0	0.0	0.0
Trade & transport	20.1	17.9	18.0	7.4	6.9	6.8	16.2	16.1	16.3
Construction	24.0	21.4	21.5	0.0	0.0	0.0	0.2	0.2	0.2
Business & finance	19.9	18.3	18.4	5.2	5.4	5.4	8.2	8.1	8.2
Government services	9.3	8.4	8.5	0.4	0.3	0.3	0.5	0.5	0.5
Total	18.1	16.3	16.3	8.6	8.3	8.2	7.7	7.1	7.1

Note: The expression w/o WTO means the case of no WTO accession and w/WTO is the case of WTO accession.

Source: Background data in Ianchovichina, Martin and Fukase (2000b).

Table A4.3 Impact of China's WTO accession on major sectors in North America (USA and Canada)

	North America's output as a share of world output (%)			North America's exports as a share of world exports (%)			North America's imports as a share of world imports (%)		
	1995	*2005*		*1995*	*2005*		*1995*	*2005*	
		w/o WTO	*w/ WTO*		*w/o WTO*	*w/ WTO*		*w/o WTO*	*w/ WTO*
Foodgrain	4.5	4.8	4.8	40.0	43.1	42.7	2.3	2.1	2.2
Feedgrain	44.1	43.3	43.5	59.8	63.0	62.9	3.8	3.6	3.6
Oilseeds	22.6	22.9	23.3	58.4	61.6	61.5	8.4	8.3	8.4
Meat & livestock	23.1	22.0	21.9	18.2	19.6	20.1	7.6	7.1	7.0
Dairy	20.6	20.9	21.0	3.6	3.9	4.0	4.6	4.8	4.8
Other agriculture	11.1	10.5	10.5	14.7	16.8	16.9	14.3	13.3	13.3
Other food	20.1	20.2	20.3	12.2	13.7	13.7	11.1	10.5	10.5
Beverages & tobacco	19.2	20.0	20.8	14.4	15.4	19.5	13.4	10.4	8.8
Extractive industries	21.1	21.1	21.2	10.9	11.2	11.1	18.9	17.7	17.8
Textiles	16.9	15.5	14.4	7.5	7.0	5.6	9.0	8.4	7.8
Wearing apparel	20.9	15.5	12.2	6.5	4.4	3.2	26.3	34.3	35.1
Wood and paper	28.3	29.7	29.8	25.6	26.8	26.3	19.4	19.8	19.6
Petrochemicals	20.4	21.1	21.1	14.9	16.6	16.3	14.3	14.0	13.9
Metals	20.2	20.7	20.9	12.5	11.7	11.6	15.7	16.8	16.5
Automobiles	28.6	30.7	31.4	24.2	26.5	25.6	30.8	32.7	31.3
Electronics	25.0	26.8	26.8	19.8	20.1	19.8	27.1	28.0	27.7
Other manufactures	24.2	24.2	24.2	18.5	17.8	17.2	21.2	22.3	21.9
Utilities	28.9	28.8	28.9	12.6	12.7	12.6	12.6	12.7	12.6
Trade & transport	28.1	29.2	29.2	17.6	16.7	17.0	14.6	15.3	15.2
Construction	24.8	26.8	26.8	0.9	1.0	1.0	2.0	2.2	2.2
Business & finance	28.3	29.8	29.8	27.0	29.6	29.8	20.3	19.9	19.7
Government services	29.4	30.1	30.1	19.7	14.7	14.8	13.2	14.7	14.7
Total	25.5	26.3	26.3	17.7	17.9	17.5	18.7	19.5	19.2

Note: The expression w/o WTO means the case of no WTO accession and w/WTO is the case of WTO accession.

Source: Background data in Ianchovichina, Martin and Fukase (2000b).

Table A4.4 Impact of China's WTO accession on major sectors in the EU

	European Union's output as a share of world output (%)			European Union's exports as a share of world exports (%)			European Union's imports as a share of world imports (%)		
	1995	2005		1995	2005		1995	2005	
		w/o WTO	w/ WTO		w/o WTO	w/ WTO		w/o WTO	w/ WTO
Foodgrain	4.9	4.5	4.5	24.6	23.5	23.3	18.8	15.6	15.5
Feedgrain	13.8	12.8	12.8	27.0	24.8	24.9	14.4	12.8	12.8
Oilseeds	6.6	5.6	5.6	10.2	10.1	10.1	46.7	43.0	43.0
Meat & livestock	30.1	26.6	26.4	47.8	45.1	44.6	47.6	41.0	40.4
Dairy	40.9	38.1	38.1	80.2	80.0	80.0	57.6	53.1	53.0
Other agriculture	16.0	13.6	13.6	28.6	26.0	25.8	47.5	41.2	41.0
Other food	26.3	24.9	24.9	43.2	40.9	40.8	41.2	38.1	38.2
Beverages & tobacco	29.5	28.4	28.9	69.7	68.5	60.0	39.8	42.0	35.5
Extractive industries	15.7	14.6	14.6	18.7	18.8	18.8	34.1	29.4	29.5
Textiles	22.1	19.6	18.7	40.5	35.4	29.7	33.7	29.0	26.2
Wearing apparel	23.3	20.3	17.6	27.1	17.8	11.7	44.3	37.4	35.1
Wood & paper	31.6	30.1	30.1	49.5	46.5	45.9	47.8	44.5	44.0
Petrochemicals	30.0	28.1	28.1	53.9	49.9	49.0	44.4	41.1	40.7
Metals	31.9	29.3	29.5	46.2	42.1	41.1	43.5	40.4	39.8
Automobiles	41.8	39.1	41.5	52.0	49.5	51.6	42.4	39.9	38.6
Electronics	21.0	19.8	19.7	30.1	28.2	27.4	37.6	34.6	34.3
Other manufactures	32.2	30.1	30.0	41.3	38.9	37.3	34.0	30.7	30.1
Utilities	33.1	31.7	31.7	71.9	69.3	68.8	73.2	72.0	71.6
Trade & transport	29.2	27.7	27.7	37.9	35.3	35.4	37.9	35.9	36.0
Construction	27.7	25.7	25.7	61.9	60.7	60.6	33.0	31.8	31.8
Business & finance	39.3	38.3	38.2	51.9	47.9	47.7	46.9	45.5	45.4
Government services	40.6	38.6	38.6	47.5	40.9	40.5	53.3	50.8	50.8
Total	32.0	30.2	30.3	42.5	39.5	38.5	39.9	36.6	35.9

Note: The expression w/o WTO means the case of no WTO accession and w/WTO is the case of WTO accession.

Source: Background data in Ianchovichina, Martin and Fukase (2000b).

Notes

1. The last census was completed in November 2000, but its results have not been made available. The figures for 2000 are estimates based on medium variant projections.
2. In conventional national output calculations, China's gross national product (GNP) in 1999 was estimated at US$ 980 billion, the seventh largest in the world. In purchasing power parity terms it was ranked second, with an estimated US$ 4.1 trillion, half that of the USA, but a third larger than Japan's.
3. China also reached an agreement with the EU in May 2000.

4. It is well-established that imports of intermediate inputs and capital goods are exempted from duty if they are used for export processing or for other export-related activities. As a result, the actual tariff collected is much smaller than what the stated tariff rates would imply. The pre-WTO tariff rates summarized in Table 4.2 are the stated rates on imports that do not benefit from duty exemptions and, hence, overstate the actual rates of protection. When we assess the quantitative impact of China's WTO accession we explicitly consider duty exemptions in the GTAP model. For the GTAP model see the following end-note 5.

5. The GTAP model (Hertel, 1997) is used widely for trade policy analysis. It is a standard global general equilibrium model that assumes perfectly competitive markets and constant returns-to-scale technology. A representative household that allocates disposal income between consumption and savings according to a Cobb–Douglas utility function governs each country's final demand. Land, labour, capital and natural resources in a country are fixed and fully employed, though they are mobile (except for natural resources) across sectors within a country. The returns to these factors of production accrue to the households (that is factor owners) in the country in which they are employed. Product differentiation among imports from different countries and between imports and domestic goods allows for two-way trade in each product category, depending on the ease of substitution between products from different countries. The GTAP model is solved in order to determine the changes in output and trade flows as a result of the proposed trade policy changes. The model maintains all of the restrictions imposed by static economic theory: global savings equal global investment and are allocated across countries in order to equate expected rates of return (without affecting capital stock); changes in consumer demand add up to changes in total spending; each country's total exports equal total imports of these goods by other countries, less shipping costs; and each country's income consists of consumption, investment, government spending and net exports.

6. Although there is nothing technically wrong with the models applied so far to the quantification of WTO effects, none of them are based on information regarding the actual commitments made by China. Several rely on heroic assumptions subsequently disproved by new data. See Wang (1997), People's Republic of China (1998), Rosen (1999), Huang and Chen (1999) Ianchovichina, Martin and Fukase (2000a, b) and Ianchovichina and Martin (2001) for some of the more useful estimates.

7. This assessment is in contrast with that of Zhai and Li (2000) who estimated that about 13 million workers would be released in rural areas over the next five years, mainly producing wheat (5.4 million), cotton (5.0 million) and rice (2.5 million). However, these figures appear to be exaggerated because their computation does not take into account: the protective nature of the TRQ bind; the low price of rice in the domestic market; the ease with which farmers shift their product mix away from those negatively affected by WTO accession towards those positively affected (such as non-grain, non-cotton crops, livestock, fruit, flowers and vegetables); and the availability of off-farm income-earning opportunities.

8. Some examples of such firms are the television manufacturers TCL Holdings Co., Ltd. and Konka Group, Ltd., the automotive manufacturers Qingling Motor Company, Ltd. and Brilliance China Automotive Holdings, Ltd., and Legend Computers LLC, China's leading manufacturer of personal omputers.

9. There are, however, serious measurement problems. Many producer services are wrongly attributed to manufacturing-sector value added. Although this is a common problem for national account statistics all over the world, it is especially troublesome in China. Firms in this country have traditionally performed a range

of functions in-house that in more developed or market-oriented economies would be delivered by specialized services sector enterprises (for example, sales, marketing, logistics management).

10. In manufacturing, there are no transparency commitments required for policies currently in place related to investment, nor are there any principles of non-discriminatory treatment or protection from expropriation without compensation. In services, the agreed performance requirements for the goods-producing sectors with respect to minimum standards of treatment, non-discriminatory treatment, transfer of funds or transparency may not apply. National treatment of foreign firms is only substantive in the GATS.

11. One important property of the baseline scenario is the rapid growth of China's output shares in the global market for almost all agricultural products. This is based on the assumptions of high rates of population growth (0.83 per cent per year), strong income growth (7.4 per cent per year), and high income elasticities of demand for agricultural commodities and food.

12. If Taiwanese firms choose to relocate production sites to China, however, Taiwan may not benefit in terms of output and export expansion as much at least in the short to medium term. Because of its comparative static nature, the current GTAP model does not capture the impact of additional FDI flows that may be induced by trade policy changes.

13. Strictly speaking, the estimates are welfare changes expressed in US\$ millions at 1995 prices. The estimates are derived from the GTAP model that incorporates duty exemptions (Ianchovichina, Martin and Fukase, 2000a and b).

References

Addonizio, E. and D. Bhattasali (2000) *The Impact of WTO Entry on China's Agricultural Sector*, Beijing: World Bank Resident Mission in Beijing.

Frazier, M.W. (1999) *Coming to Terms with the 'WTO Effect' on US–China Trade and China's Economic Growth*, mimeo, Seattle: National Bureau of Asian Research.

Hertel, T.W. (1997) *Global Trade Analysis: Modelling and Applications*, Cambridge: Cambridge University Press.

Huang, J. and C. Chen (1999) *Effects of Trade Liberalization on Agriculture in China: Commodity Aspects*, CGPRT Centre Working Paper No. 43, Bogor: CGPRT.

Ianchovichina, E. and W. Martin (2001) *Trade Liberalization in China's Accession to WTO*, mimeo, Washington, DC: World Bank.

Ianchovichina, E., W. Martin and E. Fukase (2000a) *Comparative Study of Trade Liberalization Regimes: The Case of China's Accession to the WTO*, paper presented at Third Annual Conference on Global Economic Analysis, Melbourne: Monash University, Melbourne.

— (2000b) *Assessing the Implications of Merchandise Trade Liberalization in China's Accession to WTO*, paper presented at Roundtable on China's Accession to the WTO, Shanghai: Chinese Economic Society and the World Bank.

Martin, W. (1999) *WTO Accession and China's Agricultural Trade Policies*, mimeo, Washington, DC: World Bank.

Martin, W., B. Dimaranan and T.W. Hertel (1999) *Trade Policy, Structural Change and China's Trade Growth*, mimeo, Washington, DC: World Bank.

McKinsey & Company (2000) *China in the WTO: What Will Really Change – A Perspective for CEOs*, Beijing: McKinsey & Co.

Naughton, B. (2000) *China's Trade Regime on the Eve of WTO Accession: Achievements, Limitations and Implications for the US*, mimeo, UC Davis.

Nolan, P.H. (2000) *China and the WTO: The Challenge for China's Large-scale Industry*, paper presented at Conference 2000, 21st Century Forum of the CPPCC, Beijing.

People's Republic of China (1988) *The Global and Domestic Impact of China Joining the World Trade Organization*, Beijing: Development Research Centre of the State Council.

Rosen, D.H. (1999) 'China and the World Trade Organization: An Economic Balance Sheet,' *International Economic Policy Briefs*, no. 99–6, Washington, DC: Institute for International Economics.

United States Government (China Trade Relations Working Group) (2000) *Summary of US–China Bilateral WTO Agreement*, Washington, DC: China Trade Relations Working Group.

United States Senate (Joint Economic Committee) (2000) *The US Economy and China's Admission to the WTO*, Washington, DC: Joint Economic Committee.

Wang, Z. (1997) *The Impact of China and Taiwan Joining the World Trade Organization on US and World Agricultural Trade: A Computable General Equilibrium Analysis*, Technical Bulletin no. 1858, Washington, DC: US Department of Agriculture.

Zhai, F. and S. Li (2000) *The Implications of Accession to WTO on China's Economy*, paper resented at Third Annual Conference on Global Economic Analysis, Melbourne: Monash University.

5
Japan's Role in China's Industrialization

Markus Taube

Introduction

In an historical perspective, Japan played a prominent role in China's industrialization process. During the Qing dynasty and the ensuing first years of the Republic, China failed to create a substantial industrial sector as Japan did in the same historical period (Kasper, 1994, pp. 30–2). The first time a Chinese region went through a modern integrated industrialization process dates back to the Japanese occupation of northeast China. During a period of nearly 20 years from the late 1920s until the end of Japanese presence in China, Japan invested considerable resources in building heavy industry in Manchuria (Lardy, 1987, p. 148).

Yet in the long term, Japan's efforts in Manchuria had only a minor effect on the industrialization of China. In the aftermath of the Second World War, the Soviet Union dismantled large parts of the Manchurian industrial complexes. Classified as Japanese reparation payments, machinery and whole plants were transferred to the Soviet Union to strengthen its own postwar industrialization process.

During the ensuing three decades, China pursued an industrialization policy initially modelled on the Soviet example, and then turning more and more towards self-developed approaches that were heavily influenced by ideological considerations. Japan played no role in China's industrialization during this period. It was only after the rise to power of Deng Xiaoping in the late 1970s that it was possible for Japan to influence China's industrialization process, both on a political and institutional level.

To evaluate the role of Japan in China's contemporary industrialization process, five areas must be examined:

1. Industrial policy: did Japanese industrial policy serve as a model for Chinese policy-makers?
2. Official development assistance (ODA): did Japanese ODA disbursements have an impact on Chinese industrialization in terms of its speed and direction?

3. Transfer of technology without equity participation: to what extent did plant and technology contracts between China and Japan contribute to industrial upgrading in China?

4. Foreign direct investment (FDI): did the (aggregate) engagement of Japanese companies in the Chinese economy exert a substantial influence on the build up of industrial structures?

5. Corporate governance and business concepts: did Japanese companies exert influence on the corporate governance structures and business concepts of their Chinese partners?

The following five sections examine these areas in more detail.

Japanese industrial policy as a model for China

Industrial policy in China historically had a strong bias towards an industrially active and interventionist government (Wellington and Chan, 1980; Malik, 1997; Meyer, 2000). When China opened itself to the world economy and started transformation into a market-oriented system during the 1980s, the Japanese model of strong government may well have been sympathetic to Chinese decision-makers and economic-policy advisors. It apparently offered a third way between the – obviously inefficient – 'all-state' model of economic planning and the 'no-state' model of neo-liberal coinage (Yanagihara, 1998). The model of industrialization underlying the economic take-off Japan experienced during the 1950s and 1960s has therefore been widely discussed and mostly favourably evaluated by Chinese academics and policy-makers (Taylor, 1996, p. 27).

When China entered the era of economic reform in the late 1970s, the measures taken were at first only meant to improve the performance of the existing command economy by partially introducing market-economy elements. It was not until 1985/86 that the group around Zhao Ziyang committed itself to a market-based economic system (Naughton, 1997, pp. 187, 196) and that China's economic policy was designed to transform the economic system. It was also in 1986 that China applied for (re-)admission to GATT. Since then, and especially since the start of serious membership negotiations in 1992, Chinese politics and industry became sensitive to the consequences such a move might exert on the Chinese enterprise sector and looked for ways to prepare Chinese enterprises for the world market (Marukawa, 2001, p. 1). Hence, traces of a market-based industrial policy in China and Japanese influences in particular are only evident from the mid-1980s onward.

Industrial policy Japanese style is composed of the two realms of industrial structure policy (*sangyô kôzô seisaku*), aimed at influencing the allocation of resources and industrial organization policy (*sangyô soshiki seisaku*), targeting the size and number of individual enterprises competing in the same industry (with a bias towards oligopolistic structures), and the creation of cross-industry organizations (Pascha, 1997a, p. 4). Japanese industrial policy itself has gone through a process of adaptation to its environment, with the forces of market competition having grown in importance for the allocation of resources (Komiya, 1986, pp. 61–2). Hence, this account focuses on the main characteristics of the Japanese model of industrial policy (see Figure 5.1).

The main instruments of Japanese industrial policy are understood to be, firstly, direct interventions, as exemplified by the restriction of business behaviour by law and the provision of subsidies, and, secondly, instructive guidance, as exemplified by the provision of investment incentives via taxation or policy-oriented finance, the provision of industrial structure visions and the adjustment of production and capital investment through administrative guidance (Ifo/Sakura, 1997, p. 214).

China's industrial structure policy in the 1990s was certainly influenced by Japanese policies. At its core were two strategy papers on industrial development published by the State Council in 1989 and 1994 (Song, 1999). Both papers identify industries that should be promoted, while investments in others were discouraged. A special emphasis lay on agriculture, energy and transport as well as the metallurgic and the petrochemical industries. But the programme of 1989 was characterized by such a broad range of industries eligible for governmental protection and promotion that in the end no single industry received a genuine priority treatment. Most incentives, subsidies and preferential measures were distributed quite evenly among all industries, thereby diluting the allocative impact the programme could exert on the economy's industrial structure.

It was only after Chinese economic policy went through a radical change of strategy (Naughton, 2001) that industrial policy became truly focused. In the programme of 1994 the number of industries with priority status was drastically reduced. Instead, certain key industries were identified that were meant to lead the economy to higher stages of economic development. Mirroring the priorities formulated by MITI in the 1960s, these industries included electronics, machinery, petrochemicals, automobiles and construction (Song, 1999; Taylor, 1996, p. 39; Marukawa, 2001).

Various instruments were applied to promote these industries: the formulation and implementation of new laws and administrative guidelines, subsidies in the form of tax concessions, distorted prices and soft-budget-constraints, the provision of financial means for research and development, establishment of complementary financial institutions to promote the operations of these industries, protection of key business fields against foreign competition, and in certain areas promotion of foreign equity participation to acquire state-of-the art technologies (Lo, 1997; Nolan, 2001; Song, 1999). These instruments show an obvious similarity to the various instruments put to use by Japan in the course of its industrial structure policy.

The closest resemblance of Japanese policies can probably be found in the realm of industrial organization policy. Striving to secure a leading position in the world economy, the Chinese government took recourse to strategies

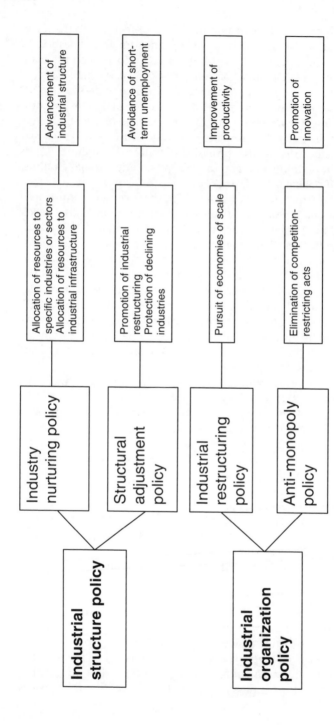

Figure 5.1 Structural characteristics of industrial policy in Japan

Source: Ifo Institute for Economic Research; Sakura Institute of Research (1997, p. 215).

very similar to those formulated during the 1950s and 1960s in Japan. The central idea is that a nation needs a certain number of large enterprises and enterprise groups that hold a considerable share of the world market in order to project its influence on a global scale. In order to make its enterprise sector fit for the world market and compete with the established multinationals, the Chinese government selected (or constructed by means of mergers and acquisitions) a group of large-scale enterprises that received support from various industrial policy instruments (Nolan, 2001), including:

- preferential treatment for loans from the state banking system;
- privileged access to national and international capital markets;
- preferential treatment regarding joint venture projects;
- protection against national contenders by means of prioritized issuance of licenses and business permits; and
- protection against international competition by means of tariff and non-tariff barriers.

Recently, however, the Japanese model of large conglomerates (*kigyô keiretsu*) and the Korean *chaebol* (designed after Japan's prewar *zaibatsu*) have been discredited in the wake of the Asian crises.

Despite the various features of Chinese industrial policy that resemble policies developed in Japan, conditions peculiar to China have prevented a more comprehensive replication of the Japanese model:

- Successful industrial policy needs an institutional framework that guarantees macroeconomic stability and prevents isolated policy measures from causing distortions that may affect the whole economic process. Precisely such an macroeconomic leveler has been lacking in China (Singh, 1992, pp. 15–6). This institutional deficit has first of all been caused by the frictions caused by the transformation of a planned in a market economy. It has arisen whenever regulation requirements have come out of step with regulation capacities of older institutions created for more plan-oriented economic processes. But also a lack of control of the central government over local government and decentralized institutions has inhibited the execution of central industrialization policies. Local governments have had considerable leeway to follow their own – locality centred – industrial development policies. The central government was not able to effectively coordinate the various local initiatives in order to bring about a macro-economic balance; instead, once the central government had proclaimed certain industrialization targets, local actors tried to benefit from the preferential policies of the centre without concerning themselves with the actions of other localities. As a result, the Chinese economy has been cyclically bogged down by overcapacities (Taube, 1997, p. 255). In this analysis the Chinese attempts of Japanese style industrial policy have created just the phenomenon, the prevention of which has been one of the guiding principles in the formulation of Japan's industrial policy: 'excess' competition.

- China's policy towards its large-scale state-owned enterprises is burdened by the legacy of the planned economy with its inconsistent goals. The same enterprises that must compete with multinational corporations that have streamlined their organizations in decades of fierce competition in the world market are at the same time obliged to fulfill social welfare functions. As a result, the introduction of incentive-based remuneration systems is obstructed and resources are absorbed by inefficient organizational structures and processes.

- China has been trying to apply features of industrial policy that have been created by a Japanese economy much further advanced than China's is at present. Chinese enterprises intending to compete on the world market encounter insufficient demand for their sophisticated, high-value-added products in the domestic market. Thus, they cannot realize economies of scale in their protected home market before entering the global market and competing with the already established players.

- Industrial policy measures must be unambiguously tied to the goal of economic development and growth to have positive welfare effects for society at large (Pascha, 1997b, p. 206). But since industrial policy measures are usually accompanied by preferential treatment, they are prone to be abused by rent-seeking and corruption. China has not been able to neutralize such detrimental behaviour and this has greatly diminished the impact of policy on the creation of industrial structures and has led to a misallocation of resources.

The Japanese model of industrial policy has not been the only influence on China's policy- and decision-makers. From the early 1980s on, China has been heavily influenced by the IMF and the World Bank, which have accompanied the process of economic restructuring with their expertise and a substantial volume of soft loans, since the acceptance of China to these organizations in 1980. Not only does the paradigm of developmental policy propagated by these organizations differ markedly from the Japanese model, the latter has lost much of its attraction in the run of the prolonged crises Japan entered in the early 1990s – just when China was beginning to seriously formulate an industrial policy in the framework of a market-oriented economic system.

Effects of Japanese official development assistance (ODA) to China

Japan is by far the largest contributor of bilateral ODA to China (see Chapter 6 for statistical details). On average, Japanese ODA is nearly two times as high as that of the second most generous provider of ODA to China, Germany, and about 10 times as high as that from the third most generous,

France (Jin, 2000, pp. 194, 215). With this substantial transfer of resources, for two decades Japan has been making an important contribution to economic development and the Chinese industrialization process in particular.

In terms of its sectoral distribution, Japanese ODA has been concentrated in transport infrastructure, electricity generation and gas supply. Only in the 1990s has agriculture become a target of Japanese ODA to China and has now assumed a prominent position. Most recently, environmental issues and the development of the Chinese hinterland have become a focus of Japanese ODA. Of the 28 projects scheduled for the years 1999 and 2000, 18 were directed at the Chinese hinterland.

While there is no doubt that the substantial Japanese ODA provided a strong impulse to the build-up of industrial structures in China, it is also worth examining the extent to which Japanese ODA also had an impact on the style and direction of China's industrialization process. We assume that the choice and development of industrial policies and industrial organization in China may be prone to influences originating from the selective provision of ODA by the Japanese government, and that there are at least two independent channels by which Japanese ODA might be used to influence the Chinese industrialization process.

Firstly, Japanese ODA to China may have functioned as an instrument of an active transnational industrial policy. Adhering to the model of a flying-geese-type regional industrialization process (see note 2 of Chapter 1), Japanese ODA might have been used to prepare neighbouring economies for their role in this common development process and pave the way for Japanese FDI (or such from second- or third-tier economies).

The implication of such a transnational strategy has been severely inhibited by the fact that the Chinese government has always been highly suspicious of Japanese efforts to establish itself as a regional power and enlarge its sphere of influence. Japanese ODA programmes that were interpreted as instrumental to such aspirations of the Japanese side, such as the highly ambitious regional industrialization programme (New Asian Industries Development Scheme) conceived by MITI in 1988, have therefore been rejected by China (Hilpert, 1997, p. 41).

Also with respect to 'regular' ODA disbursements, China has institutionalized some mechanisms that strongly inhibit the capacity of Japan to exert influence on the direction of the Chinese industrialization process. Between 1980 and 2000 Japanese assistance loans, which constitute about three-quarters of total Japanese ODA to China, have been an integral part of the Chinese five-year plans. (From 2001 on, Japanese ODA to China will be granted on a yearly basis, which is the standard approach practiced with all other beneficiary countries.) Insofar as during these two decades all Japanese assistance loans have gone into projects that had been included in the Chinese plans, Japan did not exert any influence on the quality of the Chinese industrialization process. Instead, Japanese ODA enabled the Chinese government to extend its plan balances.

Secondly, Japan might try – openly or informally – to tie its ODA disbursements to the condition that Japanese products are bought or Japanese companies are entrusted with an ODA-financed project. By this means Japan might succeed in establishing systemic solutions in the Chinese market and via industrial standards strengthen the dependence of Chinese industries on industrial structures in Japan. (Systemic solutions imply that once a decision is made for a certain system and its industrial standards, complementary goods will automatically be requested by the host country, while other systems and their complementary products remain excluded.)

Japan's development aid has traditionally been closely connected to the economic self-interest of Japan (Seitz, 2001, pp. 35, 42). Not only has it been instrumentalized to guarantee Japan access to the natural resources it is lacking, but it has also been used to establish the kind of infrastructure that facilitates Japanese FDI in the host country. With respect to the promotion of Japanese suppliers and industrial standards, Japanese development aid was very successfully instrumentalized in the 1970s (not strictly ODA but with the same aims) and 1980s. Key technologies that Japanese corporations supplied to China and which for years set the standards for its industrial development were financed with subsidized loans provided by Japanese government agencies.

In line with other DAC donor countries (OECD's Development Assistance Committee), during the 1990s Japan increasingly abstained from the practice of tying the provision of ODA to the procurement of goods and services from Japan (Jin, 2000, p. 206). During the 1990s, an increasing share of ODA was provided on an untied basis, that is without the condition that the money be used for purchases in Japan. In 1993/94 less than one-third of yen loans provided to China under ODA terms were actually spent in Japan (Yokoi, 1996a, p. 152). What the data do not tell us, however, is the extent to which companies located outside Japan but which are members of Japanese enterprise networks (*kigyô keiretsu*) have profited from ODA. It is just such companies that would be the logical transmitter of Japanese technology and production processes to the flying geese in the next tier, in this case China.

To sum up, Japanese ODA has certainly served as an lubricant for economic relations with China. In this way it has promoted the industrialization of China's economy and helped to strengthen the position and influence of Japanese companies in comparison to companies of other nationalities. But Japan did not succeed in leaving its imprint on the style and direction of the Chinese industrialization process, nor was it able to integrate China in its transnational development strategy for East Asia.

Industrial upgrading by means of plant and technology contracts

Plant and technology contracts are defined as the provision of whole plants, key facilities, collaborative manufacturing arrangements, technical licenses and technological services. They constitute a mode of economic cooperation that is more intensive than anonymous trade, and may be understood as a preliminary stage to foreign direct investment.

The utilization of this mode of economic cooperation as an element of China's foreign economic exchange dates back to the pre-reform era. While the overwhelming majority of plant and technology contracts in the 1950s and early 1960s were concluded with Socialist bloc economies, Japan became the most important partner in the 1970s. Of the US$ 12.5 billion worth of plant and technology imports realized by China during the fourth (1971–75: US$ 3.1 billion) and fifth five-year plans (1976–80: US$ 9.4 billion), Japanese companies provided more than 50 per cent. During this decade Japan made a substantial contribution to the technological upgrading and modernization of various Chinese industries, including iron and steel, electric-power generation, non-ferrous metals, petrochemicals, fertilizers, synthetic fibres, electric equipment and electronics. Key industrial complexes established in China by means of plant and technology contracts concluded with Japanese companies in this period include the Baoshan Iron and Steel Complex in Shanghai, the Daqing Petrochemical Complex in Heilongjiang Province, the Qilu Petrochemical Complex in Shandong Province, and the Yangzi Petrochemical Complex in Jiangsu Province (Yokoi, 1996b, pp. 130–1).

The strong emphasis on petrochemical projects in this list points to one of the most important motives for Japanese companies to conclude – and the Japanese government to support – plant and technology contracts with Chinese partners: securing access to Chinese natural resources in general and oil in particular. This constellation of interests is also mirrored in the Long-term Trade Agreement between Japan and China of February 1978. The agreement called for China to export coal and oil to Japan and receive plants and technology as well as construction materials in return. The planned trade flows were to amount to US$ 10 billion in each direction during a five-year period beginning in 1978. This barter trade, however, was in operation for three years only. From 1981 on, Chinese exports of coal and oil expanded steadily while the provision of plants and technology from Japan stagnated (Yokoi, 1996b, pp. 135–6).

While Japanese companies had played a dominant role in the 1970s, they lost in relative importance in the 1980s owing to North American and European companies intensifying their activities in China, the yen appreciating substantially in the latter half of the 1980s, and the Chinese government – in the face of increasing trade deficits with Japan – discouraging Japanese imports. During the 1980s, not only did the Japanese share in such contracts shrink to about one-fifth of China's total contract value and fall to less than 8 per cent in 1988, but the absolute volumes also declined. It was only in the early 1990s that a rebound could be observed and Japanese companies once again commanded a substantial share (20–30 per cent) in China's plant and technology contracts (Yokoi, 1996a, p. 151).

The transfer of technology that Japanese companies provided under the auspices of plant and technology contracts has doubtlessly made a very valuable contribution to the build-up of industrial capacities in China and has promoted its industrialization process. At the end of the 1980s, for example, 80 per cent of the total Chinese ethylene production capacity came from the six ethylene plants provided by Japan by such contracts. But the substantial impact Japanese technology transfer had on the Chinese industrialization process is perhaps best exemplified by the Baoshan Iron and Steel Complex. Baoshan Iron and Steel is a nearly exact replica of Kimitsu Works of Nippon Steel Corporation, which at the time of the signing of the contracts in 1978 was the most modern steel producer worldwide. The arrangement of buildings was exactly copied, and the equipment, including the basic oxygen technology, the continuous caster furnaces and computerized control systems was brought in from Japan. Thus, when Baoshan went into production in 1985 the Chinese steel industry had undergone an unprecedented time-jump. This rapid modernization would not have happened without Nippon Steel's willingness to transfer its technological know-how and the substantial financial assistance from the Japanese government which provided subsidized loans amounting to about US$ 1.5 billion.

The technology employed by Baoshan was not in line with the comparative advantage of the Chinese economy at that time; that would have demanded a much more labour- and less capital-intensive technology. But it conformed to an industrialization strategy based on government-induced industrial upgrading *vis-à-vis* the economy's contemporary factor endowment.

Impact of Japanese FDI on industrialization in China

The initial legal and institutional basis for FDI in China was established only in the late 1970s and early 1980s. Until then there was virtually no FDI allowed to enter China. FDI inflows picked up slowly in the 1980s, with truly substantial amounts of FDI being recorded only since the early 1990s. Between 1995 and 1999 China absorbed 7.5 per cent of global FDI flows, and about one-quarter of all FDI flows directed towards developing countries. In the years 1993 to 1996, China was host to more than one-tenth of global FDI (UNCTAD, various years). And although the massive inflow of FDI (and other forms of capital imports) has not been employed to expand the build-up of industrial capacity beyond the degree that could have been financed by domestic savings (Lardy, 1995, p. 1073; Taube, 2001), China has also been able to take advantage of many of the positive impulses FDI offers a host economy (Khan, 1991, p. 2).

The major contribution of FDI inflows to China's economic development and industrialization can be seen in reducing the technological gap (Khan, 1991, pp. 13–15; Lardy 1995, pp. 1073–5). In the majority of cases domestic and foreign investments cannot be substituted at will in China. Foreign direct investments are linked with the creation of a considerably more modern capital stock, which is additionally administered by superior management techniques, reducing inefficiencies and bringing the new technologies to full use. Over time, this constellation brings about an improvement of human capital, as Chinese engineers and managers are trained in modern technology and management practices.

Foreign Invested Enterprises (FIEs) have created a substantial number of jobs; at the turn of the century the total number of people employed by FIEs is reported to have been in excess of 20 million (Xie, 2000, pp. 7–9). This does not mean that FIEs have created a net amount of 20 million new jobs. FIEs are responsible for streamlining most industries, which has led to the dismissals of a considerable number of workers, thereby transforming hidden unemployment into open unemployment. All in all it can be presumed that FIEs had a positive effect on the labour market, although this effect was quite different depending on the time period and the various segments of the labour market. FIEs have certainly eased the strains on the market for unskilled labour. New ventures and the growth impulses originating from FIEs have been creating new jobs (on a net basis) for an abundant pool of workers. With respect to qualified labour, FIEs competed – especially in the 1980s – with local companies for scarce (human) resources, and because they could pay higher wages and provide superior working conditions have been able to crowd out local competitors. Over time FIEs with their job training programmes have also made a considerable contribution to the enlargement of the pool of qualified labour in China.

One further important growth impulse of FIEs for the Chinese economy stems from the competitive pressure these companies exert on local enterprises. Faced with FIEs' superior technology and management, local enterprises are forced to improve their operations to maintain their place in the market. Chinese enterprises are known to have closely studied management practices of their joint venture partners and foreign competitors. This competitive pressure has often been weakened, however, as artificial barriers have been erected in various industries to protect Chinese enterprises. The strong political bias in favour of export-oriented FIEs has especially led to a strong segregation of the markets in which local enterprises and FIEs operate.

FDI has contributed greatly to the development of an export-oriented industry in China. Starting from a minuscule share in China's total exports, FIEs commanded more than 40 per cent of China's exports during the late 1990s. In this way they have contributed to the development of a growth-inducing industrial structure and have improved the availability of foreign exchange in China. Export-oriented development strategies are generally accepted as growth enhancing and superior to policies relying on import substitution, but it should be noted that the strong reliance on export processing as the main mode of exports by FIEs in China has also led to a low intensity of backward linkages and has thereby been reducing the spillover effects of technological innovations introduced by FDI to other areas of the economy.

In order to isolate the impact of Japanese FDI on the Chinese industrialization process from the general developments described above, it seems justified to differentiate between the 1980s and 1990s as the investments of Japanese companies in these two periods show distinctive differences (see Chapter 4).

Throughout the 1980s the absolute volume of Japanese FDI directed towards China was small and mostly directed towards non-manufacturing ventures. Especially during the first half of the 1980s, by far the largest part of Japanese FDI was directed towards services, hotels and leasing companies (Ono, 1993, p. 19). Up to 1987 Japanese investments in the manufacturing sector amounted to only one-sixth to one-third of those in services.

This feature can be explained to some extent by the historical setting. In the period under discussion, growing Japan–US trade frictions forced Japanese companies to shift production plants to America. With resources bound by this endeavour a simultaneous, strong commitment in China was out of the question. But the initial low-key engagement of Japanese companies in the Chinese market may also be understood as the first stage of a long-term strategy to enter the Chinese market. In the first years of China's reforms and opening to the world market the general trading houses (*sôgô shôsha*) acted as a vanguard. They invested in information networks, explored potential areas for more intensive forms of engagement, and tried to gain experience in doing business under the local circumstances (Campbell, 1994, p. 132; Hilpert, 2001 p. 2). At the next stage, various investors in construction, financial services and logistics entered the Chinese market and prepared the physical and business infrastructure until finally transplants were established in the manufacturing industries (Bassino and Teboul, 1999, p. 82).

This pattern of a multistage market-entry strategy fits perfectly well to the changes in volume and composition of Japanese FDI during the 1990s. The volume of Japanese FDI flows to China increased substantially and was accompanied by dramatic changes in their sectoral composition. In the second half of the 1990s, about three-quarters of Japanese FDI was directed towards manufacturing.

Further important elements for the increase of Japanese FDI in China are the improvement of the legal system and the publication of a comprehensive set of laws and regulations governing the activities of FIEs during the late 1980s and early 1990s, as well as the signing of the Japan–China Investment Protection Pact in August 1988. The positive impact of these new institutions on the risk perception of potential Japanese investors, however, was temporarily neutralized by the Tiananmen incident in 1989.

Since the early 1990s the contribution of Japanese companies to China's overall FDI inflows has been quite impressive. According to Chinese data

Japanese companies provided 8 per cent of all FDI China attracted during 1989 to 1999. We can therefore assume that by their volume alone the impact Japanese FDI exerted on the Chinese industrialization process was very substantial during this period. This consideration applies first of all to the build-up of production capacities and the creation of jobs.

Seen from the Japanese perspective, however, China is far less important as a destination for Japanese FDI. Despite of its geographical vicinity China gathered only about 3 per cent of Japans (statistically registered) FDI outflows. This phenomenon is not as unusual as it may seem at first sight. Like the other industrial economies in the European Union and Northern America, the bulk of Japan's FDI outflows are directed towards the triad, that is other industrialized economies.

With respect to technology content, Japanese FDI was probably less 'modern' than FDI from other industrialized economies. Due to the dominant role small and medium-sized enterprises command in Japanese FDI in China – in contrast to the composition of FDI originating in Europe and Northern America – the technology content, on average, is comparatively low. Moreover, during the latter half of the 1990s the main thrust of Japan's manufacturing FDI in China has been constituted of labour-intensive industries that have become non-competitive in Japan – therewith inducing strong export flows from Chinese production sites to the Japanese home market. However, many smaller Japanese enterprises that moved to China have closed their production facilities in Japan, while remaining firmly integrated in their supplier-customer networks. Therefore, the Chinese ventures are characterized by a high export content, while permanent industrial upgrading is assured.

While the technology content of Japanese FDI in China may have been comparatively minor, Japanese enterprises have certainly acted as the single most important role model with respect to management systems. Management concepts developed in Japan like the total quality control (TQC) initiative, *kaizen*, *kanban* and so forth have been received with much interest by Chinese companies.

The discussion thus far has focused on national data, but a regional differentiation may also be instructive. Japanese FDI possibly concentrates in certain areas where it exerts a strong influence on local industrialization. As a matter of fact, a concentration of Japanese FDI can be observed in the coastal provinces. An above-average share is detectable in the provinces Shandong, Liaoning and Jilin in northeast China, which profit from their geographical proximity to Japan. But this phenomenon constitutes no substantial deviation from the overall pattern of FDI distribution in China (Guojia tongjiju [National Bureau of Statistics], various issues). With the slight exception of a strong presence of Japanese companies in the northeastern provinces, the regional distribution of Japanese FDI in China follows the same pattern as overall FDI inflows; that is, after having emphasized export-oriented ventures in southern China during the early 1990s the focus of interest has now moved towards ventures directed at the local market and stationed in the eastern and northeastern provinces (Konomoto, 1998, p. 36–8).

In an even more disaggregated analysis, the city of Dalian, a major industrial centre located at the coast of Liaoning province, can be identified as an location whose economic development and industrialization has been especially influenced by Japanese FDI. At certain periods, FDI originating in Japan has commanded a share of nearly 50 per cent of total FDI actually used in the city. More than 10 per cent of all Japanese enterprises with operations in China are said to be present in Dalian in one form or another (Whitla and Davies, 1996, p. 22).

One potential channel by which Japanese FDI may have exerted an impact on the industrial development in China is China-directed FDI originating from companies in Southeast Asia which had been founded as joint ventures with Japanese companies and employ their technologies and organizational structures (see Chapter 10). It is impossible to quantify the impact that has been exerted on the Chinese industrialization process via this indirect mechanism as investments by Japanese corporations that are conducting their FDI in China via their transplants in Southeast Asia do not enter the statistics under the label 'Japan'. But, as such, a time-spanning transmission of technology and production lines constitutes an integrated element of the Japan-directed, flying-geese industrialization process of East Asia, and we may conclude that it is not without influence. It can be assumed that technologies and production processes that have been developed in Japan have been transferred in this way to China. But whereas in Japan they are no longer in use and therefore cannot be transferred directly from Japan to China, they are now introduced to China via the Southeast Asian economies, including Taiwan, just at the point in time when in China the corresponding conditions (factor proportions) have been established. This pattern of an indirect transmission of Japanese technology and industrial organization has been especially widespread with regard to Taiwanese companies. Many Taiwanese enterprises that had originally received technology and know-how from Japanese partners and have adapted this technological and organizational know-how to the Chinese enterprise culture have, from 1985 on, been transferring this know-how to their partners and transplants in mainland China. One such case that has been documented in detail is the Taiwanese China Motor Corporation Ltd. (CMC) which is now transferring Mitsubishi technology to China (Chen, 1999, pp. 189–223; Chen, 2000).

Japanese governance structures and business concepts as models for Chinese corporations

Corporate governance structures in China stand mostly in the tradition of either the former state-owned enterprises (SOEs) or the traditional family enterprise. The so-called township-village enterprises, which have been the object of intense academic debate, are not really a type of their own but rather constitute a group of very heterogeneous enterprises scattered along the whole range between the two extremes of the SOEs and the family enterprise. These corporate structures have evolved organically over time and show no close relation to Japanese models. Since the idea of modelling Chinese enterprise groups after the pattern of the Korean *chaebol* – which themselves had been modelled along the lines of Japan's prewar *zaibatsu* – was discredited by the Asian crisis, and efforts to implement a Japan-inspired main-bank system had to be aborted as the Chinese banking system proved to be too frail, we may conclude that the Japanese model of corporate governance has not found a strong echo in China's corporations. One major exception may be seen in the concept of general trading houses as exemplified by the Japanese *sôgô shôsha*. In the above-mentioned drive to establish large conglomerates and trading houses which are expected to be able to compete successfully in the world market, the first foreign trade joint venture of China, Dongling Trading Corporation, was set up in Shanghai in 1997. The idea to take the Japanese *sôgô shôsha* as a model for this venture is reflected in the participation of Mitsubishi Shôji which commands the second largest equity share, amounting to 27 per cent (Hilpert, 2001, p. 12).

In comparison to the sphere of corporate governance, the impact of Japanese companies on the evolution of business concepts in China and the way Chinese companies adapted to the world market has been very substantial. China's larger corporations are known to have studied and adapted Japanese innovations in the fields of industrial organization and management (Hao, 1999). One example of Japanese influence on industrial organization in China is the introduction of the Toyota Production System to the Chinese automobile industry as exemplified by its first adoption by First Automotive Works (*Diyi qiche jituan gongsi* – FAW) (Lee, 2000). Until then, employing a Ford-style production system based on a highly vertical organized production process, FAW started to gather information about alternative systems in the late 1970s: study groups were send abroad (mainly Japan) and Japanese top-management personnel were invited to visit own production sites. In the early 1980s, elements of Toyota-style process management were eventually introduced in the FAW plants, greatly improving their productivity. These included measures introduced under *kaizen* and *kanban* such as just-in-time production, multi-machine handling, process synchronization, reduction of in-process stock, process-integrated quality control, and so forth. The positive results of this new organization of production processes were quickly propagated to a wider public by various publications and workshops. But, still, a comprehensive adoption of the Toyota production system was not yet implemented. This was realized only after establishing a new transmission plant in the latter half of the 1980s, which under the guidance of the Japanese Hino Motor Company (a member of the Toyota group) established an integrated Toyota style production system.

Conclusion

This analysis has presented an overview of how Japan may have exerted influence on the Chinese industrialization process and its actual impact. The conclusion is warranted that Japan certainly did play an important role in China's industrialization process over the last two decades. The Japanese influence has been exerted over various channels, none of which played a dominating role by itself; Japan's impact on China's industrialization has to be understood as the combined effect of various influences.

China did not copy the Japanese model of industrial policy but has selectively chosen certain elements and tried to integrate them in an eclectic approach of systemic transformation and industrial upgrading. While the high speed of the Chinese catching-up process is the result of an enormous transfer of resources by numerous private and governmental actors from East and Southeast Asia, Europe and North America as well as supra-national organizations, Japan certainly made a decisive contribution to this process. By means of ODA, plant and technology contracts, and in the 1990s FDI, there has been a continuous transfer of modern technology and know-how from Japan to China that enabled the Chinese economy to significantly reduce the development gap to the industrialized economies. In addition, Japanese-style management concepts have been widely accepted by Chinese companies.

References

Bassino, J.-P. and R. Teboul (1999) 'The Dynamics and Spatial Distribution of Japanese Investment in China', in S. Dzever and J. Jaussaud (eds), *China and India: Economic Performance and Business Strategies of Firms in the mid-1990s*, Basingstoke: Macmillan – now Palgrave, pp. 73–94.

Campbell, N. (1994) 'Japan's Success in China', in H. Schütte (ed.), *The Global Competitiveness of the Asian Firm*, London and New York: St Martin's Press.

Chen, C.-C. (1999) 'Taiwanese Investment in China – Don-Nan Automobile Company', in M. Taube and A. Gälli (eds), *China's Wirtschaft im Wandel. Aktuelle Aspekte und Probleme*, ifo Forschungsberichte der Abteilung Entwicklungsländer no. 88, Munich, Bonn, London: Weltforum Verlag, pp. 189–223.

— (2000) 'Taiwanese Technology Transfer to China – The Automobile Industry as a Case Study', paper presented at the 19th Annual Hōsei University International Conference Japanese Foreign Direct Investment and Structural Change in the East Asian Industrial System: Global Restructuring for the 21st Century, 30 October–1 November 2000. Tokyo: Hōsei University.

Guojia tongjiju [National Bureau of Statistics] (various years) *Zhongguo tongji nianjian* [China Statistical Yearbook], Beijing: China Statistical Publishing House.

Hao, Y. (1999) *Chûgoku no keizai hatten to Nihon teki seisan shisutemu* [China's Economic Development and the Japanese Production System], Tokyo: Minerva.

Hilpert, H. G. (1997) 'Japan und China im ostasiatischen Wirtschaftsraum: Komplementaritäten und Konflikte', in M. Taube and A. Gälli (eds), *Chinas Wirtschaft im Wandel. Aktuelle Aspekte und Problem*, ifo Forschungsberichte der

Abteilung Entwicklungsländer, no. 88, Munich, Bonn, London: Weltforum Verlag, pp. 29–66.

— (2001) *The Strategies of the Japanese General Trading Houses in the China Market*, paper presented at the DIJ–FRI Conference, Japan and China Economic Relations in Transition, 18–19 January 2001, Tokyo: FRI.

Hilpert, H. G. and M. Taube (1997) 'Deutsch–japanische Unternehmens kooperationen in Drittmärkten', *ifo Studien zur Japanforschung*, no. 12, Munich: ifo Institut für Wirtschaftsforschung.

Ifo Institute for Economic Research and Sakura Institute of Research (1997), *A Comparative Analysis of Japanese and German Economic Success*, Tokyo: Springer Verlag.

Jin, X. (2000) *Riben zhengfu kaifa yuanzu* [Japan's Official Development Assistance], Beijing: Shehui kexue wehzhai chubanshe.

Kasper, W. (1994) *Global Competition, Institutions, and the East-Asian Ascendancy*, San Francisco: ICS Press.

Khan, Z. S. (1991) *Patterns of Foreign Direct Investment in China*, World Bank Discussion Papers, no. 130, Washington, DC: World Bank.

Komiya, R. (1986) 'Industrial Policy in Japan', *Japanese Economic Studies*, vol. 14 (4), pp. 52–81.

Konomoto, S. (1998) 'Industrial Policy in China and the Strategies of Japanese Transplants', *Nomura Research Institute Quarterly*, vol. 7 (3), pp. 36–47.

Lardy, N. R. (1987) 'Economic Recovery and the 1st Five-year Plan', *The Cambridge History of China*, vol. 14 (1), pp. 144–84.

— (1995) 'The Role of Foreign Trade and Investment in China's Economic Transformation', *The China Quarterly*, vol. 144, pp. 1065–82.

Lee, C. (2000) 'Technology Transfer of the Toyota Production System in China', paper presented at the 19th Annual Hōsei University International Conference, Japanese Foreign Direct Investment and Structural Change in the East Asian Industrial System: Global Restructuring for the 21st Century, 30 October–1 November 2000, Tokyo: Hōsei University.

Lo, D. (1997) *Market and Institutional Regulation in Chinese Industrialization, 1978–1994*, Basingstoke: Macmillan – now Palgrave.

Malik, R. (1997) *Chinese Entrepreneurs in the Economic Development of China*, London: Westport.

Marukawa, T. (2001) 'WTO, Industrial Policy and China's Industrial Development', paper presented at the IDE–JETRO International Symposium, China Enters WTO: Pursuing Symbiosis with the Global Economy, 17 January 2001, Tokyo.

Meyer, M. (2000) 'Wirtschaftspolitik und State-Building. Die nationalchinesische Industriepolitik in historischer Perspektive', paper presented at the 1st conference of the Arbeitskreis für Sozialwissenschaftliche Chinaforschung at Witten, 17–18 November 2000, Witten.

Naughton, B. (1997) *Growing out of the Plan. Chinese Economic Reform, 1978–1993*, Cambridge: Cambridge University Press.

— (2001) 'Changing Horses in Mid-Stream? Explaining Changing Political Economy Regimes in China', paper presented at the DIJ–FRI Conference, Japan and China Economic Relations in Transition, 18–19 January 2001, Tokyo: FRI.

Nolan, P. (2001) *China and the Global Business Revolution*, Basingstoke: Palgrave.

Ohno, K. (1998) 'Overview: Creating the Market Economy', in K. Ohno and I. Ohno (eds), *Japanese Views on Economic Development. Diverse Paths to the Market* Routledge Studies in the Growth Economies of Asia 15, London and New York: Routledge, pp. 1–50.

Ono, S. (1993) 'Sino–Japanese Economic Relationships. Trade, Direct Investment and Future Strategy', *World Bank Discussion Papers*, no. 146, Washington, DC: World Bank.

Otsuka, K., L. Deqiang and M. Naoki (1998) *Industrial Reform in China. Past Performances and Future Prospects*, Oxford: Oxford University Press.

Pascha, W. (1997a) 'Industrial Policy in Japan and the Policy Choices for Central and Eastern European Countries – A Commentary on Some Controversial Issues', Duisburg Working Papers on East Asian Economic Studies, no. 37, Duisburg: Institut für Ostasienwissenschaften.

—(1997b) 'Nachholende wirtschaftliche Entwicklung in Japan und Südkorea: Die Rolle der Industriepolitik', *List Forum für Wirtschafts- und Finanzpolitik* 23 (2), pp. 192–213.

Seitz, C. (2001) 'Konditionierte Entwicklungshilfe? Politische Flexibilität japanischer Entwicklungshilfe', *Asien*, vol. 79 (4), pp. 33–49.

Singh, I. (1992) 'China: Industrial Policies for an Economy in Transition', *World Bank Discussion Papers*, no. 143, Washington, DC: World Bank.

Song, X. (1999) *Wirtschaftliche Entwicklung und Systemtransformation in China*, mimeo, Duisburg.

Taube, M. (1997) 'ökonomische Integration zwischen Hongkong und der Provinz Guangdong, VR China. Der chinesische Transformationsprozess als Triebkraft grenzüberschreitender Arbeitsteilung', *ifo Studien zur Entwicklungsforschung*, no. 31, Munich, Cologne, London: Weltforum Verlag.

—(2001) 'Fit für das nächste Jahrhundert? Die Wachstumsfaktoren der chinesischen Volkswirtschaft auf dem Prüfstand', in G. Schubert (ed.), *Konturen einer Übergangsgesellschaft auf dem Weg ins 21. Jahrhundert*, Hamburg: Mitteilungen des Instituts für Asienkunde 344, pp. 135–81.

Taylor, R. (1996) *Greater China and Japan. Prospects for an Economic Partnership in East Asia*, London and New York: Routledge.

UNCTAD (United Nations Conference on Trade and Development) (various years) *World Investment Report*, Geneva: UNCTAD.

Wellington, K. and K. Chan (1980) 'Government, Merchants and Industry to 1911', in *The Cambridge History of China*, vol. 11 (2), pp. 416–62.

Whitla, P. and H. Davies (1996) 'Japanese and Overseas Chinese Investment in the Chinese Economic Area', *JETRO China Newsletter*, no. 125, pp. 20–4.

Xie, S. (2000) 'Nuli zuohao xiehui gonzuo wie liyong waizi fazhan jingji fuwu' [Strive to make good work in the association and serve the utilisation of foreign capital and economic development], *Zhongguo waizi*, vol. 2 (2), pp. 7–9.

Yanagihara, T. (1998) 'Development and Dynamic Efficiency: "Framework Approach" versus "Ingredients Approach"', in K. Ohno and O. Izumi (eds), *Japanese Views on Economic Development. Diverse Paths to the Market*, Routledge Studies in the Growth Economies of Asia 15, London and New York: Routledge, pp. 70–6.

Yokoi, Y. (1996a) 'Major Developments in Japan–China Economic Interdependence in 1990–1994', in C. Howe (ed.), *China and Japan. History, Trends, and Prospects*, Oxford: Clarendon Press, pp. 147–54.

—(1996b) 'Plant and Technology Contracts and the Changing Pattern of Economic Interdependence between China and Japan', in C. Howe (ed.), *China and Japan. History, Trends, and Prospects*, Oxford: Clarendon Press, pp. 127–46.

6
Japan's ODA: Its Impacts on China's Industrialization and Sino–Japanese Relations

Juichi Inada

Introduction

Japan's official development assistance (ODA) policy can be regarded as one of the main pillars of Japan's foreign policy in the post-Second World War era. Contrary to the frequent criticism that Japan's ODA was primarily motivated by economic interests (Ensign, 1992; Arase, 1995), a remarkable change both in motives and structure has occurred since its official beginning in 1954 (Inada, 1989, 1993; Yasutomo, 1986). Japanese ODA in the 1960s was marked by postwar reparations, and in these early programme stages, economic assistance was linked to the expansion of Japan's exports through tied aid. At first almost all ODA consisted of assistance loans (so-called 'yen loans') and focused almost exclusively on the Asian region. Similarly, after the first oil shock in 1973, the securing of steady supplies of energy and other resources became a major motive of its aid policy as well.

Along with the increasing importance of the Japanese economy, the international community expected Japan to contribute more to the promotion of global peace and prosperity, and thus in 1978 the Japanese government announced a three-year plan to double its ODA disbursements. Since then, appropriations for ODA have grown rapidly. Total Japanese ODA passed that of the United States in 1989, and since 1991 Japan has become the world's largest ODA donor. Accordingly, the Japanese government regards its ODA programme as a main pillar of Japan's contribution to international burden sharing. With the changed objective of ODA, the promotion of economic interests through aid has become less important as well. In recent years, almost all Japanese assistance loans became untied (1999: 96.4 per cent), the share of grant aid increased to almost half of all bilateral ODA (1999: 52.8 per cent), and aid to other regions than Asia increased to more than half in total bilateral ODA distribution (1997: 53.5 per cent).[1] However, the latter share decreased again to 36.8 per cent in 1999 as a consequence of the large financial aid by Japan to the countries affected by the Asian financial crisis (MoFA, 2000a).

China is the largest recipient of Japanese ODA after Indonesia. Whereas China received a cumulative total of US$ 14.4 billion from 1979 until 1999, Japanese ODA to Indonesia had already started in 1969 and amounted to a total of US$ 16.3 billion until the year-end of 1999. Thus China has been the main recipient in the last 20 years, except in 1999 when China fell back to second place as Japan's aid to Indonesia was especially large in response to the severe impact of the Asian economic crisis in the largest country of Southeast Asia.

Aid to China consists of both assistance loans and grants. The latter can be rendered either as grant aid or as technical cooperation. Looking at the cumulative totals from 1979 to 1999, the share of the assistance loans is 91 per cent, the share of grants only 9 per cent. But the latter share has risen in recent years. Thus in the latest year under review (1999) the share of assistance loans in total ODA disbursements to China has come down to 66 per cent, whereas the share of technical cooperation has grown to 28 per cent and the share of grant aid to 5 per cent (MoFA, 2000a).

Japan's ODA to China lies at the core of the bilateral Sino–Japanese relationship, and it has strong political, diplomatic and economic implications. The following outlines the importance of Japan's ODA for the Chinese economy as well as its impacts on Chinese society and China–Japan relations, and points out the key issues for the future direction of Japan's ODA to China.

The characteristics of Japan's ODA to China

The beginnings of Japanese ODA to China

What were the circumstances under which the first yen loans were offered? After the ratification of the Japan–China Peace Treaty in August 1978, Prime Minister Ohira of Japan visited China in December 1979. On the occasion of this visit the Japanese government promised to assign ODA to China for the first time. In China, Deng Xiaoping had returned to power, an event which proved to become a turning point in China's political and economic history. The industrial and economic modernization process was launched and China's economy opened up to the Western world. On the political scene the cold war between the West and the Soviet Union continued, but diplomatic relations between China and the USA were restored.

Within this international political framework the general purpose of Japan's aid to China was, ostensibly, the improvement of bilateral relations. China, with its low per capita income and large population, had substantial development needs. On the Japanese side, officials from the Ministry of International Trade and Industry (MITI) speculated on the future potential of the Chinese market and the prospect of China becoming a major supplier of raw materials to Japan. In the Ministry of Foreign Affairs (MoFA) it was hoped that the new pragmatic regime in China could be stabilized and strengthened through support for its modernization policy. Thus China could be attracted to the West (RIPS, 1985, pp. 171–3).

In short, at its starting point Japan's ODA disbursement to China was highly politically motivated both by the donor and the recipient countries; China opened up its economy and accepted foreign capital for its modernization. Japan decided to support China's reform and modernization process and recognized China as a partner of the West in a new strategic framework. In addition, some Japanese political leaders thought Japan should promote the economic development of China instead of offering war reparations,[2] since China had officially renounced its claim for reparations. Moreover, along with the first disbursements of ODA to China in 1979, Japan had to reconcile this move with her other international political commitments.

Thus the so-called 'Ohira Three Principles' were established as effective criteria for aid provision to China. These criteria read as follows: first cooperation with Western nations, second consideration for a distribution balance between China and other Asian nations, especially those of the ASEAN community, and third no military assistance. Japan's Western partners, who were also looking eagerly to the future potential of the Chinese market, asked Japan to offer untied aid to China, that is untied to Japanese companies. Japan agreed to these demands, and, in the case of China, this general principle of Japanese ODA applied from 1979 onwards. Southeast Asian countries, anxious that China's modernization might result in an increasing Chinese industrial competitiveness, were afraid that the expansion of Japanese ODA to China might lead to corresponding aid reductions to Southeast Asia (Tanaka, 1991, pp. 112–3). In response, Japan declared its intention to strike a relative distribution balance between China and Southeast Asia. Since then Japan has aimed at a 1:3 ratio of ODA between China and the ASEAN countries.

After this start in a difficult international political environment, Japanese ODA to China exerted overall positive economic effects both on Japan and on China. In spite of the untied nature, Japanese assistance loans improved the environment for Sino–Japanese trade and Japanese FDI to China. Although Japan's ODA disbursements stagnated temporarily in the early 1980s, when the Chinese reform process reached a standstill, it can be assessed that the ODA had an overall positive impact on the Chinese reform process throughout the 1980s.

Volumes and structures of the Japanese ODA to China from 1979 to 1999

Japanese ODA disbursements to China from 1979 to 1999 amounted to yen 2688 billion, of which yen 2453 billion was assistance loans (91.3 per cent), yen 118 billion for grant aid (4.4 per cent) and yen 116 billion for technical assistance (4.3 per cent). From 1979 to 1999, Japanese ODA to China accounted for almost 15 per cent of total Japanese ODA of that period. Table 6.1 shows the volumes and structures of Japanese ODA to China. Unlike other recipient countries, China has been receiving Japanese ODA in the form of 'batches' or 'rounds', which comprise five to seven years. Thus China did not need to negotiate for its aid each year anew and could reckon with Japanese disbursements within the framework of its five-year development plans. In addition to the ODA disbursements outlined above, the former Export–Import Bank of Japan (JEXIM), which was integrated into the Japan Bank for International Cooperation (JBIC) in 1999, has allocated various other untied loans to China, which fell under the 'other official flows' (OOF) category.[3] These untied loans by JEXIM amounted to a total of yen 3428 billion up to 1999.

Table 6.2 shows the flows of ODA to China since 1991 by major bilateral and multilateral sources, and thus relates the Japanese contributions to the efforts of other donors. It can be seen that the Japanese ODA contributions dominate. They amount to almost half of all bilateral aid to China – Germany, the second largest bilateral donor, reached at most half of Japan's disbursements – and to nearly a third of the total amount of ODA to China, which includes also multilateral aid.[4] The high Japanese shares are even more noteworthy in the light of the fact that China became the largest ODA recipient country worldwide in the 1990s.

Table 6.3 shows the flows of ODA and OOF from Japan, the World Bank and the Asian Development Bank (ADB) to China on a pledge basis. The

Table 6.1   The shifting focus in the Japanese assistance loans to China, 1979–98, %

Sector	First batch (1979–83)	Second batch (1984–89)	Third batch (1990–95)	Fourth batch (1996–98)[1]	Total (1979–98)
Transportation[2]	60.7	53.3	38.8	37.2	42.4
Energy (power plants)	0.0	15.9	22.3	28.3	19.1
Communication	0.0	6.5	7.2	4.0	5.2
Water supply	0.0	5.7	3.6	7.4	4.5
Industries	0.0	13.0	3.8	0.0	4.5
Agriculture	0.0	0.0	13.1	3.1	5.5
Environmental protection	0.0	0.0	0.0	16.2	4.1
Commodity loans	39.3	0.0	0.0	0.0	5.7
Others	0.0	5.7	11.1	14.3	9.0
Total	100.0	100.0	100.0	100.0	100.0
of which interior regions	0.0	28.7	52.0	76.5	45.1

Notes: [1]The fourth batch consisted of a former three years and a latter two years part. The ODA extended in the latter part (1999 and 2000) is not included here. [2]The transportation sector comprises railroads, ports and airports.

Source: OECF (1999a) *Outline of Yen Loans to China.*

Table 6.2 ODA and OOF flows to China by sources from 1991–98 (US\$ millions)

Source	Type of ODA and OOF	1991	1995	1997	1998
Japan	ODA loans gross	424	1216	557	1084
	Grants	194	388	267	340
	Total	618	1604	824	1424
	ODA net disbursement	585	1380	577	1158
Germany	ODA loans gross	65	599	323	273
	Grants	94	129	134	136
	Total	159	728	456	409
	ODA net disbursement	107	684	382	321
France	ODA loans gross	127	81	39	17
	Grants	11	11	11	16
	Total	139	91	50	33
	ODA net disbursement	139	91	50	30
Bilateral total	ODA loans gross	859	2084	993	1450
	Grants	483	741	600	700
	Total	1342	2825	1592	2150
	ODA net disbursement	1253	2531	1229	1732
World Bank	IBRD[1]	538	1107	1211	1078
	IDA[2]	610	798	687	554
	Total (ODA + OOF) net disbursement	1148	1905	1898	1632
ADB[3]	Total (ODA + OOF) net disbursement	182	527	545	722
UNDP[4]	Grants	50	29	27	14
Multilateral total	Total (ODA + OOF) net disbursement	1442	2628	2620	2503
Bilateral and multilateral total	ODA net disbursement	1999	3534	2040	2359

Notes: [1]IBRD = International Bank for Reconstruction and Development; [2]IDA = International Development Association; [3]ADB = Asian Development Bank; [4]UNDP = United Nations Development Programme.

Source: OECD (2000) *Geographical Distribution of Financial Flows to Aid Recipients*.

contribution of the World Bank is considerable, but the IDA portion decreased in the second half of the 1990s. In 1999 China even lost its eligibility for IDA loans. It can also be seen from Table 6.3 that the financial contributions of the ADB and of Japan have been quite large, too. In particular the official flows from the former JEXIM have been substantial, though their activities are less well-known.

The lending conditions of the assistance loans of the Overseas Economic Cooperation Fund (OECF)[5] are extremely concessional. OECF yen loans require an interest rate of around 2 per cent, they normally have a 10-year grace period and a 30-year redemption period, whereas IBRD loans have to be

Table 6.3 ODA and OOF to China (pledged basis; US$ millions)

Donor	1992	1995	1997	1998
World Bank total	2 526	3 000	2 744	2 616
IDA[1] (ODA)	949	630	254	293
IBRD[2] (OOF)	1 578	2 370	2 490	2 323
Asian Development Bank total	903	1 201	656	1 464
ADF[3] (ODA)	0	0	0	0
OCR[4] (OOF)	903	1 201	656	1 464
Japan total[5]	2 573	6 262	2 691	n.a
OECF (ODA)	1 084	1 503	1 677	1 589
JEXIM (OOF)	1 489	4 759	1 014	n.a.

Notes: [1]IDA = International Development Association; [2]IBRD = International Bank of Reconstruction and Development; [3]ADF = Asian Development Fund; [4]OCR = Ordinary Capital Resources; [5]Conversion from yen into US dollars based on yearly average exchange rates.

Sources: World Bank, ADB and JEXIM.

repaid with an interest rate of usually around 6 to 7 per cent. In recent years, along with the generally low interest rates in Japan, the untied loans from the former JEXIM could also be offered at such low interest rates of around 2 per cent with a redemption period of 10 to 15 years. Thus the JEXIM untied loans became almost as favourable as the OECF assistance loans and contributed equally positively to the build-up of infrastructure in China.

However, the favourable lending conditions notwithstanding, the assistance loans, which had been extended in the 1980s, may prove to be more expensive for China than calculated initially, as the yen, which was worth 180–250 per US dollar in the early 1980s, appreciated substantially after 1985. For the Chinese borrowers the effective interest rate, measured in US dollars or in Chinese renminbi (RMB) may turn out to be very high in the end. However, these early assistance loans have to be repaid in 30 years, and thus it may be still too early for final conclusions.

The macroeconomic impacts of the Japanese ODA to China

Both the OECF and the JICA[6] have carried out a great number of ODA project evaluations in China (OECF, 1999b; JICA, 2000). According to these self-evaluations most aid projects reached the expected effects in terms of capacity increase in transportation, communication, utility infrastructure and the like. However, there are hardly any objective analyses examining the total impacts of Japanese ODA on the Chinese economy and society and on Sino–Japanese economic relations. Such an evaluation is the task of this section. At the outset, it should be noted that the quality of statistical data in China is quite often poor or the necessary data is not available. However, some examinations of the macroeconomic impacts of ODA are possible and cautious conclusions on the relative importance of Japan's ODA for the Chinese industrialization process can be drawn.

Impact on China's investment–saving balance

Table 6.4 shows the importance of the Japanese assistance loans relative to the total amount of China's capital inflows from 1986 to 1995, comprising both foreign loans (that is ODA and OOF) and foreign direct investments (FDI). As seen in the table, the yen loans account for almost 10 per cent in the total of all foreign loans to China. However, their relative importance in China's capital inflows has decreased since 1992 along with the rapid increase of inward FDI to China.

But what has been the macroeconomic contribution of the yen loans to China? It is a well-known fact that China, despite being a developing country, is not suffering from any balance of payments problems – and for this simple reason it does not receive structural adjustment loans from the World Bank or the International Monetary Fund (IMF). Correspondingly, China is not affected by a domestic investment–savings gap. Along with the expanding Chinese trade surplus China has accumulated larger and larger foreign reserves since 1992. China's domestic savings exceed its domestic investments. Since the potential macroeconomic function of foreign investments and loans is the reduction of domestic savings shortages, China does not need capital imports from abroad for reasons of balance of payment concerns. However, capital import (in form of foreign loan and grants) can enlarge the state budget and increase public spending in China.

The share of ODA in the Chinese state budget

What then is the share of ODA and OOF from abroad in China's total state budget? Unfortunately, China's state budget does not report these capital inflows as own categories on its revenue side; The figures must therefore first be taken from international statistics (World Bank, IMF, OECD) and then related to China's official revenues and expenditures. However, this method

Table 6.4 Capital inflows to China, 1986–95 (US$ millions)

Year	Total loans from abroad		FDI	Total capital inflows
	Yen loans	Other loans		
1986	472	5 014	2 274	7 760
1990	537	6 534	3 755	10 826
1992	856	7 911	11 291	20 058
1995	1 130	10 327	37 806	49 263
Total[1]	7 213	75 707	132 668	215 588

Note: [1] Total of 1986 to 1995.

Source: *China Statistical Yearbook* (1996).

Table 6.5 The share of foreign loans and Japanese assistance loans in China's state budget

		Unit	Time periods	
			1986–90	*1991–95*
1 A	Total budget expenditures	mn RMB	12 866	24 387
1 B	Economic construction in China's budget	mn RMB	6 230	10 126
1B/1A	Share of economic construction	%	48.4	41.5
2 A	Foreign loans (real)	mn RMB	643	1 576
2A/1B	Share of foreign loans in China's economic construction	%	10.3	15.6
2 B	Japanese assistance loans (real)	mn RMB	94	339
2B/2A	Share of Japanese assistance loans in foreign loans to China	%	14.6	21.5
2B/1B	Share of Japanese assistance loans in China's economic construction	%	1.5	3.3

Source: *China Statistical Yearbook* (1996), calculations by the OECF.

is confronted with significant statistical problems. At what exchange rate should the donor dollar (or yen) amounts be converted into recipient renminbi amounts? What is China's estimated purchasing power parity (PPP)? The results in Table 6.5 must thus be understood as cautious estimates rather than exact accounts. The table shows the estimated shares of foreign loans and Japanese assistance loans in China's state budget total expenditures and economic construction expenditures from 1986 to 1995. According to these calculations the share of all foreign loans in the total Chinese economic construction budget was around 10 to 15 per cent. The share of Japanese yen loans accounted already for around 1.5 to 3.3 per cent.

Based on an alternative estimate on a dollar basis carried out by the embassy of Japan in Beijing (MoFA, 1999a), the share of all ODA from abroad in China's total public expenditures accounted to almost 4 per cent in 1996, of which 2.4 per cent was from Japanese ODA and 1.3 per cent from international organizations. On the other hand, the share of all ODA from abroad in China's total domestic investment was almost 1 per cent, of which 0.6 per cent was from Japanese ODA and 0.3 per cent from international organizations.

The sectoral and social impacts of ODA to China

There is still no established method for the evaluation of the sectoral and social impacts of development aid (Sato, 1994). A standard reference is the 1995 World Bank publication *Social Dimensions of Adjustment*, but the methods applied there are not really useful in the case of Japanese ODA which follows a project-based approach. This section will look at the sectors targeted by Japanese ODA in China, examine the shift of priorities in the last 20 years, and present some specific projects.

Support of economic infrastructure building in the 1980s

Initially the basic aim of Japanese development aid to China was to build up a modern economic infrastructure. Thus the assistance loan projects in the first half of the 1980s co-financed priority infrastructure construction works within the framework of China's sixth five-year plan (1981–85). Prominent projects of that period included the expansion of the railroad between Hengyang and Guangzhou, the electrification of the railroad between Zhengzhou and Baoji, the expansion of Lianyun and Qingdao port, the construction of berths in Chinwangtao port, the upgrading of the telephone networks in Tianjin, Shanghai and Guangzhou, and the construction of the hydroelectric power plant in Tianshengqiao.

The loan conditions were favourable: a 3.25 per cent interest rate per annum for project loans and a 3 per cent rate for commodity loans, a redemption period of 30 years including a 10-year grace period. According to OECF statistics, these assistance loans contributed substantially to the build-up of new infrastructure capacities. The OECF reports that projects sponsored by Japanese assistance loans accounted for almost 38 per cent of the new construction of railroads, 15 per cent large piers of ports, 25 per cent of new production capacities of chemical fertilizers and 3 per cent of power plants (OECF, 1999a). However, these figures must be qualified since the Japanese assistance loan system usually finances development projects only partially. It is always required that 'domestic sources' in the recipient country accept more than half of the total budget costs. In other words, Japanese assistance loans supported less than half of the total costs of the projects cited above. The Japanese share usually ranges from 10 to 50 per cent for each project. Therefore, the relative figures mentioned above should be reduced accordingly.

Shifting targets in the 1990s

In the 1990s the sectoral and regional focus of Japanese assistance loans to China underwent change. The emphasis of the fourth round of yen loans (1996–2000) was on the development of China's interior regions, the improvement of the environment and the development of the domestic agricultural food production. Corresponding with the changing focus in China's own development policy on the environment, agriculture and the interior regions, the focus of Japanese ODA shifted to the objective of a more balanced development in China, too.

Table 6.6 shows the absolute volumes and the relative shares of targeted sectors of Japanese assistance loans from 1979 until the end of calendar year 1998. A look at the accumulative totals shows that Japanese ODA in China has generally focused on infrastructure building, especially in the areas of

Table 6.6   Japanese assistance loans to China by sector, 1979–98 (Yen millions and %)

Sector	Cumulative totals at year-end 1998	Shares
Project loans, of which	2 130 873	94.3
• Transport infrastructure	1 069 572	47.3
• Energy infrastructure	476 667	21.1
• Communication infrastructure	116 949	5.2
• Mining and manufacturing industries	100 999	4.5
• Agriculture and fisheries	124 024	5.5
• Social services	24 070	1.1
• Environmental protection	196 057	8.7
• Irrigation and water supply	22 535	1.0
Commodity loans	130 000	5.7
Total	2 260 873	100.0

Source: OECF Quarterly Report.

transportation (railroads, ports, airports) and energy (electrical power generation, gas supply). However, a remarkable shift of emphasis occurred over the years, as can be seen in Table 6.1. Railroads and ports were especially at the core of the first round of yen loans (1979–83), but the weight of the transportation sector has been decreasing round by round. Along with the falling share of transportation, the weight of water supplies and environmental protection has risen. The agricultural sector increased its share in the third round, but less so in the fourth round (see Table 6.1). However, although ODA to agricultural and water supply sectors has been increased, Japan's share in the total amount of China's domestic investment in those sectors is still much smaller than its share in China's transportation sector. Nevertheless, the shares of the environment, the agricultural and the interior region, which are the main focus of Japanese assistance to China in recent years, have especially increased in the last two loan rounds.

Further to the different sectors mentioned above, Japanese ODA to China also contains a relatively large human resource development programme, which finances the training of around 900 people every year (JICA, 1999b). Whereas in the 1980s this training programme focused on industrial technologies, in the 1990s the focus shifted to corporate management and 'capacity-building' in judicial and administrative systems. These activities should be recognized in view of the frequent criticism of the alleged weakness of Japanese ODA in the area of capacity-building or institution-building (OECD, 1999).

Specific Japanese ODA projects in China

The wide spectrum of Japanese ODA projects in China can be illustrated by exemplary projects, some of which have been visited by the author personally.

The capacity expansion of both the new Beijing airport and the new Shanghai airport were co-financed by Japanese assistance loans. The Japanese share accounted for 40 and 22 per cent of the total costs, respectively. It is estimated that the new Beijing airport will expand its capacity threefold to 26 million passengers per year, and the new Shanghai airport, which had enlarged from a former capacity of 13 million passengers per year to 20 million in 2000, will grow to 33 million in 2005 (MRI, 2000). The number of beneficiaries of those two projects is very large, and these infrastructure investments are expected to considerably benefit local economies.

The construction of the Beijing subway has been co-financed by a yen 19.7 billion assistance loan that covered 45 per cent of the total cost. Since its opening in the year 2000, approximately 60 000 people use the subway daily and this number is expected to rise to 110 000 people in the year 2001 (MRI, 2000). However, such large-scale assistance loans have been frequently criticized by the Japanese mass media, because the Chinese government does not acknowledge the Japanese ODA support to the Chinese public. Thus, almost nobody in China is aware of the Japanese assistance. In this respect the Japanese ODA to China seems to be useless in the diplomatic sense in spite of its large contributions to the Chinese economy (*Sankei Shinbun*, 9 February 2000; 29 February 2000).

A similar case is the construction of the railroad between Nanning and Kunming, which has been supported by Japanese ODA that covers 25 per cent of the total costs. As a result the transportation capacity expanded from 2871 to 5110 tons, so that natural inland resources such as coal, phosphorus and aluminium can be carried more easily to the coastal area. However, this project has been criticized by military experts because the railroad leading to the Vietnamese border has a very high strategic importance. Furthermore, the project contributes mainly to resource development but not to the welfare of the people (*Sankei Shinbun*, 29 September 2000).

In contrast to the large scale yen loan projects, the so-called 'grassroots grant aid' is much better recognized by the Chinese public and especially by the Chinese people in the local poor areas benefiting from it directly. No more than yen 10 million may be spent for each of these projects. Representatives of the Japanese embassy directly contact the recipients and personally offer them the project aid. This grassroots aid has targeted such sectors as water supply facilities, school-building, local bridges and training centres. Although the amount of money spent is relatively small, it has directly contributed to the improvement of local people's lives, and it is highly appreciated. In that sense, these projects seem to be very effective by all measures. Consequently, the Japanese government has substantially increased the budget for its grass-root grant aid.

Japanese ODA to China and Sino–Japanese economic relations

As mentioned above, the allocation of Japanese ODA to China is largely untied. Nevertheless, a great many of the resulting project procurement orders granted by the Chinese entities have been going to Japanese companies, so that Japan's financial assistance proved to be an important and positive factor in Sino–Japanese economic relations, promoting Japanese exports and FDI to China. Along with Japan's increasing ODA disbursements to China in the 1980s and the 1990s, Sino–Japanese trade increased and Japanese FDI in China expanded in spite of some ups and downs (see Chapter 2).

However, the share of Japanese companies in the procurements of Japanese ODA projects in China has fallen drastically in recent years. Whereas in the 1980s the Japanese ODA procurement share amounted to approximately 50 to 70 per cent, this share fell to 34 per cent in 1996, to 36 per cent in 1997, to 15 per cent in 1998 and all the way to 4 per cent in 1999, according to OECF statistics. The share of Chinese companies rose accordingly. Such a rising share of procurement orders by recipient country companies may serve the theoretical developmental objective of ODA well, but it is naturally not well-received by Japan's private companies which are eager to expand their business in China. Along with the declining share of Japanese procurement, the flow of Japanese FDI to China, which had reached its peak in 1995, also decreased in the late 1990s for various reasons (see Chapter 3).

Japanese investors who complain about the generally harsh investment environment in China and the discrimination by Chinese authorities criticize Japanese ODA policy in China as a waste of taxpayers' money. In response to this criticism, the Japanese government acknowledged the economic interests of Japanese business in China, and a change in policy occurred in 1999. The Japanese government offered 'special yen loans' to the countries affected by the Asian financial crisis. These loans carry extremely concessional conditions with an interest rate of less than 1 per cent and a 40-year redemption period. In return, the recipients are requested to place more than half their procurement orders with Japanese companies. These special loans are called 'half-tied' loans. China was included in this programme, and such special yen loans were granted for two ODA projects in Beijing and Xingyan in March 2000 (*Nihon Keizai Shinbun*, 3 August 2000). It was reported that the special loan offer was initiated by MITI with the objective of export promotion (*Sankei Shinbun*, 31 July 2000). It is not surprising that this change of policy was strongly criticized by some Japanese politicians and mass media as being inconsistent and opportunistic (*Sankei Shinbun*, 18 August 2000; *Mainichi Shinbun*, 11 August 2000).

The political and diplomatic context

Further to its impact on bilateral economic relations, Japanese ODA has also been a pillar of Japanese diplomacy towards China. Japan's ODA programme has a wide range of implications in the political and diplomatic arena of Sino–Japanese relations.

'Politicization' of Japan's ODA to China

In the changing international political environment of the post-cold-war era, structural changes in the Sino–Japanese political relationship have occurred giving rise to various frictions. Japanese ODA to China has become a political issue between both countries, in addition to the 'history problem', the Senkaku (Diaoyu) islands issue and the controversy over the Japan–US Security Alliance. Thus the 'politicization' of Japanese ODA has become visible on various occasions.

The suppression of the democracy movement in Beijing's Tiananmen Square in June 1989 put the Japanese government in a dilemma. How should Japan react to the outright abuse of human rights by a country with which it has entered into such close diplomatic and economic relations? At first, Japan halted all new assistance and shelved its previously pledged aid projects on the grounds that implementation would be difficult (Tanaka, 1990). Only one year later, in July 1990, Japan resumed its economic assistance to China (Zhao, 1993). This change was justified by two reasons. First, sanctions would not necessarily encourage the democratization process, and, second, support for China's modernization was considered necessary for internal and regional stability, while the isolation of China would be harmful (Inada, 1993). In addition to the official statement of the MoFA, a report by a JICA study group headed by Saburo Okita proposed the expansion of Japanese ODA to China to promote economic reforms (JICA, 1991).

The next incident occurred in reaction to China's nuclear testing. In protest the Japanese government suspended its grant aid to China in 1995 (Katada, 2001; RIPS, 1996, p. 131). Some members of the ruling Liberal Democratic party also called for a 'reconsideration', meaning the suspension of assistance loans to China. These demands resurfaced in March 1996 when tensions escalated in the Taiwan Straits. Later on, Japanese ODA to China became a contentious issue out of principal concern. Already in June 1992 the Japan ODA Charter had been adopted, which relates the granting of ODA to political and strategic factors such as an end to nuclear testing, a reduction in arms exports, modest military expenditures, and respect for human rights (Shimomura, Nakagawa and Saito, 2000). It is evident that in these respects China would not be eligible for ODA, and therefore principal concern about ODA to China has been raised in Japan. However, the Japanese government did not interrupt assistance loans to China for such principal reasons.

On the other hand, the new linkage of ODA to political issues did, in fact, create a negative reaction on the Chinese side, and lead to the deterioration of the Sino–Japanese relationship. Although some argued that Japan should make demands on China when they are necessary, there is a deeply rooted belief, particularly within the MoFA, that ODA to China should not be altered in light of long-term Sino–Japanese relations and the need to assist Chinese reforms (RIPS, 1997, p. 117).

Although the principal importance of ODA for Sino–Japanese relations has been heralded within Japan, the view persists that aid to China should be revised given China's rapid economic development and Japan's economic and fiscal difficulties. In response to these views, a report by the second JICA study group on aid to China proposed that Japan's aid should focus on such really necessary areas as measures aimed at the Chinese interior, the environment and capacity building, relying on the self-help of the Chinese people (JICA, 1999a). In addition, MoFA organized a 'study group on aid to China' and made a proposal to redefine the direction of Japan's ODA to China in December 2000 (MoFA, 2000a).

Systemic changes in the offer and the reception of Japanese ODA to China

The State Planning Committee (SPC)[7] is the foremost institution in China's public investment decision-making. The SPC drafts the five-year development plan and decides on almost all economic construction projects in China (Takahara, 2000). Only for politically important projects has the judgement of the politburo of the communist party to be obtained; the top leaders themselves decide on the most important ODA projects. Although the (Chinese) Ministries of Finance, of Foreign Economy and Trade, and of Science and Technology accept the multilateral and bilateral foreign aid and loans, the key overarching organization is the SPC.

In this sense Japanese ODA within the Chinese system centres on the SPC and the communist party. Thus Japanese ODA money has strengthened the power of the state bureaucracy. From the perspectives of the local entities that receive Japanese financial support for their development projects, the money comes via the decisions and the judgements of the central government, not via the decisions of the Japanese side. Through recent changes, however, the scope of influence of the Japanese donors has been extended. The procedure of project selection has shifted from the 'short list' method to the 'long list' method. Now the Japanese side can choose appropriate projects from a longer list of possible projects. In addition to this change, the scheme of Japanese assistance loans to China is now shifting from multiyear (five to seven) commitments to one-year commitments. Whereas in the third round of yen loans, project commitments had been made for a period of six years (1990 to 1995), in the fourth round of yen loans the long-term commitments were divided into a first three-year period (1996 to 1998) and a second two-year period (1999 to 2000). Finally, beginning with the fiscal year 2001, the Japanese government has been offering assistance loans to China in the form of one-year commitments only. It is argued that this scheme will enable the Japanese side to decide on the content and the amount of its ODA to China more flexibly in response to changing situations. In the end the Japanese ODA authorities have obtained more influence in the decision-making on ODA projects in China.

Changing Japanese attitudes to aid to China

The Tiananmen incident of June 1989 was a turning point in the attitude of the Japanese public with respect to ODA to China. Ever since, the public support for aid to China has dropped. The international political environment changed in the post-cold-war era and so did the domestic political situation in Japan. The LDP, especially the Tanaka–Takeshita–Hashimoto Faction, has been supporting the increase of Japan's ODA to China, but has been losing its dominant influence to Japanese policy-making in recent years. The Japanese economy has stagnated in the aftermath of the collapse of the 'bubble economy', and within this changing framework, the Japanese stance to China has become increasingly detached. At the same time the significance of ODA for China's economic development has also decreased as China's dynamic economic growth was maintained throughout the 1990s and the Chinese economy grew to a considerable size. Given the changing environment in the twenty-first century, a reconsideration of ODA is needed from the Japanese point of view (MoFA, 2000b).

Apart from the particularities of 'the China case', Japanese public opinion has become increasingly negative to the increase of ODA in general. According to the annual opinion poll made by MoFA, the share of people who think Japan's ODA should be decreased rose to 22.3 per cent in 2000 (19.3 per cent in 1999) and the share of people who think aid should be stopped rose to 4.8 per cent in 2000 (2.4 per cent in 1999). Still the majority is supportive to the status quo level of ODA (42.4 per cent in 1999, and 41.5 in 2000), but the shift in a negative direction is very clear (PMO, 1999, 2000). In accordance with the fading public support for ODA, the Japanese ODA budget has been decreased in the latest fiscal year 2001 by 3 per cent from that of the previous year. In the general cut of ODA expenses, Japanese aid to China has been no exception. Japanese public sentiment has become negative to large disbursements of ODA, especially with regard to China which has become a major Asian power not only in the military and political sense, but also economically. Such changed attitudes in Japan constitute the general background of rethinking of aid policy to China among decision-makers in the government and political parties.

Key issues for the future directions of Japan's ODA to China

Integration of the Overseas Economic Cooperation Fund (OECF) and the Export–Import Bank of Japan (JEXIM) into the Japan Bank for International Cooperation (JBIC)

In October 1999 the two major Japanese ODA and OOF financing institutions, the Overseas Economic Cooperation Fund (OECF) and the Export–Import Bank of Japan (JEXIM) merged into the Japan Bank for International Cooperation (JBIC). Through this integration a huge lending institution has been established and synergetic effects are expected. In fact, the lending activities of both institutions already became quite similar during the 1990s. In the late 1990s the interest rate of JEXIM dropped to around 2 per cent, which was almost as low as the official ODA interest rate applied by the OECF. Besides, JEXIM offered untied loans for such infrastructure projects as local airports, roads and highways in China. Since both the ODA and the OOF lending are now disbursed by the JBIC, a meaningful demarcation has to be set up for the future. In the case of China a probable and useful distinction would be the granting of concessional lending (ODA) to the poorer inland area, and of less concessional loans (OOF) to more profitable projects in the coastal area.

Stronger focus on social development in poorer areas

Along with the lost eligibility of multilateral IDA loans in 1999, China needs even more Japanese assistance loans for the development and industrialization of its western regions. As the IDA formerly focused largely on agriculture and public health projects or transportation in poorer areas, Japanese ODA should compensate for the decreasing multilateral aid in these sectors through a corresponding shift in its ODA focus; that is, a shift from infrastructure building to social development, and from the coastal area to the interior regions. As has been mentioned to the author, such a change is expected by the World Bank as well (World Bank, 1999). Already in 1999 the JICA argued for a greater emphasis on poverty alleviation and social development in its second country study report on China (JICA, 1999). However, such a shift in focus to social sectors in the poorer interior regions would require a kind of institutional learning by the Japanese ODA institutions involved. Either they will have to increase their information and research capacities in such sectors as agriculture, education and health, or they will have to cooperate more intensively with the World Bank which has acquired such expertise through its former IDA projects.

More efforts in capacity-building

As already mentioned, China's domestic savings exceed its domestic investments, and China is attracting large amounts of private FDI. Thus, there is no macroeconomic need for public ODA. However, the Chinese state budget is running a huge structural deficit which is highly unlikely to shrink in future, as China's capital markets are still immature and the tax revenues are not sufficient. Thus, China's economic development is seriously handicapped by the limited redistribution capacity of the Chinese state. China's capital allocation system must be improved so that China can employ its relatively large domestic savings efficiently in the current development and industrialization process. The tax system has to be reformed and efficient capital markets have to be developed. Japanese ODA should focus on these objectives.

The Japanese efforts in this area should be coordinated with the same kind of efforts by the World Bank and other donors. Unfortunately in the past there has been only little cooperation between OECF, the World Bank and other donors in China, but much closer coordination will be necessary in the future. It would be useful if a forum could be set up to discuss the comprehensive development strategy of China between the different donors and the Chinese authorities such as the State Planning Committee and the Chinese Ministry of Finance. In addition, it would be desirable to involve Chinese 'civil society' in these dialogues, as the international aid community has strongly advocated such a participatory approach in recent years.

Notes

1. All figures on Japanese ODA refer to fiscal years, lasting from 1 April to 31 March unless otherwise stated.
2. Although there is no clear evidence in diplomatic documents, such motives can be assumed from the memoirs and interview remarks of some political leaders of the Liberal Democratic Party (LDP) and of high ranked officials of the MoFA.
3. Other official flows (OOF) refer to official lending with grant elements of less than 25 per cent and a less concessional character than ODA.
4. The World Bank has channelled large amounts of loans to China through its main lending institutions under the ODA category through the International Development Association (IDA), and under the OOF category through the International Bank for Reconstruction and Development (IBRD). The IDA is the so-called 'Second World Bank' for the development of less-developed countries, established in 1960, and the IBRD is the main part of the World Bank, established in 1945.
5. The Overseas Economic Cooperation Fund (OECF) is the Japanese government agency responsible for the extension of government assistance loans denominated in Japanese yen. In October 1999 the OECF was integrated into the Japan Bank for International Cooperation (JBIC).
6. The Japan International Cooperation Agency (JICA) is the Japanese government institution responsible for implementing technical assistance and offering grant aid. The JICA conducts training programmes in Japan and an expert dispatch programme and provides equipment and materials.
7. The State Planning Committee (SPC) is regarded as the most influential government institution for economic management in China. In 1999 its name was changed to the State Development and Planning Committee.

References

ADB (Asian Development Bank) (1998) *Country Assistance Plan: People's Republic of China (1999–2001)*, Manila: ADB.

Arase, D. (1995) *Buying Power: The Political economy of Japan's Foreign Aid*, Boulder: Lynne Rienner.

Ensign, M. M. (1992) *Doing Good or Doing Well? Japan's Foreign Aid Programme*, New York: Columbia University Press.

Inada, J. (1989) 'Japan's Aid Diplomacy: Economic, Political, or Strategic?' *Millennium: Journal of International Studies*, vol. 18 (3), pp. 399–414.

— (1993) 'Democratization, Marketization, and Japan's Emerging Role as a Foreign Aid Donor', US–Japan Programme Occasional Paper no. 93-03, Cambridge MA.: Harvard University.

— (2000) 'The Economic and Social Impacts of Japan's ODA to China', Japan Institute for International Affairs (JIIA), *Preliminary Research on the Economic and Social Impacts of ODA to China*, Tokyo: JIIA.

JICA (Japan International Cooperation Agency) (1991) *Chûgoku: kunibetsu enjô kenkyûkai hôkokushô* [China: Report of the Country-Specific Aid Research Group], Tokyo: JICA.

— (1999a) *Chûgoku kunibetsu enjô kenkyûkai hôkokushô Dainiji* [China: Report of the Country-Specific Aid Research Group – The Second Study], Tokyo: JICA.

— Beijing Office (1999b) *Outline of JICA Projects in China*, Beijing: JICA.

— (2000) *Jigo hyôka hôkokusho* [Post Evaluation Report], Tokyo: JICA.

Jin, X. (2000) *Riben zhengfu kaifa yuanzu* [Japan's Official Development Assistance], Beijing: Shehui kexue wehzhai chubanshe.

Katada, S. N. (2001) 'Why did Japan Suspend Foreign Aid to China? Japan's Foreign Aid Decision-making and Sources of Aid Sanction', *Social Science Japan Journal*, vol. 4 (1), pp. 39–58.

Mainichi Shinbun (2000) Chûgoku e no enshakkan no bôkyo [Nonsense of Yen Loan to China], 11 August 2000.

MRI (Mitsubishi Research Institute) (2000) *Taichû ODA no kôka chôsa* [Research on the Impacts of ODA to China: Preliminary Report], Tokyo: Mitsubishi Research Institute.

MoFA (Ministry of Foreign Affairs), Embassy of Japan in Beijing (1999a) 'Recent Economic Situations in China and Japan–China Economic Relations', Research Paper, Beijing: Embassy of Japan in Beijing.

— Economic Cooperation Bureau (1999b) *Keizai kyôryoku hyôka hôkokusho* [Economic Cooperation Evaluation Report], Tokyo: MoFA.

— Economic Cooperation Bureau (2000a) *Japan's Official Development Assistance*, Tokyo: Association for Promotion of International Cooperation (APIC).

— (2000b) *Nijûisseiki nimuketa taichû keizaikyôryoku no arikatani kansuru kondankai teigen* [The Proposal of the Study Group on the Economic Assistance to China in the 21st Century], December, Tokyo: MoFA.

Naughton, B. (1995) *Growing out of the Plan: Chinese Economic Reform 1978–1993*, Cambridge and New York: Cambridge University Press.

Nihon Keizai Shinbun (2000) Chûgoku e teiri enshakkan [Low Interest Rate Yen Loan to China], 3 August 2000.

OECD (Organization for Economic Cooperation and Development), Development Assistance Committee (1999) *Development Cooperation Review*, series no. 34: Japan, Paris: OECD.

— Development Assistance Committee (various years), *Geographical Distribution of Financial Flows to Aid Recipients*, Paris: OECD.

OECF (Overseas Economic Cooperation Fund) (1999a) *Outline of Yen Loans to China*, Beijing: OECF.

— (1999b) *Enshakkan anken jigo hyôka hôkokusho 1999* [Yen Loan Projects: Post-Evaluation Report 1999], Tokyo: OECF.

PMO (Prime Minister's Office) (1999) *Gaiko ni kansuru yoron chôsa* [Public Opinion Poll Regarding Foreign Policies], Tokyo: PMO.

— (2000) *Gaiko ni kansuru yoron chôsa* [Public Opinion Poll regarding foreign policies], Tokyo.

RIPS (Research Institute for Peace and Security) (1985) *Asian Security 1985*, Tokyo: RIPS.
— (1996) *Asian Security 1995–96*, Tokyo: RIPS.
— (1997) *Asian Security 1996–97*, Tokyo: RIPS.
— (1998) *Asian Security 1997–98*, Tokyo: RIPS.
Sankei Shinbun (2000) Nihon no taichû ODA keizaikôyô ni? [Japan's ODA to China: Any Economic Effect?], 9 February 2000.
— (2000) Pekin kokusaikûkô [Beijing International Airport], 29 February 2000.
— (2000) Taichû ODA 170 okuen tsuika [Additional ODA of 17 billion Yen to China], 31 July 2000.
— (2000) Senryakunaki sirimetsuretsu no gaikô [Incoherent Diplomacy with no Strategy], 18 August 2000.
— (2000) Taichûgoku ODA no jittai sôtenken o [Examine the Reality of ODA to China], 29 September 2000.
Sato, H. (1994) *Enjo no shakaiteki eikyô* [Social Impacts of Aid], Tokyo: Institute of Developing Economies.
Shimomura, Y., Nakagawa, J. and Saito, J. (2000) *ODA taikô no seijikeizai gaku* [Political Economy of ODA Charter], Tokyo: Yuhikaku.
State Statistical Bureau of PRC (2000 and various years), *China Statistical Yearbook*, Beijing: China Statistical Publishing House.
Takahara, A. (2000) 'Chûgoku no keizai gyôsei kaikaku to Nihon no ODA' [China's Economic and Administrative Reforms and Japan's ODA], The Japan Institute for International Affairs (JIIA), *Preliminary Research on the Economic and Social Impacts of ODA to China*, Tokyo: JIIA.
Tanaka, A. (1990) 'Tenanmon jiken igo no Chûgoku wo meguru kokusai kankyô' [International Environment after the Tienanmen Incident], *Kokusai Mondai* 358 (January), pp. 30–40.
— (1991) *Nicchû kankei: 1945–1990* [Japan–China Relations 1945–1990], Tokyo: Tokyo University Press.
UNDP (United Nations Development Programme) (1999) *United Nations Development Programme in China: Sustainable Human Development*, Beijing: UNDP.
World Bank, Operations Evaluation Department (1995) *Social Dimensions of Adjustment*, Washington, DC: The World Bank.
World Bank (1997a) *China 2020: Integration with the Global Economy*, Washington, DC: World Bank.
— (1997b) *China – Country Assistance Strategy*, Washington, DC: World Bank.
— (1999) *China: Weathering the Storm and Learning the Lessons*, Washington, DC: World Bank.
World Bank (Resident Mission in China) (ed.) (2000) *The World Bank Group in China: Facts & Figures*, Beijing: World Bank.
Yasutomo, D. T. (ed.) (1986) *The Manner of Giving: Strategic Aid and Japanese Foreign Policy*, New York: St Martin's Press.
Zhao, Q. (1993) 'Japan's Aid Diplomacy with China', in B. M. Koppel and R. M. Orr (eds), *Japan's Foreign Aid: Power and Policy in a New Era*, Boulder: Westview Press.

7
Will Global Warming Affect Sino–Japan Relations?

Yasuko Kameyama

Introduction

Over the past two thousand years, Sino–Japanese relationships have not always been stable, and especially in the aftermath of the Second World War the political atmosphere of the Northeast Asian region has been chilly. Relations started to improve only in the past three decades following the resumption of diplomatic relations in 1972. The pace has been slow, however.

Japan has been attempting to achieve better political relations by strengthening economic ties with China, and there are many reasons why Japan aspires to a better relationship with its biggest neighbour. From China's point of view, however, Japan's attempt to normalize bilateral ties without resolving the historical legacy of the Second World War is unsatisfactory. Strengthened regional ties would favour Japan without acknowledgement of what it had done to the region in the past. On the other hand, by taking advantage of this situation China stands to receive more financial and technological assistance from Japan than would otherwise be the case.

The global warming problem entered international political consciousness in the late 1980s and has been influencing the conventional Sino–Japanese relationship ever since. Global warming is caused by the increasing concentration of greenhouse gases (GHG) in the atmosphere. According to the Third Assessment Report (TAR) of the Intergovernmental Panel on Climate Change (IPCC), the average global surface temperature (that is the average of near surface air temperature over land, and sea surface temperature) has increased since the late nineteenth century. Over the period 1990 to 2100, the temperature is projected to increase by 1.4 to 5.8 degrees centigrade. These results are for the full range of all 35 scenarios in the Special Reports on Emission Scenarios (SRES), based on a number of climate models. Such an increase of temperature may cause sea-levels to rise, change precipitation patterns, and increase extreme climatic events. Yields of crops are likely to be affected by the changes of temperature and water supply (IPCC, 2001).

The main focus of debate at the international level is the question of how much each country should reduce or limit greenhouse gas (GHG) emissions, especially CO_2 (carbon dioxide) emissions. Both China and Japan are great contributors to world CO_2 emissions: China's emissions are around 14.1 per cent of the world total, while Japan is responsible for around 4.9 per cent (figures for 1996). It is thus important to have both Japan's and China's involvement in mitigating climate change. On the other hand, things look different when the degree of responsibility is discussed in terms of emission per capita. As a developing country, China's CO_2 emission per capita is only 2.6 tons, while that of Japan is 9.8 tons. From these figures, it is natural to say that one Japanese person must assume more responsibility than one Chinese person. Thus, how much Japan can do together with China to reduce emissions automatically links to debates on responsibility.

The following chapter examines how global environmental problems, especially global warming, have influenced Japan's China policy in recent years. The climate change problem is not merely an environmental problem. It can also play a role as a catalyst for a new dialogue between the countries in the region. Will climate change lead to a new Sino–Japan relationship? How does Japan view climate change from the perspective of its China policy? Is China willing to accept Japan's proposal for cooperation on climate change policy? To answer these questions, this chapter reviews Japanese China policy in the past and examines how it has changed along with the emergence of the climate change problem. The chapter concludes that the international regime on climate change has influenced both Japan and China in a positive way, that the Sino–Japan relation may improve by utilizing institutions established under the climate change regime, and that success for such improvement lies significantly in the hands of China.

Evolution of a new concept of security

What is the basis of Japanese foreign policy? Perhaps most significant is Japan's perception of vulnerability and the concept of security that arises from it. Japan has always been vulnerable to changes outside of Japan, both economically and politically. As a country that relies heavily on other countries for natural resources, it is destined to be receptive to changes that occur outside of the country. In particular, changes in the supply of natural resources such as oil and other minerals are critical to Japan. In the year 1994, for instance, 94.7 per cent of Japan's total energy supply was imported from abroad (EDMC, 1996), a rate which has been fairly stable in the last two decades. The dependence on imports for natural resources is not only crucially important for the economy but also politically significant, because Japan is compelled to maintain good relations with countries which export natural resources to Japan.

Another aspect of Japan's political vulnerability is related to its military defence. Since the end of the Second World War, Japan has relied on the

United States for its military security. Japan itself, however, has been reluctant to maintain strong military forces both during and after the Cold War (Berger, 1998). Supporters for rewriting Article 9 of the Japanese Constitution, which restricts Japan in its military capacity building, are facing strong domestic political opposition. For Japan's national security the term *sôgô anzen hoshô* (comprehensive security) is the keyword. The understanding of comprehensive security, however, has shifted as circumstances have changed, and this shift has also influenced the positions of Japan on various foreign policies including its China policy.

The Japanese notion of comprehensive security may be treated theoretically in recent studies on the environment and security. Approaches that are used in studies on this topic differ, but they may be categorized in several ways (Dabelko and Dabelko, 1995; Rønneldt, 1997; Gleditsch, 1998; Ohta, 1998). Among those categorizations, one of the most distinct is a group of studies that considers environmental degradation and depletion of resources as a new type of threat to our social system, nation and/or individuals (Ullman, 1983; Thomas, 1987; Mathews, 1989; Wirth, 1989). This approach intends to elevate environmental issues to an equal status with other issues that are considered to be 'high politics' by enlarging the scope of 'security' to non-military issues such as the global environment, the economy and social problems. Japan's notion of comprehensive security is similar to studies that fall into this category. This group's argument, however, is challenged by some other studies which criticize the view that the relation between the different types of issues considered as security threats is not clear (Deudney, 1990; Levy, 1995). It is also difficult to determine priority among issues.

To overcome this challenge, other types of environment and security studies are helpful. These are studies that limit a 'threat' to conventional military conflict, and attempt to explain linkages between conflict and scarcity of resources and/or environmental degradation (WCED, 1987; Myers, 1989; Homer-Dixon, 1991; Gleick, 1993). In recent years, an increasing number of case studies have been made to establish the linkage between environmental degradation and conflict.

The differences of approach of these environment and security studies illustrate the differences between the Japanese concept of security in the 1970s and in the 1990s. These are explained in the following sections.

Sino–Japanese relations before the emergence of the climate change problem

The argument in this chapter is based on how climate change debates have influenced Japan's notions of security. As reviewed in the previous section, two categories of relationship between the concept of traditional security and other kinds of non-military risks are helpful to explain the evolution of the Japanese security concept, with issues such as energy or environment being important. In order to implement appropriate measures to turn comprehensive security into reality, however, it is necessary to recognize the relation between environmental policies and other related policies. Such relations can possibly reveal the cooperative connection between China and Japan.

Japan's notion of comprehensive security came into being in the 1970s at a time when a new era of Sino–Japanese relations began. In 1972, President Nixon visited China and normalized diplomatic relations between China and the United States. In his discussion with Mao Zedong, Nixon was assured that China would not threaten Japan or South Korea, and that it regarded the Soviet Union as the world's principal security concern (Tow, 1994). After Nixon's visit to China, Japan's Prime Minister Tanaka followed suit and diplomatic relation between China and Japan were also normalized.

By that time, Japan had regained its economic strength, achieving high rates of economic growth (9.4 per cent during the 1965–73 period; EDMC, 1996). Following the collapse of the Bretton Woods Agreement, an event to be known as the Nixon Shock in Japan, the yen appreciated significantly against the US dollar in the early 1970s, and Japan's exports of manufactured goods plunged. In addition to that, the first oil crisis hit the world in 1973 and the price of oil quadrupled. Japan's annual GDP growth rate fell to minus 0.5 per cent in 1974.

With the shift of people's concern from political tension to economic anxieties, Japanese policy-makers called for comprehensive security (Katzenstein, 1996). Thus national security consisted not only of security by means of military power for defence, but also in the existence of a favourable environment for stable economic growth. A supply of constant energy resources was considered to be of extreme importance.

The late 1960s and early 1970s were also the time of the first environmental movement at a global level. Many publications came out that suggested doomsday scenarios resulting from heavy contamination, depletion of natural resources, and population expansion (Ehrlich, 1968; Hardin, 1968); and in 1972 the United Nations Conference on the Human Environment was held in Stockholm (Tolba *et al.*, 1992). In those days, however, the focus in Japan was more on pollution at the domestic and local level, and on scarcity of resources. Japanese policy-makers believed that Japan was still in the midst of industrialization (CJEBAP, 1997), so they were not looking at Japan's foreign policy from the industrialized countries' point of view. Thus Japan along with many other countries at that time considered that a pollution abatement policy was to be implemented at the national level only; they were not interested in the establishment of international institutions. Japan's comprehensive security covered only security for Japan itself, and not security for Asia and the Pacific region.

Nevertheless, within the framework of the comprehensive security concept the relations with countries that supplied Japan with resources were considered crucial. China became an important country for Japan because of the supply of coal and agricultural products, such as soybeans. Although the normalization of relations between China and Japan contributed to increasing bilateral trade, and Japan offered large amounts of financial assistance to China, Japan did not engage in trying to solve other political bilateral problems. Thus the comprehensive security policy was effective for Japan's prosperity, but not for the political stability of the region. The notion of comprehensive security did not lead to institution-building for regional security.

During the 1980s, the price of oil dropped again and Japan regained its economic strength. Although the yen appreciated again substantially in the aftermath of the Plaza Agreement in 1985 and export activity temporarily collapsed, the economy grew vigorously at rates of around 3 to 6 per cent annually. Imports of foreign products increased, and the price of energy was kept low, so there was less incentive to be aware of energy scarcity. The economic boom ended suddenly in the early 1990s following the crash of Japan's stock and real-estate markets, and during that decade the Japanese economy never really rebounded and remained in severe stagnation.

The decisive event in international political affairs in the late 1980s and the early 1990s was the end of the Cold War, and the collapse of the centrally-planned economies of Central and Eastern European countries. The Soviet Union turned into the Russian Federation and other independent states. This era was also the time when global environmental problems started to be placed on the international political agenda, more frequently and more seriously than at the time of the Stockholm meeting in 1972. The acid rain problem was already being discussed in Europe and in North America in the early 1980s, and ozone depletion was dealt with in the late 1980s and climate change in the early 1990s. The United Nations Conference on Environment and Development was held in Rio de Janeiro in 1992 (Tolba *et al.*, 1992).

A brief history of climate change negotiations

Since climate change is of a global nature, existing institutions for combating climate change are mostly global. After global warming was recognized as an international political issue in the late 1980s, the first international treaty on climate change, the Framework Convention on Climate Change (FCCC), was adopted in 1992 (United Nations, 1992). The FCCC urged the Annex I country parties (that is the industrialized countries and countries whose economies are under transition to a market economy) to take measures aimed at returning their greenhouse gas (GHG) emissions to 1990 levels by the year 2000.[1]

In 1995, at the first Conference of the Parties (COP1) to the Framework Convention on Climate Change (FCCC), the participants discussed the adequacy of commitments under Article 4.2 (a)(b), and arrived at a conclusion that further steps were needed to achieve the ultimate objective, which is the stabilization of GHG concentrations in the atmosphere at a level that prevents dangerous anthropogenic interference with the climate system (Article 2). It was agreed that the Conference of the Parties (COP) would begin a process to strengthen the commitments of Annex I countries by elaborating policies and measures, and by setting 'quantified limitation and reduction objectives within specific time-frames, such as 2005, 2010 and 2020' for their GHG emissions, which were later called QELROs – Quantified Emission Limitation and Reduction Objectives (United Nations, 1995).

This agreement, the Berlin Mandate, initiated the second phase of the international consultation process that led to the adoption of the Kyoto Protocol in 1997 (United Nations, 1997). During the negotiation, the United States and other industrialized countries insisted that the developing countries should also set emission targets, a proposal which was strongly opposed by China and other developing countries. This group, called G77 plus China, reasoned that emissions from industrialized countries were luxurious emissions, while those of the developing countries were necessary ones. The view of G77 plus China succeeded in this debate. The Kyoto Protocol called for legally-binding targets for GHG emissions and sequestration of the Annex I countries only during the period 2008–12. For instance, Japan's annual average GHG emission from 2008 to 2012 was to be 6 per cent lower than that of the 1990 level. The United States initially agreed to lower its emissions by 7 per cent within the same timeframe.[2]

On the other hand, G77 plus China did not win the battle over 'mechanisms'. Mechanisms are the three types of institutions regulating the international cooperative actions for emission reductions, such as Joint Implementation (JI) (between Annex I countries only), the Clean Development Mechanism (CDM) and Emission Trading (ET).

Joint implementation (JI) is defined in Article 6:

> Any Party included in Annex I may transfer to, or acquire from, any other such Party emission reduction units resulting from projects aimed at reducing anthropogenic emissions by sources or enhancing anthropogenic removals by sinks or GHG.

The clean development mechanism (CDM) is similar to joint implementation (JI) but between Annex I and non-Annex I countries. Article 12 states that:

> a clean development mechanism is hereby defined [to] assist Parties not included in Annex I in achieving sustainable development and in contributing to the ultimate objective of the Convention, and to assist Parties included in Annex I in achieving compliance with their quantified emission limitation and reduction commitments.

The third mechanism, emission trading (ET), was accepted in Article 17 stating:

> The Conference of the Parties shall define the relevant principles, modalities, rules and guidelines, in particular for verification, reporting and accountability for emissions trading.

The G77 plus China were against these mechanisms which allow industrialized countries to buy emission permits from other countries. They argued that such mechanisms prevented developed countries from seriously reducing emissions domestically. However, the non-EU Annex I countries strongly requested the establishment of such mechanisms. Japan was also concerned that it might not be able to achieve its 6 per cent emission reduction target agreed in the Kyoto Protocol, and would only ratify the protocol if it were certain that it could comply with its obligations under the Protocol. GHG emissions have been on the rise in Japan since 1990, and they were expected to continue to rise by 2010 to about 20 per cent without a changed climate policy.

It was therefore important for Japan to use the Kyoto mechanisms and to acquire emission permits abroad through emission trading. Emission trading under the current Kyoto Protocol allows trading among Annex B countries only, which are basically the same group of countries as Annex I. However, the growth of emission can be curbed at most in the developing world. The clean development mechanism (CDM) is the only mechanism that involves emission limitation projects in developing countries. Thus CDM is an important mechanism to increase environmental cooperation between Japan and the developing countries especially in the Asia-Pacific region.

In order to make the mechanisms workable, the parties have to agree on principles, modalities, rules and guidelines for emission trading. In this respect, questions as to whether forest-related projects are eligible as CDM projects became one of the major contentious issues in the climate change negotiation;[3] Japan always supported the idea of including forest-related activities in CDM. Thus, reforestation activities especially in Southeast Asia and in China could be promoted.

Climate change and regional cooperation

Climate change is related to the global atmospheric concentration of GHG. Therefore, reduction or limitation of GHG in any part of the world will have an effect on the global climate. Cooperation in actions to mitigate climate change in Northeast Asia, however, has been driven more rapidly within the region than with countries outside the region. Since Japan is the only fully industrialized country in the region, most of the cooperation on climate change in the region has been initiated either by Japan or by multilateral organizations. In many cases, cooperation on climate change is part of the regional cooperation for environmental problems in general. Thus regional

(Northeast) environmental cooperation takes place both at the multilateral and the bilateral level.

Multilateral environmental cooperation in Northeast Asia

At the multilateral level there are various cooperative activities supported by Japan:

- In 1991, the Japanese Ministry of the Environment (formerly the Environment Agency) launched the Asia-Pacific Seminar on Climate Change, where experts from the Asia-Pacific region gather every year to discuss possible regional cooperation on climate change. The objective of the seminar is to support regional efforts to address climate change, to promote awareness and exchange experiences on the issue within the Asia-Pacific region, and facilitate steps to address climate change issues within the region. For this purpose, the agenda of the meetings contains topics such as the dissemination of information about recent progress in international efforts, the exchange of information relating to the preparation of national communications to be submitted to the Framework Convention on Climate Change (FCCC) secretariat, and the facilitation of cooperation among countries in the Asia-Pacific region in coping with climate change and its impacts (EAJ, 1996).
- Japan acts as the secretariat of the Asia-Pacific Network for Global Change Research (APN). The APN's objective is to foster regional-scale research programmes and to increase developing countries' participation in international research activities such as the International Geosphere-Biosphere Programme (IGBP), the International Human Dimensions Programme on Global Environmental Change (IHDP) and Systems for Analysis, Research and Training for Global Change (START).
- The Conference on Northeast Asia Environmental Cooperation was established in 1992 and consists of Japan, China, Korea, Russia and Mongolia. It gathers once a year to discuss different environment-related topics at an official and academic level.
- The Environmental Congress for Asia and the Pacific (ECO Asia) is also an annual meeting at ministerial level to discuss a variety of environmental topics. The first ECO Asia was held in 1992. Apart from ECO Asia, there are trilateral ministerial meetings that began in 1992, which include only Japan, China and Korea. These exchanges of views have not developed into further cooperation, but have been considered as an initial step for integrity of the region (EAJ, 1998).

Bilateral environmental cooperation in Northeast Asia

Other more tangible forms of cooperation are being implemented bilaterally, and Japan has especially strengthened its environmental cooperation with China.

In 1996 the 'China–Japan Environment Cooperation Comprehensive Forum' was set up, the objective of which is the exchange of views on possible collaboration in the mitigation of urgent environmental problems in China such as air pollution, water pollution and acid rain. When Prime Minister Hashimoto visited China in 1997, he emphasized Japan's willingness to cooperate with China to solve China's environmental problems. He publicly committed the Japanese government to Sino–Japan Environmental Cooperation in the 21st Century, which consists of two main pillars. First, the Environmental Information Network Plan aims at setting up computers in 100 cities in China to facilitate the dissemination of information on environmental issues. Second, within the framework of the Sino–Japan Environmental Development Model for Urban Planning, the three cities Dalian, Chongqing and Guiyang have been chosen as model cities to implement comprehensive urban policies to establish environmentally sound, economically developing cities. To support these projects financially, the interest rates of Japanese ODA assistance loans to China related to environmental projects are to be minimized.

In 1997, 15 per cent of Japanese grants and assistance loans to China, amounting to US\$ 3012 million and US\$ 309 million, respectively, were employed for environmental purposes. The environment share is likely to increase in future, while the total amount of Japanese overseas development aid (ODA) is likely to decline due to the difficult economic situation in Japan (MoFA, 1998).

Apart from ODA, the Ministry of Economy, Trade and Industry (METI, formerly the Ministry of International Trade and Industry, MITI) and the Ministry of the Environment have taken the initiative to start so-called Activities Implemented Jointly (AIJ) projects. AIJ projects are types of cooperation similar to the clean development mechanism (CDM). It was agreed at the 1995 Conference of the Parties (COP1) to start such programmes in a pilot phase to run until the end of the decade, so that the COP could then decide whether they are effective enough to be continued. Eleven projects have been accepted as AIJ projects by the Japanese government (NEDO, 1998).

In 1998, MITI accepted another 37 new projects, which were considered as feasibility studies towards effective joint implementation (JI) or CDM projects as soon as the CDM scheme was officially accepted under the Kyoto Protocol. Of these 37 projects, 20 are projects with Russia, and nine are with China. The average cost of one project will be about US\$ 450000, and large Japanese companies will be the main contributors to these projects.

Regional objectives of climate change cooperation

In spite of certain similarities in Japan's domestic and international environment in the 1970s and the 1990s, Japanese foreign policy, following the concept of comprehensive security, was markedly different in both periods.

In the 1970s, comprehensive security emphasized a stable energy supply; in the 1990s, the concept accentuated environmental problems. Japan's responses to regional security challenges were also different. In the 1970s, Japan was only interested in its national security level and did not make any efforts to build up bilateral or multilateral regimes for the discussion of regional security issues. In the 1990s, Japan was more willing to do something at the regional level in Northeast Asia. How did these differences originate?

As observed in the previous section, Northeast Asian countries have been strengthening their regional cooperative relations on global warming as well as on environmental issues in general. Several questions arise regarding this regional cooperation. First, what are the incentives of the regional cooperation on climate change for the countries in the Northeast Asia region? Second, why does cooperation occur within the region, while GHG can be reduced anywhere? Third, why is most of the regional cooperation bilateral and not multilateral? These questions may be answered within the context of the specific political and economic environment for climate change cooperation in Northeast Asia.

Effect of reducing greenhouse gas (GHG) emissions in Northeast Asia

It is generally assumed that CO_2 emission in Northeast Asia, especially from China, will rapidly increase in the coming decades. On the other hand, there is ambiguity concerning the impact of climate change in the region. Thus, efforts to reduce emissions are not likely to occur if the climate change problem is only regarded from a game-theory point of view, taking only the impact of climate change and the cost of mitigation into account. On the other hand, climatic disasters such as extraordinary rainfall can lead to severe floods in the region: in the summer of 1998, more than 3000 people were killed in China. Although this extraordinary weather was not necessarily caused by climate change, there now seems to be more awareness within the region of the serious impact of climate change. Once the impact of climate change is acknowledged, the importance of countermeasures within a region that emits nearly one-fifth of global emissions and is likely to emit twice that amount in the next decade is acknowledged as well.

Japan's participation at the clean development mechanism (CDM)

Japan's commitment of 6 per cent reduction of GHG during the 2008–12 period in the Kyoto Protocol is considered difficult, and there are various estimates of how much emission can be reduced without severely damaging economic activities (Amano, 1996). The majority view agrees that it would be less expensive to reduce CO_2 emissions outside of Japan, since the marginal costs of CO_2 reduction in Japan are even higher than in other OECD countries (OECD, 1998a). Since the clean development mechanism (CDM) is the only mechanism that allows the exchange of emission credits between Annex I and non-Annex I countries, the Japanese government and the business community of Japan have been interested in starting CDM with countries in Northeast Asia. Thus Japan's willingness to cooperate in the Northeast Asian region is driven by the mechanisms of the Kyoto Protocol.

Environmental problems other than climate change

There is a growing recognition in Northeast Asia that acid rain is a major environmental problem in the region. However, regional cooperation on the acid rain issue is still in the monitoring stage of ascertaining the sulphur content of precipitation that moves from one country to another (Brettel and Kawashima, 1998). Nevertheless, it is frequently stressed that mitigation of sulphur emission in China will be the key. Within China, local air pollution has been a serious problem in many industrial cities; in Chongqing, for instance, the atmospheric concentration of SO_x was $0.351 \, mg/m^3$ in 1992, around four times above the set air-quality standard of China (Imura and Katsuhara, 1995). There is already cooperation between Japan and China to set up desulphurization equipment within coal burning plants, but desulphurization equipment is itself expensive and consumes extra electricity when operating (MITI, 1997), and such equipment has frequently been left idle. More recent bilateral technological cooperation focuses on improvements in energy efficiency. Examples are carbon dry quenching technology and energy-efficient coal-burning power plants. These technologies are less expensive and they reduce emissions of both sulphur and CO_2 for each unit of electricity generated. Therefore, the most likely effect of the Sino–Japan Environmental Development Model for Urban Planning is to solve local air pollution, acid rain and climate change at the same time.

Energy security

Although the term *sôgô anzen hoshô* is now less popular than in the 1970s and 1980s, the basic idea still remains. In contrast to the 1970s, however, in the 1990s the concept of comprehensiveness of security also includes environmental issues. In the era of low oil prices, climate change served as an alternative impetus for Japan's foreign policy considerations of energy resources. However, apart from Japan's own energy consumption, that of neighbouring countries' also became an important matter. If China's economy continues to grow at the same rate as in the last decade, it will become a huge energy consumer. Since (South) Korea is also increasing its energy consumption, it can be easily expected that the regional energy market will become tighter and tighter. Can the regional market be regulated? A regional institute for energy policy would probably not find much support in the region because no country would accept a limit on its own energy use. In this situation, climate change policy is a useful tool to regulate energy use in China and elsewhere in the region.

Natural resources are not equally distributed in Northeast Asia, and Japan's energy demand depends almost completely on imports. In 1996

Japan imported 98 per cent of the coal and almost 100 per cent of the crude oil it consumed. The situation is similar for Korea, whose respective coal and oil import shares were 96 and 100 per cent in the same year (OECD, 1998b). On the other hand, China has a great amount of coal, but also imports crude oil. Both Japan and Korea worry that China along with its increasing oil consumption will dominate the oil market; Japan and Korea will become price takers. It is thus important for the Japanese and Korean governments to try to reduce the growth of China's oil demand, and one way is to offer technological assistance to improve energy efficiency in oil-consuming equipment such as automobiles.

Moreover, China can reduce its fossil fuel consumption through the development of its nuclear energy generation. This option is realistic for Japan but too expensive for China alone. Up to now no official bilateral cooperation has been started in nuclear power plant construction in China, but Japan has already proposed that nuclear power plant projects be made eligible for the clean development mechanism (CDM) because nuclear power plants emit less CO_2 than coal burning power plants. China supports this position.

The Japanese government and business community started an activity called the Asia Pipeline Study Group in 1997, a plan to construct a gas pipeline from Siberia down to China, Korea and Japan, with the main purpose being to secure energy for Japan (APSG, 1998). This project also attempts to refurnish old pipelines within Russia to reduce gas leakage, which may also be counted as reduction of GHG emission of joint implementation (JI) projects.

China as a new market

More and more Chinese people are earning high or medium incomes, and it is therefore quite natural that foreign business, such as the automotive or the home electric appliance industry, are becoming more and more interested in entering the Chinese market (see Chapter 9). Starting projects with the Chinese business community may mean new economic relations with the Chinese people, which will lead to more investment and economic benefits. Not only Japan and Korea but also many other countries are interested in China's large market.

Improving regional political relationships for regional security

North Korea presents a serious security problem within the region, and relations between North Korea and the other countries of the region have become increasingly tense in the last few years. Korea (South Korea) was threatened by North Korean submarines several times in 1998, and in the same year North Korea shot a missile across Japan. Both Japan and (South) Korea are wary of North Korea's intentions and ability to use military force in the region, and strengthening ties between Northeast Asian countries is a way to prevent North Korea from threatening its neighbours. For Japan, cooperation with China in nuclear plant management could be a measure to prevent the transfer of nuclear technology from China to North Korea.

The other important regional security issue is Taiwan. The People's Republic is claiming Taiwan as part of China, and when Japan and the United States revised their Guideline for US–Japan Defense Cooperation in 1997, China was highly apprehensive (MoFA, 1998). Since the Soviet Union no longer exists, China is afraid that the hypothetical enemy cited in the guideline may be China. Therefore any bilateral cooperation between Japan and China may contribute to softening tensions between the two countries on this issue.

Relations between Japan and both Korea and China are burdened by the historical legacy of the Second World War. Japan has been in a difficult position when it comes to assuming responsibility for what it did to Korea and China. Official financial aid from Japan for Korea started in 1965, and for China in 1979, soon after both countries had normalized their relations. At present China receives the largest amount of overseas development aid (ODA) from Japan (see Chapter 6). Although Japan may consider ODA as a way to compensate for its deeds, it is politically difficult for Korea and China to accept ODA as compensation.

Compared to the 1970s, Japan is assuming a more important role in the international arena in the 1990s. Whereas Japan's per capita GDP amounted to US$ 5100 in 1970 (at current exchange rates), and Japan still considered itself as an industrializing country, in 1990 Japan's per capita GDP amounted to US$ 24 800 (at current exchange rates). In the 1990s, Japan has acknowledged its status as a developed country, and is willing to do something not only for Japan but also for the region.

Progress in regional environmental cooperation in Northeast Asia in the 1990s

Comparing the 1970s and the 1990s, it can be recognized that regional cooperation has been stimulated by the climate change problem. Without this problem there would have been only little technological cooperation to improve energy efficiency in China, because the technologies are owned by private firms who would not transfer their know-how without benefits in return. The acid rain problem motivated the Japanese government to employ a part of its ODA to China for the installation of desulphurization equipment, but at first little attention was paid to the maintenance cost of this equipment. Japan had to see the benefit of the equipment for fulfilling its own obligations from the Kyoto Protocol. The development of a natural gas pipeline from Russia would also have been difficult if there had been no climate change problem. To secure natural gas supplies for energy security reasons alone would not have been a sufficient reason for constructing such pipelines; business would not have been interested in investment. Without foreign investment, Russia would not have been interested in it either.

Moreover, the size of Japan's ODA budget allocated to regional environmental purposes would have been smaller if no new regional issue had come up. When taking into account the climate change problem as well as acid rain, it was easier to convince Japanese taxpayers why regional cooperation was necessary. At the same time it is beneficial for recipient countries like China and Russia to agree to such cooperation.

In light of the various factors discussed above, it can be concluded that regional cooperation in Northeast Asia towards mitigating global warming has developed because of many factors that do not directly relate to climate change, and that regional cooperation for other issues has been stimulated by the change. Japan's new security concept has developed in the 1990s along with the development of climate change strategies, by linking environmental issues with other non-environmental issues, and by seeking benefits for the whole region.

Conclusion: stronger future cooperation?

Table 7.1 shows the costs and benefits for Northeast Asian countries in regional environmental cooperation. It can be seen that Japan has a lot of positive reasons other than environmental issues to cooperate with China and other Northeast Asian countries. For the other countries of the region, however, it is rather difficult to accept offers from Japan, knowing that such cooperation benefits Japan the most.

Whether environmental cooperation can overcome the remaining political impediments remains to be seen. The Sino–Japanese relationship and the regional security system cannot be developed by Japan alone, the willingness of other countries to cooperate is indispensable. A serious political conflict between China and Japan concerns the sovereignty over a small territory, the Senkaku Islands (Chinese: *Diaoyu*) (Katahara, 1998). There is also a worry that China is likely to use force to dominate the region as it becomes economically influential (Roy, 1998). From the viewpoint of environmental cooperation, however, it should be noted that China is facing domestic environmental problems such as air pollution, water contamination and deforestation, as well as suffering from its inefficient use of energy. As long as these problems continue, it will be beneficial for China to cooperate with Japan and (South) Korea to deal with these problems. Thus it may be said that environmental security contributes to regional military-related security as well. China has in fact been active in international meetings on environmental issues, especially since the Rio Conference in 1992, and will get the most benefits out of international environmental cooperation when it tackles its environmental problems at home and at the global level. The international cooperation, however, does not necessarily include Japan.

This unbalance of interests is likely to retard the regional cooperation process, and as can be seen in Table 7.1, China has the least incentive to

Table 7.1   Costs and benefits of regional environmental cooperation in Northeast Asia

Factors	Japan	China	Other countries (Korea, Russia etc.)
Costs:			
Costs of cooperation for climate change purposes	Financial and technological assistance	Efforts to curb GHG emission growth	Financial and technological assistance
Benefits:			
1. Reduction of GHG emissions	Benefit, but no need to cooperate in NEA region	Benefit, but no need to cooperate in NEA region	Benefit but no need to cooperate in NEA region
2. CDM and JI	Benefit to cooperate in NEA region	Benefit, but no need to cooperate in NEA region	Benefit, but no need to cooperate in NEA region
3. Other environmental problems	Benefit to cooperate in the region, especially with China	Benefit, but no need to cooperate in NEA region	Benefit to cooperate in the region, especially with China
4. Energy security	Benefit to cooperate in the region, especially with China and Russia	Benefit, but no need to cooperate in NEA region	Benefit, but no need to cooperate in NEA region
5. China as a new market	Benefit to cooperate with China	Benefit, but no need to cooperate in NEA region	Benefit to cooperate with China (Korea)
6. Improvement of regional security	Benefit to cooperate in the region, especially with China and Korea	Difficult to agree climate change cooperation as compensation of war	Difficult to agree climate change cooperation as compensation of war (Korea)

cooperate. If there are better assistance offers from countries in the region, China may choose other political and economic partners. Therefore, Japan and Korea have to keep offering more enticing projects than other countries to keep the regional cooperation process going. If it were only for the purpose of climate change mitigation, it would make no difference whether the cooperation were regional or global. Considering the positive effect of climate-related cooperation on other regional issues, however, it is favourable to uphold the regional cooperation while keeping the door open for countries outside the region as well.

It can also be expected that the nature of the cooperative relationships in Northeast Asia will evolve in future. Having been basically a donor/recipient relation between a developed country (Japan) and various developing countries, that structure is likely to change. Korea has already become an OECD member country, and the Chinese economy is growing rapidly. The Japanese economy, on the other hand, has stagnated during the past decade. Thus the nature of cooperation will gradually evolve to become an equal partnership. In that case, all countries of the region will take up cooperation efforts in a more balanced way.

Notes

1. Article 2(a) reads, 'Each of these Parties shall adopt national policies and take corresponding measures on the mitigation of climate change, by limiting its anthropogenic emissions of greenhouse gases and protecting and enhancing its greenhouse gas sinks and reservoirs. These policies and measures will demonstrate that developed countries are taking the lead in modifying longer-term trends in anthropogenic emissions consistent with the objective of the Convention, recognizing that the return by the end of the present decade to earlier levels of anthropogenic emissions of carbon dioxide and other greenhouse gases not controlled by the Montreal Protocol would contribute to such modification ...'
2. Article 3.1 of the Kyoto Protocol says, 'The Parties included in Annex I shall, individually or jointly, ensure that their aggregate anthropogenic carbon dioxide equivalent emissions of the greenhouse gases listed in Annex A do not exceed their assigned amounts, calculated pursuant to their quantified emission limitation and reduction commitments inscribed in Annex B and in accordance with the provisions of this Article, with a view to reducing their overall emissions of such gases by at least 5 per cent below 1990 levels in the commitment period 2008 to 2012.'
3. Article 12 of the Kyoto Protocol uses the term 'project activities resulting in certified emission reductions', but does not mention sequestration by sinks such as reforestation projects. Some countries argue that sequestration projects should also be certified as CDM projects, while others oppose the inclusion, saying that such inclusion may tremendously increase certified emission reductions so that Annex I countries may not reduce emissions at home.

References

Amano, A. (ed.) (1996) *Global Warming, Carbon Limitation and Economic Development*, CGER-1019-'96, Tsukuba: National Institute for Environmental Studies.

APSG (Asia Pipeline Study Group) (1998) *Wagakuni wo meguru Gas paipurain no kôsô no dôkô* [Trend of Gas Pipeline Plans in Our Country], Brochure for Asia Pipeline Study Group, Tokyo.

Berger, T. (1998) 'From Sword to Chrysanthemum: Japan's Culture of Anti-militarism', in M. Brown, S. Lynn-Jones and S. Miller (eds), *East Asian Security*, Cambridge: MIT Press.

Brettell, A. M. and Y. Kawashima (1998) 'Sino–Japanese Co-operation on Acid Rain', in M. Scheures and D. Pirages (eds), *Ecological Security in North East Asia*, Seoul: Yonsei University Press, pp. 89–113.

CJEBAP (Committee on Japan's Experience in the Battle against Air Pollution) (1997) *Japan's Experience in the Battle against Air Pollution*, Tokyo: The Pollution-Related Health Damage Compensation and Prevention Association.

Dabelko, D. D. and G. D. Dabelko (1995) *Environmental Security: Issues of Conflict and Redefinitions, Environment and Security*, International Institute for Environmental Strategies and Security, no. 1, pp. 23–50.

Deudney, D. (1990) 'The Case Against Linking Environmental Degradation and National Security', *Millennium: Journal of International Studies*, vol. 19 (3), pp. 461–76.

EDMC (Energy Data and Modelling Centre) (1996) *Enerugî keizai tôkei yôran* [Compilation of Data on Energy and Economy], Tokyo: Sho-Enerugi Senta.

EAJ (Environment Agency of Japan) (1996) *Proceedings of the Sixth Asia-Pacific Seminar on Climate Change*, Tokyo: Government of Japan.

—(1998) *Kankyô hakushô* [Environment White Paper], Tokyo: Government of Japan.

Ehrlich, P. (1968) *The Population Bomb*, New York: Ballantine Books.

Gleditsch, N. P. (1998) 'Armed Conflict and The Environment: A Critique of the Literature', *Journal of Peace Research*, vol. 35 (3), pp. 381–400.

Gleick, P. (1993) 'Water and Conflict – Fresh Water Resources and International Security', *International Security*, vol. 18 (1), pp. 79–112.

Hardin, G. (1968) 'The Tragedy of the Commons', *Science*, vol. 162, pp. 561–8.

Homer-Dixon, T. (1991) 'On the Threshold: Environmental Changes as Causes of Acute Conflict', *International Security*, vol. 16 (2), pp. 76–117.

Imura, H. and K. Katsuhara (1995) *Chûgoku no kankyô mondai* [Environmental Problem in China], Tokyo: Tôyô Keizai Shinposha.

IPCC (Intergovernmental Panel on Climate Change) (2001) *Climate Change 2001: The Scientific Basis*, Cambridge: Cambridge University Press.

Katahara, E. (1998) 'Japan', in C. Morrison (ed.), *Asia Pacific Security Outlook 1998*, Tokyo: Japan Centre for International Exchange.

Katzenstein, P. (1996) *Cultural Norms and National Security*, Ithaca: Cornell University Press.

Levy, M. (1995) 'Is the Environment a National Security Issue?' *International Security*, vol. 20 (2), pp. 35–62.

Mathews, J. (1989) 'Redefining Security', *Foreign Affairs*, pp. 162–77.

Meadows, D., D. Meadows, J. Randers and W. Behrens III (1972) *Limits to Growth*, New York: Universe Books.

MoFA (Ministry of Foreign Affairs) (1998) *The ODA White Paper for 1998*, Tokyo: Government of Japan.

MITI (Ministry of International Trade and Industry) (1997) *Ajia to kankyôtaisaku kenkyûkai hôkokusho* [Report of Environmental Policies in Asia Study Group], Tokyo: Government of Japan.

Myers, N. (1989) 'Environment and Security', *Foreign Policy (Spring)*, pp. 23–41.

NEDO (New Energy and Industrial Technology Development Organization) (1998) *Kyôdô jisshi kiso chôsa* [Preliminary Survey of Joint Implementation], Tokyo: NEDO.

OECD (Organization for Economic Cooperation and Development) (1998a) *Economic Modelling of Climate Change: OECD Workshop Report*, Paris: OECD.

—(1998b) *Energy balances of OECD countries 1995–1996*, Paris: OECD.

Ohta, H. (1998) 'Anzen hosho no gainen to hankyo mondai [Security and Environmental Problems]', *Kokusai Seiji*, no. 117, pp. 67–84.

Rønneldt, C. F. (1997) 'Three Generations of Environment and Security Research', *Journal of Peace Research*, vol. 34 (4), pp. 473–82.

Roy, D. (1998) *Hegemon on the Horizon?* M. Brown, S. Lynn-Jones and S. Miller (eds), *East Asian Security*, Cambridge: MIT Press, pp. 113–32.

Thomas, C. (1998) *In Search of Security: The Third World in International Relations*, London: Lynne Rienner.

Tolba, M., K. Osama, A. El-Kholy, E. El-Hinnawi, M. H. Holdgate, D. F. McMichael and R. E. Munn (eds) (1992) *The World Environment 1972–1992: Two Decades of Challenge*, London: Chapman & Hall.

Tow, W. (1994) 'China and the International Strategic System', in T. Robinson and D. Shambaugh (eds), *Chinese Foreign Policy: Theory and Practice*, Oxford: Clarendon Press, pp. 115–57.

Ullman, R. (1983) 'Redefining Security', *International Security*, vol. 8 (1), pp. 129–53.

United Nations (1992) *United Nations Framework Convention on Climate Change*, New York: UN.

—(1995) *FCCC Document Decision 1/CP.1*, New York: UN.

—(1997) *United Nations Kyoto Protocol to the Framework Convention on Climate Change*, New York: UN.

—(1998) *FCCC Document Decision 1/CP.4*, New York: UN.

Wirth, D. (1989) 'Climate Chaos', *Foreign Policy (Spring)*, pp. 3–22.

World Bank (1998) *Global Development Finance: Country Tables*, Washington, DC: World Bank.

WCED (World Commission on Environment and Development) (1987) *Our Common Future*, Oxford: Oxford University Press.

8
Japanese Business Strategies towards China: A Theoretical Approach
René Haak

Introduction

The People's Republic of China has gained increasing importance as a market and production base for the internationally active Japanese industry. At the same time, Japanese companies represent one of the most important supports of China's economic and technological development. A look at the strategic management of internationally active Japanese manufacturers shows that investments currently being made in China are shaped by the current trends of globalization and intensified international competition.

In this chapter, first the role of China as a new and important business operation base for Japanese companies is discussed. The analysis will focus on the question of why Japanese companies are attracted to China. Subsequently, basic trends in research on the main motives of Japanese internationally active companies towards China are summarized, with a particular focus on the apparel industry, adding some examples from other industrial fields.

This chapter provides a new summarized framework based on and drawing from the theories of Porter (1980, 1985), Bartlett and Ghoshal (1989, 1995) and Sydow (1993), with the aim of delivering a solid basis for further analysis and discussions about the various forms of Japanese business strategies towards China. From the practical research standpoint of strategic management, the theories will be examined and applied to the research subject of Japanese business strategies. In theory, Japanese companies can use six basic strategies for entering Chinese markets: an export strategy, an international strategy, a multidomestic strategy, a global strategy, a transnational strategy and a collective strategy. We then discuss the different strategies that Japanese firms can theoretically use when competing internationally, competing in the Chinese market, and the pros and cons of these strategies.

Emergence of China and the offshore movement

China has become in the last two decades a new and important business operation base for Japanese companies. China's 'open-door' policy and its various reforms have gained momentum, and Japanese companies have begun forming joint ventures with state and local enterprises, and building wholly-owned factories in various locations in China (Naughton, 1997a, b; Taylor, 1996; Haak, 2001a, p. 46; Li and Li, 1999).

In any discussion of Japanese business strategies towards China, we will be aware of one basic question which arises almost naturally: why are Japanese companies attracted to China, despite differences in language and culture, political uncertainties, an unsure legal system, and the inadequate development of transportation, communications and other infrastructure in most areas of the country? As a general answer we can say that ever-growing globalization of production and markets provides the main impetus for internationally active Japanese manufacturing firms to go to China (Beechler and Bird, 1999; Teranishi and Yamasaki, 1995; Fieten *et al.*, 1997; Welge, 1990). Firms want, for instance, to shift parts of their value chain (Porter, 1980) and in most cases their production processes to various locations in China to take advantage of national differences and/or to establish new distribution channels and service stations to promote products manufactured in China, Japan or elsewhere in Southeast Asia.

This general answer, however, is not really satisfying. For a more detailed answer we should closely examine the internationalization motives of Japanese companies in order to get a deeper understanding of their business strategies towards China.

Traditional motives for companies to internationalize can be classified as resource-seeking and market-seeking (Bartlett and Ghoshal, 1995). We can understand resource-seeking as a behaviour driven by the desire of the company either to access key supplies – such as energy, minerals and scarce natural resources – or to lower costs in factors of production such as labour. These motivations are dominant in industries in which competitive advantage (Porter, 1985) is based on access to or control of key resources. This is the case, too, in industries in which competitive advantage is enhanced by driving down costs by the employment of a large pool of unskilled labour, often in the mass-manufacturing industries like the apparel industry. Market-seeking behaviour is a logical characteristic of companies in mass-manufacturing industries which seek to exploit economies of scale and scope in production in order to generate a source of competitive advantage over other competitors, especially domestic competitors. According to the main motives, market-seeking and resource-seeking, we should perhaps formulate the main question in other words: Why are Japanese companies attracted to China as a manufacturing base (resource-seeking) and/or attracted to China as a huge and promising marketplace (market-seeking)?

One of the main motives is, of course, that China has a huge supply of inexpensive labour, which enables Japanese companies to cut their costs, especially their production costs (Konomoto, 1997, pp. 70–3, see also Ohmae, 2001; Köllner, 1997; and Chapter 3).

In the last decade Japan's economy has been facing various problems, and the maturing economy has been slowing down since the early 1990s. Japan's domestic demand is weak, the yen is appreciating steadily, and import competition is growing. Traditional pricing systems in Japan are under strong pressure as imports become cheaper and numerous Japanese retailers switch to discounting strategies to stimulate demand in Japan. The downward pressure on prices extends all the way from the retailers back to the manufacturers, making cost-cutting the single most important issue, and Japanese manufacturing companies are accelerating most of their offshore facilities, particularly to China, in an effort to cut cost, especially in labour-intensive industries. Labour costs in China in the early 1990s were only one-twentieth of the cost of Japanese labour – though of course differences existed depending on the particular industry and business areas – which made China extremely attractive to Japanese companies struggling to reduce costs (Konomoto, 1998, p. 39). During the 1980s, most Japanese companies setting up abroad tended to set up operations in south China.

China is not a homogeneous economy; commerce and purchasing power are concentrated mainly in the coastal regions where most of the international companies have established themselves. The old areas of heavy industry are in the north, a modern centre for technology and services is developing in Shanghai in the east, and since the formation of the first special economic areas the southern regions are emulating the model of the former British crown colony Hong Kong, now a special administrative region of China, in their economic development.

In the 1990s, direct investment by Japanese companies has been concentrated in the Dalian area, in 'Greater Shanghai', and also in the area around Beijing. An outstanding factor for Japanese investment in China over recent years has been the powerful allure of China's potential market growth. The income of the population is increasing, particularly where industry is concentrated, and a new consumer class with a lot of purchasing power needs to be supplied with high-quality consumer goods. During the first half of the 1990s, Japanese companies focused on the new Chinese market itself, and tended to set up operations in east China in the area around Shanghai and Suzhou. Shanghai opened up to foreign business in 1984 and has been a priority area for government infrastructure investment (Toga, 2001). Major Japanese construction machinery manufacturers, for example, have moved into the Chinese market. Komatsu, the largest Japanese producer of construction machinery, established a wholly-owned subsidiary in Shanghai in February 2001 to oversee its Chinese operations, and Hitachi Construction Machinery Corp., the leading manufacturer of hydraulic shovels, is keeping full-capacity operations at its Chinese manufacturing subsidiary. These moves are apparently aimed at establishing a greater market presence in China where demand for construction equipment is expected to grow due to major construction projects in western regions. All these business plans have involved investing capital in mainland China on the one hand for off-shore production, and on the other hand to penetrate Chinese markets.

A good example that illustrates the motives of the movement to China and also the specific forms of Japanese business strategy is provided by the apparel industry. The movement of Japanese apparel makers to China has proceeded in two waves – the first in the 1980s, and the second in the 1990s. The first wave in the 1980s was prompted by rapid growth in Japan's domestic apparel demand, the low labour costs in China, and difficulties in attracting labour in Japan (NRI, 1995; Abo, 1989). In an industry where labour costs represent most of the costs of goods sold, the cost benefits of moving labour-intensive operations from Japan to China are quite substantial. Some manufacturers in this industry have been able to improve their gross margins in certain products by more than 10-percentage points by shifting production to China.[1] Most of the offshore business operations that Japanese apparel makers set up at this time were concentrated in south China, near the earlier offshore locations of Japanese apparel makers established in the 1970s, in Taiwan and South Korea.

The second wave in the 1990s was much larger and qualitatively different. In the 1990s in Japan, apart from the continuing problems of attracting workers to the industry, the apparel industry was facing new challenges in the form of increasingly price-conscious Japanese consumers, a rising level of apparel imports and international price competition, and new types of apparel retailers that emphasized discount pricing – a new business environment threatening the survival of the Japanese apparel industry. The Japanese apparel market was maturing, and China had become increasingly alluring to Japanese apparel companies (see also Chapter 9). China's apparel market promised enormous growth potential, and mid-sized as well as large Japanese apparel firms developed sales channels in the Chinese market. Some Japanese mid-sized apparel makers overcame their size limitations in capitalization, human resources, distribution and marketing by forming joint ventures with local Chinese partners. Other Japanese companies formed joint ventures with foreign investors in order to strengthen their market position (Yoda, 2001; Konomoto, 1998). Beyond the apparel industry, business cooperation in general and cooperative arrangements between companies have become increasingly popular for business organization in China. Strategic alliances, joint ventures, cooperative projects – all varieties of collective strategies as a special form of strategy towards China – have become an essential part of business strategy for Japanese and other companies in today's Chinese markets, and in other industries besides the apparel industry (Haak, 2000a, pp. 113–16; Haak, 2001b).

Apparel manufacturing involves a number of different tasks, including product planning, material procurement, production, inspection, distribution and marketing. For the most part, Japanese companies in the 1980s and the early 1990s shifted only production operations – sewing and stitching – to China, as shifting these labour-intensive operations out of Japan generated the largest cost-savings. Some production operations remained in Japan simply because the techniques and materials were not available in China. During the 1990s, however, a new trend arose in Japanese strategies (NRI, 1995); some apparel makers began to perform procurement, inspection, distribution and marketing activities locally in China, while all their product planning was still being done in Japan. The technical capabilities of Japanese joint ventures in China in the textile field were improving, and local sourcing of liner fabric is also increasing nowadays.

Many Japanese companies decided to expand their offshore capabilities by pursuing local marketing. In fact, most offshore operations by Japanese apparel makers are joint ventures with local partners, precisely because of the expectations of ultimately selling to the Chinese market. China's coastal region, in particular, has become an important apparel market, and is still gaining importance as a base for inspection and distribution operations in today's China.

Improving a firm's profitability, and the supreme role of business strategy

Why are Japanese companies proceeding in the way outlined in the previous section, one that many might say is decidedly risky, with direct investment into China? Basic theoretical understanding tells us that a company must manufacture a product that is valued by consumers in order to make profits. Thus we say that companies engage in the activity of value creation. Firms can increase their profits basically in two ways: first, by adding value to a product so that consumers are willing to pay more for the product, the so-called differentiation strategy; and second, by lowering the costs of value creation, the so-called low-cost strategy (Porter, 1980).

For example, a business company adds value to a product when it improves the product's quality, provides an additional service to the consumer, or customizes the product to consumer needs. The consumer is then willing to pay more (differentiation strategy). On the other hand, firms lower the costs of value creation when they find ways to perform value creation activities more efficiently (low-cost strategy). These are the two basic strategies for improving a firm's profitability (*ibid.*).

For a theoretical approach to the complex subject of business strategies, to take account of Japanese strategies toward China, it is useful to think of the company as a value chain composed of a series of distinct value-creation activities including production, marketing, materials management, research and development (R&D), human resources management, information systems, and the firm's infrastructure. We can categorize these value-creation activities as primary activities and support activities (Porter, 1985).

The primary activities of a firm have to do with creating the product, marketing and delivering the product to the buyers, and providing them with support and after-sales services. Efficient production can reduce the costs of creating value and can add value by increasing product quality, which facilitates premium pricing. Efficient marketing can also help the firm reduce its costs of creating value, and add value by helping the firm customize its product to consumer needs and differentiate its products from competitor's products.

Business support activities provide the inputs that allow the primary activities of production and marketing. For example, the materials management function controls the transmission of the physical materials through the value chain, from procurement through production and into distribution. In addition, an effective materials management function can monitor the quality of inputs into the production process. This results in improved quality of the firm's outputs, which adds value and thus facilitates premium pricing (*ibid.*). Both the primary and the support activities are important to improve a firms' profitability: business strategy is the key. It is the most important consideration that the company and its employees have to bear in mind in order to attain the fundamental objective of any business, to make profits.

A firm's business strategy is defined as the actions that managers take to attain the objectives of the company (Porter, 1986), actions that seek to reduce the costs of value creation (low-cost strategy) or to differentiate its product (differentiation strategy) (Porter, 1980, 1985).

If we are following Porter's theoretical understanding, expanding to international markets (in our case to China) allows companies (in our case Japanese companies) to increase their profitability in ways not available to purely domestic enterprises. Therefore Japanese firms are able to earn a greater return from their distinctive skills, or core competencies, and realize greater experience curve economies which reduce the costs of value creation. Also, Japanese companies can realize location economies by dispersing particular value-creation activities to those locations in China where they can perform such activities most efficiently – for example labour-intensive industries in western China with a huge supply of unskilled and inexpensive labour. The term 'core competence' refers to skills within the firm that competitors cannot easily match or imitate (Hamel and Prahalad, 1989). These skills may exist in any of the firm's value-creation activities, that is R&D, production, human resource management, marketing, general management, information system and technology, and so on. Such skills are typically embodied in products that other firms find difficult to match or imitate: it is difficult, for example, for Chinese companies to imitate products, production technology or the management know-how from Japanese companies operating in the Chinese market. Once again, according to Porter's (1985) theoretical view, the core competencies are the bedrock of a firm's competitive advantage. They enable a firm to reduce the costs of value creation and/or to create value in such a way that premium pricing is possible.

For example, Toyota Motor Corp. has a core competence in the manufacturing of cars, especially in production technology and work organization. It is able to manufacture high quality, well-designed cars at a lower delivered cost than competitors. The skills that enable Toyota to do so seem to reside primarily in the firm's production, material and human resource management areas. For firms such as Toyota, global expansion in China is a way of further exploiting the value-creation potential of their skills and product offerings by applying those skills and products in a larger market.

What does all this mean for an internationally operating Japanese company that is trying to be successful in China? In brief, it means, that the Japanese firm will benefit by shifting each value-creating activity it performs to the location in China where economic, political and cultural conditions, including relative factor costs, are most conducive to the performance of that particular activity. Therefore, locating a value-creation activity in an optimal location in China can either lower the cost of value creation and help the firm to achieve a low-cost position – in the Chinese market, in Japan or elsewhere – or it can enable a firm to differentiate its products. In theory, a company that applies location economies by dispersing each of its value-creation activities to its optimal location should have a competitive advantage *vis-à-vis* a firm that bases all its value-creation activities at a single location (Hill, 1997). In a world where competitive pressure is increasing, such a way of doing business may well become an imperative for survival for Japanese companies.

For a certain number of Japanese companies the optimal location to perform manufacturing operations in the field of consumer electronics, textile and apparel is China, whereas in most cases the optimal location for design operations and R&D is Japan (NRI, 1995; Beechler and Stucker, 1998). Japanese firms, especially in the textile, apparel and consumer electronics industry, have often configured their value chain accordingly; by doing so they hope to be able to simultaneously lower their cost structure and differentiate their products. Such was the management behaviour first for the Japanese and the United States markets, but in recent years for the Chinese market (McMillan, 1996). This seem likely to continue in the future.

Strategic choices for Japanese companies

In a theoretical view, Japanese companies have six main business strategies that they can use to enter the Chinese market and compete in the international environment in the age of globalization. They are:

1. an export strategy;
2. an international strategy;
3. a multidomestic strategy;
4. a global strategy;
5. a transnational strategy (Bartlett and Ghoshal, 1989); and
6. a collective strategy (Sydow, 1993).

Each of these strategies has specific advantages and disadvantages for Japanese companies competing in China. The appropriateness of each strategy varies with the extent of pressure for cost reductions and local responsiveness in China.

Export strategy

Most Japanese manufacturing firms began their global expansion to China as exporters, which in the early years of expansion had two distinct advantages. It avoided the cost of establishing manufacturing operations in China, and exporting also helped Japanese firms to achieve experience-curve effects. By manufacturing the product in a centralized location in Japan and exporting it into the Chinese market, the firm could realize substantial scale economies from its global sales volume (Abegglen and Stalk, 1985).

On the other hand, exporting has a number of drawbacks. First, exporting from the home base in Japan may not be appropriate if there are lower-cost locations for manufacturing in China. Thus, particularly for firms pursuing global or transnational strategies, it may be preferable to manufacture in a location where the mix of the factor conditions is most favourable from a value-creation perspective. Many Japanese companies, especially electronic firms, moved some of their manufacturing to China, even shifted whole production lines, due to the availability of low-cost and well-trained labour. These companies export from the Chinese production (value-creation location) to the rest of the world, and especially to Japan.

A second drawback for Japanese companies pursuing an export strategy to China is that high transport costs can make exporting uneconomical. An important point in the current business relationship between Japan and China, that has negative effects on the export business, relates to tariff barriers. This situation exists in a lot of business fields, and it is impracticable, for example, to export Japanese cars to China due to high tariff barriers. Only 1 per cent of Japan's auto exports go to China.

A third drawback for Japanese firms in exporting arises when a firm delegates its local marketing activities to a local agent (Hill, 1997). Such behaviour is common for Japanese companies that are just beginning to export to China, but foreign agents often carry the products of competing firms and so have divided loyalties. There are, however, ways to avoid this problem. One is to set up a wholly owned subsidiary in China to handle local marketing directly, and this is the most common method used by Japanese companies to enter the Chinese market after their first year of exporting or operating as a joint venture.

International strategy

Apart from the export strategy, an international strategy is the most common focus of Japanese companies doing business in China. Japanese firms that pursue an international strategy try to create value by transferring valuable skills, qualifications, products or production technology to the Chinese market where indigenous competitors lack these assests (Hill, 1997; Dülfer, 1991; Bartlett, 1989; Harzing, 1999; Champell and Burton, 1994).

Numerous Japanese firms have followed the international strategy and created value by transferring differentiated products developed in Japan to new markets in China. Accordingly, these Japanese companies tend to centralize product development functions and the development of production technology at the workfloor level in Japan, mainly in the head office of R&D (McMillan, 1996; Ôuchi, 1979). However, most Japanese firms in China also tend to establish manufacturing and marketing functions locally, such as product customization and localization of communication (Konomoto, 2000).

Ultimately, in most international Japanese companies that follow an international strategy, the head office (in Japan) retains tight control over marketing and product strategy in China. One of the main characteristics of Japanese subsidiaries in China in the frame of international strategy is that the subsidiaries are rigidly managed by the parent company in Japan, and the organisation in general is bureaucratic. The decision-making process for Japanese offices in China is one-way and therefore the style of management is top-down rather than bottom-up. Japanese companies in China control their employees carefully and monitor everything they do (Konomoto, 2000, p. 4; see also Kopp, 1994; Harzing, 1999). In such a rigid atmosphere, employees cannot be expected to engage in active discussion or to volunteer opinions. The local personnel become concerned that the company has too many complicated rules and regulations that only make it more difficult for the employees to do their jobs (Kawashima and Konomoto 1999; Child 2000; Roth and Nigh 1992).

The international strategy makes sense for Japanese firms, with a valuable core competence that indigenous competitors in China lack, which faces relatively mild pressures for local responsiveness and cost reductions. In such circumstances an international strategy can be very profitable (Harzing 2000). However, when pressure for local responsiveness is strong, Japanese firms pursuing this strategy lose out to firms that place a greater emphasis on customizing the product offering and marketing strategy to the local Chinese market conditions.

Multidomestic strategy

As far as the multidomestic strategy is concerned, firms orientate towards achieving maximum local responsiveness (Bartlett and Ghoshal, 1989, Sydow, 1993). In contrast to firms pursuing an international strategy which tends to transfer skills and products developed at home to China, Japanese companies pursuing a multidomestic strategy extensively customize both their products and their marketing strategy to the different local conditions in China. Consistent with this strategy, they have also a tendency to establish a complete set of value-creation activities in China – including production, marketing, and R&D.

When there is high pressure in various Chinese markets for local responsiveness, and low pressure for cost reductions, a multidomestic strategy generally makes sense. The high-cost structure associated with the duplication of production facilities, however, makes this strategy inappropriate in industries where cost pressure is intense (Hill, 1997). There is currently no major evidence of Japanese companies choosing the multidomestic strategy, and in fact another weakness of this strategy has to be stated. The experiences of Western companies in China shows us that many multidomestic firms have developed into decentralized federations in which each subsidiary functions in a largely autonomous manner. As a result of this, after a certain time subsidiaries begin to lack the ability to transfer their qualifications and products to other facilities in the Chinese market, or to their other subsidiaries around the world.

Global strategy

Japanese firms that follow a global strategy focus on increasing profitability by reaping the cost reductions that come from experience-curve effects and location economies; these companies are pursuing a low-cost strategy (Dunning, 1993; Elger and Smith, 1994). The R&D activities, production and marketing of firms pursuing a global strategy are concentrated in a few favourable locations. Global firms tend not to customize their product offers and marketing strategy to local Chinese conditions because customization raises costs. Instead, companies that concentrate on the global strategy prefer to market a standardized product worldwide, not only in China, so they can achieve the maximum benefits from the economies of scale that underlie the experience curve. And some companies tend to use their strong cost advantage to support aggressive pricing in the markets (Bartlett and Ghoshal, 1989; Sydow, 1993).

This strategy makes most sense for Japanese companies in those cases where there is strong pressure for cost reductions and where demand for local responsiveness is minimal. These conditions exist in various industrial-good industries. Especially in the semiconductor industry, global standards have emerged that have created enormous demands for standardized global products. Accordingly, firms such as NEC Corp. pursue a global strategy with strong production bases in mainland China and also in Taiwan. These special conditions cannot be found in most consumer-goods markets where demands for local responsiveness in China remain high. Rising production of information and telecommunication equipment such as cellphones has been driving up demand for semiconductors in China. Meanwhile, the Chinese government, which gives priority to chip-making as one of the key industrial sectors, lends support to foreign-owned manufacturers that build new factories or upgrade existing ones.

NEC Corp., as Japan's largest semiconductor manufacturer, follows the global strategy. The company is planning to step up operations in China in response to growing demand there for its product, and will expand output capacity by 50 per cent at its chip-making joint venture with the Shanghai municipal government at a cost of yen 35 billion (US$ 301 million). NEC aims to increase the supply of system chips to locally made cellular phones and home appliances.

Transnational strategy

The significance of the transnational strategy (Bartlett and Ghoshal, 1989) is that in the modern multinational enterprise, distinctive competencies do not just reside in the home country; core competencies can be developed in any of the firm's worldwide operations. In this sense the flow of skills and products should also be from foreign subsidiary to home country, and from foreign subsidiary to foreign subsidiary – a process Bartlett and Ghoshal refer to as 'global learning'. In their view, the transnational strategy makes sense when a firm faces high pressures for cost reductions and high pressures for local responsiveness. Companies that pursue a transnational strategy are trying to simultaneously achieve low cost and differentiation advantages.

This strategy implies serious difficulties as pressures for local responsiveness and cost reduction put conflicting demands on a firm (Porter, 1980). According to Porter it seems to be better to decide on one clear strategy – whether a low-cost or differentiation strategy – to respond to the pressure of the market.

The transnational strategy seems to have no empirical value in the case of Japanese companies in China. At this juncture it might be noted that Bartlett and Ghoshal may be overstating the case for the transnational strategy, which they present as the only viable strategy in international markets. As has been illustrated by the case of the semiconductor industry, pressures for local customization in China are minimal and competition is purely a cost game, and in such a scenario it is not sensible to concentrate on a transnational strategy.

Collective strategy

Last but not least the collective strategy is highly important for most Japanese companies to enter the Chinese market. Collective strategies (Sydow, 1993) are a traditional and yet modern organizational form used to enter a market or international markets. In practice they appear as strategic alliances, regional and global networks, joint ventures, value-adding partnerships, inter-firm networks and consortia (Haak, 2001b; Hammes, 1993). Collaboration between companies, joint development, production and marketing, exchange of components and technology are, as part of international cooperation and decentralised production to ensure a global presence, fundamental factors in strategic management for success (Buckley and Casson, 1988). Faced with increasingly dynamic, competitive and complex environments, more and more organizations are being advised to concentrate on their core competencies. To implement such a strategic orientation, organizations prefer an intelligent 'downscoping' to straightforward downsizing or demassing of their activities. For example, in some Japanese industries – such as automotive, electronics or retailing – vertically and horizontally-integrated organizational business systems (*keiretsu*) are shifted to China. Small and medium-sized firms in particular engage in networking in order to gain the advantages of large size while keeping the flexibility of small size (Haak, 2001b).

An empirical view of engagements of firms in the last decade shows that the most popular business form used to enter the Chinese market is the joint venture. This entails establishing a firm that is jointly owned by two or more otherwise independent firms. The most typical joint venture is the 50:50 arrangement, in which of two parties each holds a 50 per cent ownership stake and contributes a team of managers to share operating control. Joint ventures have a number of advantages. First, a firm is able to benefit from a local partner's knowledge of the host country's competitive conditions, the cultural situation, language, political and business systems (Balling, 1998). Second, when development costs and/or risks of opening a foreign market are high, a firm might gain by sharing these costs and/or risks with a local partner. Third, in some special industries in China, political considerations make joint ventures the only feasible entry mode (Hill, 1997; Haak, 2001b).

There are two major disadvantages with Japanese–Chinese joint ventures in China. First, just as with licensing, a firm that enters into a joint venture risks giving control of its technology to its partner. One option here is to hold majority ownership in the joint venture, allowing the dominant partner to exercise greater control over its technology. A second disadvantage is that a joint venture does not give a firm tight control over subsidiaries, which stands in sharp contrast to traditional Japanese management overseas and at home.

A substantial amount of research has been devoted to a better understanding of the circumstances under which Japanese firms find it beneficial to cooperate with Chinese firms, and it is a fact that joint ventures and cooperative projects, in other words specific forms of collective strategies, have become an essential part of business strategy for Japanese companies in today's Chinese markets. Most research projects in the field of strategic management have focused on the cooperative strategies between one Japanese and one Chinese (local) firm, and little is known about the collective strategies between two foreign firms in an overseas market, particularly with regard to 'Japanese firm–Foreign firm' business cooperation (Haak, 2001b). Third-market business cooperation as a specific form of the collective strategy, offers substantial economic advantages for entering the Chinese market. Investments and risks are shared; marketing, distribution and production knowledge from two or more foreign companies can be used; and other resources like human resources and finance are also beneficial for market entry or for market penetration activities of a third-country business cooperation. It seems that third-market cooperation can lower costs and risks more than any other of the market entry options.

From another point of view, however, there are also numerous problems associated with third-market business cooperation. For example, issues of management control, local and international sourcing and technology transfer. The performance of a third-market business cooperation, in our case a Japanese company with a foreign company such as a German or French firm in China, depends mainly upon qualitative variables such as cooperate culture and structure, individual personality of the management, and the basic philosophy of two or more parent companies. Third-market business cooperation as a special form of the basic collective strategy to enter the Chinese market is an outstanding field of research which should be pursued.

Conclusion

During the 1980s and in the early 1990s, most Japanese firms in the field of production adopted a strategy intended to lower their cost structure: shifting production from high-cost locations in Japan to low-cost locations in China. Later, Japanese manufacturing companies in China adopted a strategy intended to differentiate basic products to enable them to charge a premium price. These strategies involved strong investment of capital in China, both for offshore production and to penetrate Chinese markets.

We can classify the motives for Japanese companies to develop and implement business strategies towards China as resource-seeking and market-seeking. These two basic motives stand behind the fundamental purpose of any business firm to make profits. We have also considered the two basic business strategies of reducing the costs of value creation (low-cost strategy), or differentiating products (differentiation strategy). In this chapter I have reviewed the academic field of strategic management from a professional discipline perspective, and discussed the pros and cons of six basic business strategies in order to give a summarised frame for ongoing analysis and discussion: the export strategy, the international strategy, the multidomestic strategy, the global strategy, the transnational strategy and the collective strategy.

What kind of strategy is successful in the Chinese market? As my preceding discussion has demonstrated, there are advantages and disadvantages associated with the business strategies of Japanese companies towards

China. Their success depends on deciding on the right strategy or the right strategy mix bearing in mind the particular circumstances of Chinese markets. Different factors influence the decision-making process, such as new competitors, strong suppliers, new technologies, and so forth (Porter, 1980). Based on this theoretical understanding, the main objective of Japanese companies should be to focus on capability-building that aims for better technology and quality. At the same time, Japanese companies should develop their strategic management in order to make the most of their long-term capability-building; strategic ideas and concepts, such as the six business strategies discussed here, will become more and more important to carry out cooperate reforms more strategically. However, the most important question for a successful business strategy of Japanese companies towards China still concerns whether China's economy will continue to develop against the background of difficulties in the political and social system.

Note

1. There is also another example, which shows that China has not only attracted Japanese companies in the field of textiles and other relatively simple manufacturing products, but has also attracted mass-production for export back to Japan or for the Chinese market itself. This example concerns one of the biggest players in the world of entertainment and consumer electronics, Sony Computer Entertainment Inc. Sony Entertainment plans to contract production of its PlayStation2 game consoles to Chinese firms as soon as possible for export to Japan. The company aims to raise competitiveness through low-cost manufacturing in China as competition is certain to intensify with the entry of the US software giant Microsoft Corp. into the game machine market.

References

Abegglen, J. C. and G. Stalk (1985) *Kaisha: The Japanese Corporation*, New York: Basic Books.

Abo, T. (1989) 'The Emergence of Japanese Multinational Enterprise and the Theory of Foreign Direct Investment', in K. Shibagaki, M. Trevor and T. Abo (eds), *Japanese and European Management*, Tokyo: University of Tokyo Press, pp. 3–17.

Balling, R. (1998) *Kooperation. Strategische Allianzen, Netzwerke, Joint Ventures und andere Organisationsformen zwischenbetrieblicher Zusammenarbeit in Theorie und Praxis*, 2nd edn, Frankfurt am Main: Lang Verlag.

Bartlett, C. A. and S. Ghoshal (1989) *Managing Across Borders. The Transnational Solution*, Boston, MA: Harvard Business School Press.

—and— (1995) *Transnational Mangement*, 2nd edn, Chicago: Irwin.

Beechler, S. L. and K. Stucker (1998) *Japanese Business*, London and New York: Routledge.

—and A. Bird (eds) (1999) *Japanese Multinationals Abroad – Individual and Organizational Learning*, New York and Oxford: Oxford University Press.

Buckley, P. J. and M. Casson, (1988) 'A Theory of Cooperation in International Business', in F. J. Contractor and P. Lorange (eds), *Cooperative Strategies in International Business*, Lexington, MA and Toronto: Lexington, pp. 31–53.

Champell, N. and F. Burton (eds) (1994) *Japanese Multinationals. Strategies and Management in the Global Kaisha*, London and New York: Routledge.

Child, J. (2000) 'Management and Organizations in China: Key Trends and Issues', in J. T. Li, A. Tsui and E. Weldon (eds), *Management and Organizations in the Chinese Context*, Houndmills, Basingstoke: Macmillan – now Palgrave, pp. 33–62.

Dülfer, E. (1991) *Internationales Management*, Munich: Oldenbourg.

Dunning, J. H. (1993) *Multinational Enterprises and the Global Economy*, Wokingham, UK: Addison-Wesley.

Elger, T. and C. Smith (1994) 'Introduction', in T. Elger and C. Smith (eds), *Global Japanization*, London and New York: Routledge.

Fieten, R., F. Werner and B. Lageman (1997) *Globalisierung der Märkte – Herausforderungen und Optionen für kleine und mittlere Unternehmen, insbesondere für Zulieferer*, Stuttgart: Schäffer-Poeschel.

Haak, R. (2000a) 'Kollektive Internationalisierungsstrategien der japanischen Industrie – Ein Beitrag zum Management internationaler Unternehmungskooperationen', *Zeitschrift für wirtschaftlichen Fabrikbetrieb (ZWF)*, vol. 95 (3), pp. 113–6.

—(2000b) 'Zwischen Internationalisierung und Restrukturierung – Kooperations-management der japanischen Industrie in fortschrittlichen Technologiefeldern', *Industrie-Management*, no. 6, Globalisierung und Regionalisierung, pp. 64–8.

—(2001a) 'Strategisches Management in Dynamischer Umwelt – Markt- und Technologieführerschaft in der chinesischen Automobilindustrie', *Zeitschrift für wirtschaftlichen Fabrikbetrieb (ZWF)*, vol. 96 (1/2), pp. 46–51.

—(2001b) 'Japanese–German Interfirm Networks in China', in Fujitsu Research Institute (ed.), *Conference Papers, Japan and China. Economic Relations in Transition*, 18–19 January 2001, paper 18, Tokyo: Fujitsu Research Institute.

Hamel, G. and C. K. Prahalad, (1989) 'Do You Really Have a Global Strategy?' *Harvard Business Review*, vol. 63 (5), pp. 139–48.

Hammes, W. (1993) *Strategische Allianzen als Instrument der strategischen Unternehmensführung*, Wiesbaden: Gabler Verlag.

Harzing, A. W. (1999) *Managing the Multinationals – An International Study of Control Mechanisms*, Cheltenham: Edward Elgar.

—(2000) 'An Empirical Analysis and Extension of the Bartlett and Ghoshal Typology of Multinational Companies', *Journal of International Business Studies*, vol. 31 (1), pp. 101–20.

Hill, C. W. L. (1997) *International Business: Competing in the Global Marketplace*, USA: Hoffmann Press.

Kawashima, I. and S. Konomoto (1999) 'Time for More Autonomy: Problems of Japanese Companies in East and Southeast Asia', *Nomura Research Institute Quarterly*, vol. 8 (3), pp. 18–31.

Köllner, P. (1997) 'Japans Rolle in der industriellen Arbeitsteilung in Ostasien: Theorie und Praxis', *Japan aktuell Wirtschaft Politik Gesellschaft*, vol. 5 (4), pp. 171–7.

Kobayashi, N. (ed.) (1997) 'Management: A Global Perpective', Tokyo: *The Japan Times*.

Konomoto, S. (1997) 'Japanese Manufacturing in Asia. Time for a Reassessment', *Nomura Research Institute Quarterly*, vol. 6 (3), pp. 70–83.

—(1998) 'Industrial Policy in China and the Strategies of Japanese Transplants', *Nomura Research Institute Quarterly*, vol. 7 (3), pp. 36–47.

—(2000) 'Problems of Japanese Companies in East and Southeast Asia', *Nomura Research Institute Papers*, no. 18, Tokyo: Nomura Research Institute

Kopp, R. (1994) 'International Human Resource Policies and Practices in Japanese, European, and United States Multinationals', *Human Resource Management*, vol. 33 (4), pp. 581–99.

Kwan, C. H. (1997) 'The Rise of Asia and Japan's Hollowing Out Problem', *Nomura Research Institute Quarterly*, vol. 6 (1), pp. 58–75.

Li, F. and Li, J. (1999) *Foreign Investment in China*, Houndmills, Basingstoke: Macmillan – now Palgrave.

McMillan, C. J. (1996) *The Japanese Industrial System*, Berlin and New York: Walter de Grüyter.

Naughton, B. (1997a) 'The Emergence of the China Circle', in B. Naughton (ed.), *The China Circle – Economics and Electronics in the PRC, Taiwan, and Hong Kong*, Washington DC: Brookings Institute Press, pp. 3–37.

— (1997b) *Growing out of the Plan. Chinese Economic Reform, 1978–1993*, Cambridge, MA: Cambridge University Press.

NRI (Nomura Research Institute) (1995) 'Going Offshore: Asian Strategies of Mid-Sized Japanese Companies. Management Research and Consulting Section', *Nomura Research Institute Quarterly*, vol. 4 (2), pp. 34–61.

Ohmae, K. (2001) 'Asia's Next Crisis: Made in China. Rapid Evolution of Chinese Economy Threatens Regional Status Quo', *The Japan Times*, Tokyo, 30 July 2001.

Ôuchi, W. G. (1979) 'A Conceptual Framework for the Design of Organizational Control Mechanisms', *Management Science*, vol. 25 (9), pp. 833–48.

Perlmutter, H. V. (1969) 'The Tortuous Evolution of the Multinational Company', *Columbia Journal of World Business*, no. 1, pp. 9–18.

Porter, M. E. (1980) *Competitive Strategy: Techniques for Analyzing Industries and Competitors*, New York: Free Press.

— (1985) *Competitive Advantage: Creating and Sustaining Superior Performance*, New York: Free Press.

— (1986) *Competition in Global Industries*, Boston: Harvard Business School Press.

— (1990) *The Competitive Advantage of Nations*, New York. Free Press.

Prahalad, C. K. and Y. L. Doz (1987) *The Multinational Mission*, New York: Free Press.

Roth, K. and D. Nigh (1992) 'The Effectiveness of Headquarter Subsidiary Relationships: The Role of Coordination, Control, and Conflict', *Journal of Business Research*, vol. 25 (4), pp. 277–301.

Sydow, J. (1993) 'Strategie und Organisation international tätiger Unternehmen – Managementprozesse in Netzwerkstrukturen', in H.-D. Ganter and G. Schienstock (eds), *Management aus soziologischer Sicht*, Wiesbaden: Gabler, pp. 47–82.

Taylor, R. (1996) *Greater China and Japan. Prospects for an Economic Partnership in East Asia*, London and New York: Routledge.

Teranishi, K. and M. Yamasaki (1995) 'Going Offshore: Japan's Electronics Industry in Asia', *Nomura Research Institute Quarterly*, vol. 4 (3), pp. 22–43.

Toga, M. (2001) 'Beijing Pushes Industry Expansion Guides', *The Nikkei Weekly*, 9 July 2001.

Toyo Keizai (2000) *Kaigai shinshutsu kigyô sôran '00, kigyôbetsu-hen* [General Survey of Japanese Companies Abroad '00, Volume by Firms], Tokyo: Toyo Keizai Shinposha.

Welge, M. (1990) 'Globales Management', in M. Welge (ed.), *Globales Management. Erfolgreiche Strategien für den Weltmarkt*, Stuttgart. C. E. Poeschel, pp. 1–16.

Yoda, N. (2001) 'Relocation and Reorganization of Japanese Industries: Textiles', in FRI–MIT–SOFI Conference: Can Japan be a Global Player? 28 June 2001, Tokyo: Fujitsu Research Institute.

9

Japanese FDI and China's Industrial Development in the Automobile, Electronics and Textile Industries

Tomoo Marukawa

Introduction

Japanese foreign direct investment (FDI) to China rose sharply after 1991, reached a peak in 1995, and then suddenly dropped (Figure 9.1). One of the plausible explanations for this sharp rise and sudden drop is that most Japanese enterprises interested in investing in China had established their operations by 1995. The figure shows that the newly-pledged investments have diminished while the stock of investments is still increasing. Others may attribute this drop to the financial difficulties of Japanese business corporations, caused by the long, lingering depression of the Japanese economy. But this factor cannot explain the entire drop, because the portion of FDI to China to Japanese FDI to all countries has also shown a significant drop (Table 9.1). It does not seem either that China lost its attraction as a host country of FDI for all foreign companies, for the portion of Japanese FDI to all incoming FDI to China has also dropped (for Japanese FDI in China see also Chapter 3).

What is behind the absolute and relative contraction of Japanese FDI to China? The reason may lie both in the limit of Japanese firms' internal resources, and in their low evaluation of market conditions in China. The former is linked to the continuing stagnation of the Japanese economy. Some Japanese banks and brokerages which were very aggressive up to the mid-1990s downsized their activities in China in the late 1990s due to internal financial difficulties, and many potential investors abandoned plans to invest in China. In addition, Japanese companies' evaluation of the profitability of China's market environment is low compared to other host nations in the world. A recent survey of 472 Japanese firms conducted by the Japan Bank for International Cooperation (JBIC) (Kaburagi, Noda and Ikehara, 2000) indicates that Japanese firms' assessments of the profitability, sales, localization and overall performance of their FDI operations in China were the lowest

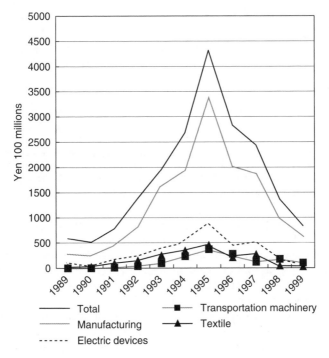

Figure 9.1 Japanese FDI to China

Note: Based on reports from firms to the government. All years are fiscal years (April–March).

Source: Ministry of Finance, Japan (2000, Internet).

Table 9.1 Relative shares of Japanese FDI in China, %

	1990	1992	1995	1997	1998	1999	2000
Share in total outward Japanese FDI	0.6	3.1	8.7	3.7	2.6	1.1	2.0
Share in total inward Chinese FDI	6.9	3.7	8.3	6.7	5.3	6.3	–

Source: Ministry of Finance, Japan (2000, Internet) and National Bureau of Statistics (2000), MOFTEC China (2000, Internet).

among selected regions and countries, including also NIEs, ASEAN-4, the USA, Canada, the EU, Latin America and Central Europe (Table 9.2). Although the statistical significance of the difference is questionable, it is striking that the evaluations of China are the lowest in all four aspects.

Two factors may have led to this low appraisal, the first being the investment environment. In response to the survey question regarding the concerns

Table 9.2   Assessment of the performance of FDI operations by Japanese firms (average score)[1]

	China	NIEs[2]	ASEAN-4[3]	USA & Canada	EU	Latin America	Central Europe
Profitability	2.61	3.07	2.74	2.97	2.78	2.67	3.00
Sales	2.59	3.12	2.89	3.21	3.00	2.81	3.07
Localization	3.01	3.45	3.27	3.57	3.50	3.31	3.21
Overall performance	2.72	3.23	2.96	3.19	3.09	2.87	3.00

Notes: [1]Self-evaluation is based on a 5-point scale, ranging from 1 insufficient, 2 somewhat insufficient, 3 in-between, 4 somewhat sufficient, 5 fairly sufficient. [2]NIEs: Hong Kong, Korea, Singapore, Taiwan. [3]ASEAN-4: Indonesia, Malaysia, Philippines, Thailand.

Source: Kaburagi, Noda and Ikehara (2000).

in undertaking FDI to China, 64.7 per cent of the Japanese firms indicated 'Frequent and abrupt changes in local legal system'; 60.8 per cent marked 'Ambiguous application of local legal system'; 53.6 per cent selected 'Local infrastructure'; and 53.6 per cent marked 'Frequent and abrupt changes in local taxation system'. This result is in striking contrast to Japanese firms' responses about their concerns in other developing countries, where their worries are 'Local political and social situation'; 'Local infrastructure'; and 'Stability of currency'. The second factor is the market environment. The low evaluations for China on 'Profitability' and 'Sales' in Table 9.2 suggest that Japanese-invested companies in China suffer from severe competition and low profitability.

The purpose of this chapter is to examine the behaviour and performance of Japanese companies in three important industries in China: the automobile industry, the consumer-electrical electronics and appliance industry, and the textile and apparel industry. Japanese firms in these three industries face different types of markets. The Chinese automobile industry is basically a domestic market-oriented industry, whereas the other industries cater to both domestic and foreign markets. Government control of production and investment is relatively strict in the automobile industry, but in the consumer-electrical electronics and appliance and textile and apparel industries it is relatively weak, albeit not without controls. By shedding light on Japanese firms in different types of markets, we can identify the behavioural characteristics of Japanese firms that lead to their low appraisal of their performance.

Japanese firms in the Chinese automobile industry

Japanese automobile companies have a strong presence in ASEAN countries, occupying 90 per cent of the Thai market, 95 per cent of the Indonesian market and more than 80 per cent of the Philippine market. But this is not the case in China. Cars made in China that are technologically of Japanese origin, including those made by Sino–Japanese joint ventures and by domestic car-makers that bought technology from Japan, accounted for only 29 per cent in 1999, whereas those of German origin accounted for 58 per cent (Figure 9.2). The share of Sino–Japanese joint ventures in Chinese domestic truck production was even smaller: only 9 per cent. What accounts for these low figures?

The small share of Japanese-origin trucks can be explained by the existence of many domestic truck producers; they can produce trucks that cost less than half of those made by Sino–Japanese joint ventures. Although the maximum speed of Japanese-origin trucks is greater than domestic trucks, the poor road conditions in China do not allow Japanese-origin trucks to demonstrate their advantage over domestic trucks.

In the passenger car market, on the other hand, Japanese car-makers yielded the market to Western rivals, although Japanese auto-makers were not late in approaching China. Toyota Motor Corporation made its first contact with Chinese auto-makers in the late 1970s: it assisted First Auto Works (FAW) (China FAW Group Corporation) in renovating its rusty production technology, also introducing some methods of the Toyota production system (Lee, 1997). But the first Western auto-maker to establish a production site in China after the reform was American Motors Corporation (AMC), which was later acquired by Chrysler Corporation (the present DaimlerChrysler AG). AMC established a joint venture in Beijing in 1983. Although its initial purpose was to renovate the antiquated off-road vehicles of the Beijing auto-maker using AMC's technology (Mann, 1989), the joint venture later started to produce Cherokees which were classified as passenger cars according to the Chinese classification, and thus became the first foreign auto-maker to produce passenger cars in China.

The second Western auto-maker to establish a joint venture in China was Volkswagen AG (VW), which set up a joint venture with Shanghai Automobile Works in 1984. The Chinese government wanted to modernize the

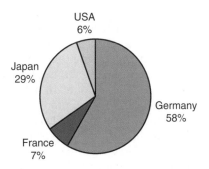

Figure 9.2 China's car production classified by the origin of technology, 1999
Source: *China Automobile Industry Yearbook*, 2000.

passenger car technology of the Shanghai factory which had been producing sedans since the late 1950s. Volkswagen was chosen in 1981 from among seven Western auto companies, including General Motors Corporation (GM), Ford Motor Company, Nissan Motor Co., Ltd, Renault Group and PSA Peugeot Citroën. Volkswagen's production technology and its favourable terms, made possible by the company's clear intention to set a foothold in Asia, were most attractive to the Chinese (Chen, 2000).

When the Chinese government decided to set up two more large joint ventures to produce passenger cars in 1987, it was again the European auto-makers that acquired the tickets to the Chinese car market. The two largest state-owned auto-makers, FAW and Dong Feng Motor Corporation, were designated as the next sites for passenger car production. FAW decided to set up a joint venture with Volkswagen, and Dong Feng with Citroën. Volkswagen provided the most favourable conditions to FAW, allowing the latter to take 60 per cent of the joint venture's share, even though most of the equipment of the joint venture was provided by Volkswagen. This was made possible because Volkswagen had an idle car plant in the United States, forced to stop operation in 1988 after severe competition with Japanese car-makers, that could be provided cheaply to the joint venture. In the case of Dong Feng, the fact that the French government pledged to provide preferential loans to the project was a great advantage in Citroën's selection as partner.

Shanghai, FAW and Dong Feng having been designated as the 'production base' for passenger cars in 1987, the Chinese government approved three more car plants in 1988, namely Beijing Jeep Corporation Ltd, Guangzhou Peugeot Automobile Co. Ltd and Tianjin Auto. The latter three car plants were called the 'Small Three' in contrast to the former 'Big Three', mainly because the approved size of their investments was smaller than the latter. The actual size of their production, however, was not always smaller than the Big Three (Table 9.3).

Japanese auto-maker Daihatsu Motor Co. Ltd supplied the technology and key components to one of the Small Three, Tianjin Auto. This company is the only company among Big Three and Small Three that have not elevated the status of cooperation from mere technology transfer to joint venture. It was not that Daihatsu had no interest in investing. As a matter of fact, Daihatsu and Tianjin had been negotiating the issue of establishing a joint venture for a long time but never came to terms. The Tianjin side wished to have a grandiose plant with the latest equipment, whereas Daihatsu insisted on economizing the investment in order to produce cheap cars.

The main reason why Japanese car-makers failed to establish joint ventures with the Big Three and Small Three is that the Japanese side was not as eager as their European partners to invest in China. After many trips by Chinese leaders and automobile factory managers to Japan, the Chinese had come to admire the Japanese automobile production technology and invited the Japanese to invest in China. It is widely believed that Chinese authorities

Table 9.3 Production volume of car-makers in China

Name of enterprise	Firm type	Brand name	1983	1989	1992	1995	1998	1999
Shanghai Volkswagen Automotive Company Ltd	JV with Volkswagen AG	Santana	0	15 688	65 000	131 070	126 292	–
		Santana 2000	0	0	0	29 000	108 708	230 946
		Audi100	0	0	0	0	0	0
Shanghai Automobile Works	SOE	Shanghai	5 607 438	5 518	–	–	–	–
		Santana		0				
Tianjin Automobile Industrial (Group) Corporation	TT from Daihatsu Motor Co., Ltd	Charade 7100	0	1 274	30 150	65 000	82 240	83 115
		Charade 7130	0	0	0	0	17 781	18 713
Beijing Jeep Corporation, Ltd	JV with Daimler-Chrysler AG	Cherokee	0	6 630	20 001	25 127	8 344	8 121
Guangzhou Peugeot Automobile Co., Ltd	JV with PSA Peugeot Citroën	Peugeot	0	4 494	15 666	6 939	2 246	–
Guangzhou Honda Automobile Co., Ltd	JV with Honda Motor Co.	Accord	0	0	0	0	344	10 008
China FAW Group Corporation	TT from Volkswagen AG	Audi	0	1 922	15 127	17 961	208	–
		Hongqi CA7560		0	2	7	0	15 731
		Hongqi CA7220		0	0	1 749	14 743	–
FAW–Volkswagen Automotive Company, Ltd	JV with Volkswagen AG	Jetta	0	0	8 062	20 001	60 085	75 566
		Audi		0	0	0	3 837	–
		AudiC3V6		0	0	0	2 178	6 636
Chang An Automobile Liability Co., Ltd, Chongquing Chang An Suzuki Automobile Co., Ltd	TT from Suzuki Motor Corporation, JV with Suzuki Motor Corporation	Alto	0	0	5 565	13 180	35 555	44 583

Table 9.3   continued

Name of enterprise	Firm type	Brand name	1983	1989	1992	1995	1998	1999
Qingchuan Machinery Works	TT from Suzuki Motor Corporation	Alto	0	0	82	2 790	5 008	5 306
Jiangnan Machinery Works	TT from Suzuki Motor Corporation	Alto	0	0	0	1 568	1 012	700
Jiangbei Machinery Works	TT from Suzuki Motor Corporation	Alto	0	0	176	425	518	487
Dong Feng–Citroën Automibile Co., Ltd	JV with PSA Peugeot Citroën	CitroenZX	0	0	0	1 314	36 240	40 200
Dong Feng Motor Corporation	SOE	CitroenZX	0	0	801	3 797	0	0
Guizhou Aviation Industry Corp./ Guizhou Yunque Automobile Ltd	TT from Fuji Heavy Industries, JV with Fuji Heavy Industries	Rex	0	0	93	7 105	1 064	1 529
FAW-Shunde Automobile Works	a subsidiary of China FAW Group Corporation	GolfASS13	0	0	0	3 985	194	1
FAW-Hainan Automobile Works	a subsidiary of China FAW Group Corporation	CA7160 etc.	0	0	0	0	0	725
Shanghai General Motors Co., Ltd	JV with General Motors Corporation	Buick	0	0	0	0	0	23 290
Total Car Production			6 045	35 526	160 725	331 015	506 597	565 657

Note: JV = joint venture, TT = technology transfer, SOE = state-owned enterprise.

wanted to have Toyota invest in China the most, but Toyota was never seriously interested in investing during the 1980s.

There are three main reasons why Japanese auto-makers were not as eager as European auto-makers (see also Watanabe, 1996). First, Japanese auto-makers were too occupied coping with trade frictions with the United States to seriously consider the Chinese market, which was much smaller than the US market. The USA imposed 'voluntary export restraints' on Japanese auto-makers in 1981, which pressured them to start operations in the United States. Honda Motor Corporation started to produce cars in Ohio in 1982, Toyota Motor Corporation, Nissan Motor Co. Ltd, Mitsubishi Motors Corporation, Mazda Motor Corporation, Fuji Heavy Industries Ltd, and Isuzu Motors Ltd followed suit (Hiraoka, 2001). Japanese auto-makers may have exhausted their internal resources of international production by setting up factories in the United States and had no resource left to invest in China. The fact that Daihatsu was the only Japanese car-maker that showed a willingness to invest in China during the 1980s, though not realized, may be related to the fact that Daihatsu was the only Japanese car-maker that didn't invest in the United States.

Secondly, the large amount of exports and large share of Japanese cars in the Chinese market during the first half of the 1980s (Table 9.4) might have led Japanese auto-makers to be optimistic about the possibility of conquering the Chinese market through exports.

Thirdly, Japanese auto-makers were skeptical about the growth potential of the Chinese car market, a skepticism strengthened by experiences in the

Table 9.4 Automobile exports from Japan and their share in China's automobile market

	Automobiles (trucks and passenger cars)		Passenger cars	
	Volume (units)[1]	Share (%)[2]	Volume (units)[1]	Share (%)[2]
1980	28747	11	12591	50
1985	226640	28	70721	64
1988	24517	3	13405	14
1990	18796	3	5270	7
1993	99740	6	45927	11
1996	25887	2	19421	4
1998	36084	2	23069	4
1999	28244	2	18970	3

Notes: [1]The export volume is according to Japanese Custom Statistics. [2]The share is calculated as follows: (Japan's export volume by Japanese statistics) / {(China's domestic production) + (China's imports by Chinese statistics) − (China's exports)}.

Source: China Automobile Industry Yearbook; China Customs Statistics; Japan's White Paper on International Trade; MITI.

mid-1980s. After the import boom in 1985, auto imports and the auto market of China suddenly shrank because of strict import restrictions and austerity policies imposed in 1986, and, accordingly, auto exports from Japan contracted to 24 per cent of the 1985 level, and car exports contracted to only 5 per cent (see Table 9.4).

In the early 1990s, however, Japanese auto-makers changed their skeptical attitude towards the Chinese market. The fact that vehicle (truck and passenger car) sales in China almost tripled between 1990 and 1993, and car sales more than quintupled during the same period, led virtually all the Japanese auto-makers to think seriously about setting up operations in China. Shanghai Volkswagen seemed to enjoy a first-comer's advantage, quintupling its production volume, while high car prices caused by the high protection rate of the Chinese domestic market enabled the enterprise to earn lucrative profits: the profit rate (that is profit and taxes in relation to total assets) of the joint venture reached 56 per cent in 1993. The Chinese government's policy to protect and promote domestic automobile production and to restrict the number of production sites, which was announced in its Automobile Industry Policy (1994), further increased the interest of Japanese companies to invest in China. This policy meant that Japanese auto-makers would lose the chance to have access to the Chinese market unless they had production sites within the Chinese border.

Minor Japanese auto-makers were faster than the major ones in their move to China, and Isuzu was the first to invest there. Isuzu established a small joint venture in Chongqing in 1985 with only 10 per cent of share ownership, and its plant engaged in the small-scale assembly of Isuzu trucks with a capacity of several hundred units a year. The plant's capacity, however, was expanded in the 1990s to 50 000 units a year. In order to enlarge the local supply of components, Isuzu, together with its related component makers, established five joint ventures in 1995 that produce axles, moulds and plastics in Chongqing.

Suzuki Motor Corporation set up a joint venture in Chongqing in 1993 to produce light passenger cars with an artillery maker, the latter being one of only two plants that received government approval to produce light passenger cars in 1992. The government had made it clear in 1988 that no other plants except for the Big Three and Small Three would be allowed to produce cars, but under pressure from the military industry bloc, which was in desperate need of new lines of business to cope with excess capacity and overstaffing, the government specially approved two more car plants in 1992 to promote the conversion of the munitions industry. Suzuki and Fuji Heavy Industries became the foreign counterparts of these newly-approved car plants. Fuji, however, had more trouble than Suzuki in establishing a joint venture and the plant has been less successful than that of Suzuki, as can be seen in Table 9.3.

Toyota was as eager as Suzuki and Isuzu to have a production site in China, but it had to struggle for a foothold in the Chinese car market. The Chinese government closed the door again after approving the two additional light passenger car plants in 1992. The ban was finally lifted in 1996, but the government approved only one additional plant. During the period of the ban China's auto market grew most rapidly, and all the major auto-makers of the world were interested in investing in China and struggled to get the last available slot. Toyota remained one of the two final candidates for the foreign partner of the new car plant, but it gave way to GM.

Japanese auto-makers then started to make use of existing car-makers in China. As the growth rate of the Chinese car market decelerated from the staggering 43 per cent a year during the first half of the 1990s to -1.5 per cent in 1996, some of the existing car plants in China encountered difficulties. Guangzhou Peugeot, one of the Small Three, was among them, and after Peugeot had abandoned it Honda took over the plant in 1997. Toyota, on the other hand, decided to negotiate setting up a joint venture with Tianjin Auto, a company to which Daihatsu had been transferring technology. Toyota tried to persuade the Chinese government that it was not trying to set up another new car plant but was only inheriting an existing operation by its subsidiary, Daihatsu. In order to make the relationship between the two Japanese companies clear, Toyota even raised its capital share at Daihatsu from 16.8 per cent to 51.2 per cent (Chen, 2000).

Turning now to Japanese investments in the automobile components industry, we find that Japanese components suppliers have a larger presence in China compared to Japanese auto-makers. Among the 69 foreign-invested automobile components suppliers, excluding engine-makers, listed in Wang (2000), 25 are joint ventures with Japanese components suppliers. A brief look at the spatial distribution of Japanese-invested components suppliers reveals an interesting locational pattern. They tend to locate near the automobile plant established by the auto-maker of the same industrial group or *keiretsu*. Japanese-invested suppliers are concentrated in Tianjin where Toyota has a plant, and Chongqing where Isuzu has a plant.

There are exceptions, however. Shanghai Koito Automotive Lamp Co. Ltd, a joint venture with Japanese lamp-maker, Koito, was established to supply automobile lamps mainly to Shanghai Volkswagen, responding to the call from Volkswagen. The Japanese-invested suppliers in Tianjin and Chongqing, on the other hand, were established to supply components to Toyota and Isuzu's operation. Toyota and Isuzu asked the component suppliers to make investments in the vicinity of their operations in order to raise the local content of their automobiles. Compared to Japanese components suppliers, American and German suppliers have a tendency to locate in the provinces that have large automobile production, rather than in the provinces where auto-makers from their home country are located.

The story of Japanese auto-makers' investments in China sheds light on some of their characteristics. For example, they are more risk-aversive than their European and American counterparts. They didn't decide to invest until they had confirmed that the Chinese auto market was sure to grow. Not having taken risks, Japanese auto-makers lost the first-comer advantage which Shanghai Volkswagen had enjoyed, but they avoided the fate of Beijing Jeep and Guangzhou Peugeot. On the other hand, although they may be slow in deciding on investments, once decided they will not change their mind even if the situation changes. Honda and Toyota, for example, signed an agreement to invest even after the growth rate of the auto market had decelerated.

Having once decided to build a large plant in a foreign country, Japanese auto-makers also take the trouble to create a local supplier network of components, mainly by asking components suppliers of the same *keiretsu* to invest in the vicinity of the plant. Taking the large initial cost of setting up a supplier network in the host country into consideration, it is understandable that Japanese auto-makers do not easily decide to invest.

Minor Japanese auto-makers such as Isuzu and Suzuki, however, do not seem to share the risk-aversive attitude of the large companies. Their unfavourable position in other markets made it inevitable that they would take a chance in a new market.

Japanese firms in Chinese consumer electronics and electric appliance industries

Chinese consumer electronics and electric appliance industries have experienced spectacular growth since the reform: the annual production volume of colour television sets grew from 4000 in 1978 to 42 million units in 1999, that of refrigerators from 28 000 to 12 million, and air conditioners grew from zero to 13 million. China has become the world's largest producer of these items. Japanese consumer electronics companies contributed in various ways to this growth. Most consumer electronics and electric appliance makers in China imported production lines from Japan. 'Duplicative introduction of technology' became a major problem in the 1980s, as Chinese state-owned enterprises rushed to Japanese electronics makers to buy production lines of colour television sets, refrigerators, washing machines and air conditioners. Japanese FDI, however, played only a minor role in this development. This is mostly because the Chinese government did not allow foreign enterprises to invest in these industries except for a few export-oriented joint ventures. The domestic market was reserved for domestic state-owned enterprises, and virtually closed to foreign companies.

Hitachi Ltd and Sanyo Electric Co. Ltd were the exceptional foreign enterprises allowed to make investments. Hitachi established a joint venture in Fuzhou to produce colour TV sets in 1980. Hitachi first intended to sell colour TV sets to the domestic market, but as the Chinese authorities allowed only a limited amount of domestic sales, the joint venture did not enjoy first-comer's advantage such as Shanghai Volkswagen did. Sanyo started a joint venture in Shenzhen in 1984, but this didn't succeed in penetrating the domestic market either.

Japanese FDI's presence was small in the end-product manufacturing of consumer electronics and electric appliances, but they played a major role in the production of their key components. The fact that a huge amount of foreign exchange was needed to maintain production was a major problem for the industry in the 1980s, because the industry had to import a huge amount of key components from abroad. Localization of key components became the top priority of the industry. The production of key components, however, required a large amount of initial investment and more sophisticated manufacturing technology than the assembly of end products. Chinese authorities had no choice but to encourage FDI to achieve the localization of key components.

Take the case of colour televisions. Cathode ray tubes (CRTs), which account for half of the material costs of colour television sets, were in short supply during the 1980s. In order to keep the existing colour television plants in operation, China had to import a lot of cathode ray tubes, spending a huge amount of foreign currency – 11 million tubes in 1988 at a cost of US$ 720 million. There was only one domestic colour cathode ray tube maker then, a state-owned enterprise that bought technology from Hitachi and Asahi Glass Company. The Chinese government launched a plan to expand the annual production capacity of cathode ray tubes by 8 million units in 1985; the existing cathode ray tube plant in Xianyang was to be expanded, and three new plants were to be built. Among the four projects, Japanese electronics companies bid for three (Zhongguo xianxiangguan hangye minzhu guanli xiehui, 1992). The recent situation of the cathode ray tube industry is shown in Table 9.5; of the total production, 27 per cent is produced by joint ventures with Japanese firms. Makers that introduced technology from Japan now supply 77 per cent of Chinese cathode ray tube production.

In the case of videocassette recorders (VCRs), a Sino–Japanese joint venture in Dalian became the sole supplier of key components in China. China's videocassette recorder production started in the early 1990s with the assembling of imported knocked-down components. Eleven domestic companies started production, but only on a small scale. The Ministry of Machine and Electronics Industry then came up with an idea that could increase the local content of videocassette recorders and realize scale economies of component production at the same time. The Ministry asked the 11 companies to establish a joint venture which would produce key components of videocassette recorders: cylinder heads and chassis. The Ministry then looked for a foreign partner that could supply the technology for these components.

Japan's Matsushita tendered for this project and the new company, China Hualu Matsushita AVC Co. Ltd, was established in 1994 to become the sole supplier of videocassette recorder components in China. The success in acquiring this project, however, did not bring about financial success to

Table 9.5   Characteristics of major colour cathode ray tube (CRT) makers of China

	Type of enterprise	Origin of technology	Production (1998) (thousand units)	Sales (1998)
Caihong Colour CRT Works	State-owned enterprise	Hitachi, Ltd, Asahi Glass Company, Toshiba Corporation	6 460	7 310
Beijing Matsushita Colour CRT Ltd	JV with Matsushita Electric Industrial, Co., Ltd	Matsushita Electric Industrial, Co., Ltd	4 162	4 296
Shanghai Novel Colour Picture Tube Co., Ltd	JV with Novel Colour Picture Tube Co., Ltd (Hong Kong)	Toshiba Corporation	3 777	3 797
Guangdong Colour Picture Tube Co.	JV with Fuminfa Corporation (Hong Kong)	Hitachi, Ltd	3 285	3 294
Huafei Colour Monitor Ltd	JV with Royal Philips Electronics and Novel Colour Picture Tube Co., Ltd	Royal Philips Electronics	3 213	3 214
Shenzehn SEG Ltd	JV with Hitachi, Ltd	Hitachi, Ltd	2 784	2 784
LG Shuguang Electronic Ltd	JV with LG Electronics Inc.	LG Electronics Inc.	2 657	2 704
Shanghai Suoguang Video Ltd	JV with Sony Corporation	Sony Corporation	445	430
Tianjin Samsung SDI Co., Ltd	JV with Samsung SDI Co., Ltd	Samsung SDI Co., Ltd	255	253
Foshan Colour CRT Corporation	JV	Thomson Multimedia	40	100

Note: JV stands for joint venture.

Source: *China Electronics Industry Yearbook*, 1999; Zhongguo xianxiangguan hangye minzhu guanli xiehui (1992).

Matsushita. Videocassette recorder sales in China plunged soon after the joint venture went into full operation in 1994. More than 3 million recorder units were sold in China in 1993, including 2.5 million smuggled units, but sales diminished to only 0.8 million in 1996. Chinese citizens lost interest in videocassette recorders when a cheaper alternative, the video CD player, was introduced. Initially the joint venture was intended to supply the expected ever-growing production of videocassette recorders in China, but when the JV went into full operation it was discovered that the demand of the original 11 recorder makers was not enough. The joint venture then started to produce videocassette recorders on its own, while exporting a part of their production.

Japanese companies also play a major role in the supply of compressors, the most important component of refrigerators and air conditioners. In the case of compressors for air conditioners, Sino–Japanese joint ventures account for 90 per cent of domestic production. Toshiba, Matsushita, Sanyo, Daikin Industries Ltd, Mitsubishi Electric Corporation and Hitachi all produce compressors in China.

The above observations regarding the colour TV, videocassette recorder and air conditioner industries illustrate the technological advantage Japanese consumer electronics companies have in key components. This advantage, however, is not reflected in their shares in the market for end products; as shown in Table 9.6, Japanese brands have only small shares in the Chinese television set market.

All of the top seven brands in 1999 were made by domestic enterprises including several state-owned enterprises. The highest Japanese brand's ranking in market share had dropped from number one in 1994 to number eight in 1999. We can hardly say that this is the result of protectionism, since, after 1994, the Chinese government started to allow Japanese electronics companies to establish joint ventures with ailing state-owned television makers and sell the products to the domestic market. Matsushita, Sony, Victor Company of Japan Ltd and Toshiba all established production sites in China after 1995. The shortage of foreign exchange, which confined the ability of foreign-funded enterprises to sell their products to the domestic market, had disappeared.

The falling market shares of Japanese brands indicates the disadvantage of Japanese firms in marketing their products in China. This disadvantage is caused partly by the fact that FDI is still restricted in the wholesale and retail industries, but a more important reason is the rising competitiveness of Chinese domestic television makers. The quality and functions of domestic-made sets are now approaching the level of those of Japanese sets, while their prices have declined sharply: the price of 21-inch colour sets fell more than 60 per cent in nominal value during the 10 years since 1989. Japanese electronics companies, while competing with Chinese makers in the end product market, supported the technological improvement of domestic makers by providing cathode ray tubes and integrated circuits to domestic makers and by assisting their circuit design. Most Japanese electronics companies are multidivisional giants, comprising various end products and components. The components division's interest is to sell as many components as it can, and this sometimes assists competitors of the end product divisions of the same company.

A similar situation can be found in the air conditioner market. Although Japanese-funded enterprises supply 90 per cent of compressors for air

Table 9.6   Market shares of top colour television brands in China, %

Brand name	Maker	1993	1994	1996	1997	1998	1999
Changhong	Changhong Electric Co., Ltd	4.2	5.0	20.5	25.0	33.7	13.2
Konka	Konka Group, Ltd	13.4	11.0	12.2	15.1	13.7	15.9
Haier	Haier Group Company	–	–	–	–	7.9	7.8
TCL	TCL Holdings Co., Ltd	–	–	6.2	9.5	7.8	11.0
Panda	Panda Electronics Group Co., Ltd	11.2	11.0	4.6	3.9	5.6	2.9
Hisense	Hisense Electronic Co., Ltd	1.9	–	–	3.1	5.6	8.5
LG	LG Electronics	–	–	–	–	3.6	–
RGB	Shenzhen Chuangwei-RGB Electronics Co., Ltd	–	–	–	4.4	2.6	4.5
Philips	Philips Consumer Electronics of Suzhou	–	–	–	4.5	2.4	–
Matsushita	Shandong Matsushita Television and Visual Co., Ltd	10.7	14.7	13.3	6.7	2.3	–
Sony	Shanghai Suoguang Electronics Co., Ltd	–	3.5	5.5	–	2.3	3.6
Toshiba	Dalian Toshiba Television Co., Ltd	2.1	–	4.2	–	2.1	–
Jinxing	Shanghai Guangdian Electric Group Corporation	4.2	3.7	2.7	4.5	2.0	2.8
Xoceco	Xiamen Overseas Chinese Electronics Co., Ltd	3.3	–	2.7	3.8	2.0	6.5
Beijing	Tianjin Tongguang Samsung Electronics Co., Ltd	5.4	4.0	7.1	–	–	–
Share of top ten brands		56.5	52.8	79.0	80.5	85.2	76.7

Source: *China Market Statistics Yearbook; China Electronic News.*

conditioners, Japanese brands occupy only a small portion of the end product market (see Table 9.7).

Our observations regarding colour TVs, videocassette recorders and air conditioners leads us to the conclusion that in the Chinese consumer electronics and electric appliance market, Japanese firms have shown competitiveness only in the area where their core competence resides: the production of key components. Chinese domestic enterprises, including several state-owned enterprises, have succeeded in assimilating the technology of assembling

Table 9.7 Characteristics of air conditioner makers in China

Name of enterprise	Production volume in 1997 (thousand units)	Sales in 1997 (billion yuan)	Market share in 1999 (%)
Haier Group Company	1 100	3.42	27.0
Shunde Midea Group Ltd	906	1.83	8.8
Shanghai Sharp Electric Ltd	467	1.48	7.3
Shanghai Hitachi Electrical Appliances Co., Ltd	183	0.84	7.1
Chunlan (Group) Corporation	1 167	5.33	5.5
Guangdong Kelon Electric Ltd	670	1.46	3.8
Zhuhai Glee Electric Ltd	1 183	4.42	3.2
Hisense Electronic Co., Ltd	–	–	6.3
LG Electronics Tianjin Appiances Co., Ltd	–	–	5.4
Changhong Electric Co., Ltd	–	–	5.0
Guangdong Huabao Air Conditioner Factory	785	1.82	–
Ningbo Sanxing (Group) Co., Ltd	339	0.95	–
Guangzhou Hualing Air-conditioning and Equipment Co., Ltd	278	1.4	–
Guangdong Zhuoyue Air Conditioner Factory	233	1.11	–
Hangzhou Jinsong Group Co., Ltd	233	0.75	–

Source: *China Light Industry Yearbook*, and various sources.

end products, their technological progress being achieved with continuous assistance by Japanese firms. Chinese enterprises are not only able to catch up with Japanese firms in producing the latest products, but also in doing so more cheaply. In marketing, Japanese firms proved not to have special skills that could be applied successfully in China.

The production of key components, however, which requires precision machining, was not easily assimilated in China. Although China localized the production of linear integrated circuits used in colour television sets in the late 1980s, in recent years Chinese television set makers have been importing integrated circuits from Japanese electronics companies because domestic integrated-circuit makers cannot catch up with the latest technology. The growth in production volume and competitiveness of the Chinese consumer electronics and electric appliance industry is remarkable, but at the same time its dependence on the Japanese electronics industry for key components supply is increasing.

Japanese firms in Chinese textile and apparel industries

China is the largest exporter of textiles and clothing in the world, and accounted for 8.8 per cent of world exports of textiles and 16.2 per cent of clothing in 1999 (WTO, International Trade Statistics 2000). China's actual share may be several per cent higher than these figures if re-exports through Hong Kong are added.

Japan contributed in many ways to China becoming the world's largest textile and apparel exporter. First, Japan provided the largest market for Chinese clothing. According to Chinese customs statistics, Japan is the largest importer of Chinese clothing, accounting for 31.4 per cent of China's clothing exports, and, if we include re-exports through Hong Kong, the share may be even higher. If we compare Japanese import statistics from China with Chinese export statistics, Japan absorbed 38 per cent of China's clothing exports and 13 per cent of China's textile exports in 1999. Sixty-three per cent of Japanese imports of clothing was from China in 1998 (see Table 9.8), and one out of four pieces of clothing sold in Japan in 1996 was made in China. The ratio seems to have further increased since then.

Secondly, Japanese FDI to China promoted the expansion of Chinese apparel exports to Japan. Japanese companies started to produce clothing in China in the early days of reform mainly in the form of processing trade, which is not counted as FDI by Chinese authorities. In processing trade the foreign side provides most of the materials and equipment to a factory in China and takes back all the products processed by the factory. A processing factory is virtually a foreign-invested enterprise that is controlled by foreign managers. Since 1987, Japanese FDI in the apparel industry to China started to increase because of the appreciation of the yen, the labour shortage in Japan, and the depreciation of the renminbi. According to the data of Toyo Keizai (1999), there were 302 Japanese-affiliated enterprises in the Chinese textile and apparel industries in 1998.

The textile and apparel trade between Japan and China consists mostly of trade between the companies in Japan and Japanese-invested enterprises in China, if we include the factories engaging in processing trade in the latter. In the near future, however, it is likely that more and more Chinese domestic companies will be involved in bilateral trade. We can justify this conclusion if we examine the nature of the division of labour between the two countries in detail.

Table 9.8 Japan's textile and apparel trade, 1999 (US$ millions)

	Exports		Imports	
	World	*China*	*World*	*China*
Textile materials	994	269	1015	151
Yarn	1039	138	1003	203
Fabrics	4057	1827	1226	382
Textile articles	1817	345	18716	12660
Textiles and textile articles (total)	7981	2585	21960	13396

Source: White Paper on International Trade, MITI.

There are four types of companies in the Japanese apparel industry: trading companies sell fabric to apparel makers; apparel makers make the design and pattern of clothing, and provide them with the materials to sewing companies; sewing companies make clothing according to orders from the apparel makers; apparel makers pay a processing fee to sewing companies, take back the clothing and resell the clothing to retailers.

The role of sewing companies was transferred to China from the late 1980s, and thus exports of fabrics from Japan to China and imports of clothing from China to Japan increased. What changed was not just the location of apparel factories, but also the division of labour between the companies. The clothing factories in China are not only run by Japanese sewing companies but also by trading companies and apparel makers. Some sewing companies are assuming a part of the role which has been played by apparel makers, such as designing and patterning, while trading companies and apparel makers are assuming the role of sewing companies in China. Although the new division of labour among firms seems complex at first glance, all actors seem to be heading for a similar type of division of labour. In the former division of labour, clothing reached customers after being handled by four types of firms: trading companies, apparel makers, sewing companies and retailers. In the new division of labour, the steps are reduced to two: a maker and a retailer. Some retailers, such as Uniqlo (First Retailing Co. Ltd), design the clothing and send them directly to factories in China. Some apparel makers design clothing and produce them at factories they own in China and sell them to retailers. Price competition in the Japanese market is the driving force that reduced the steps in the division of labour.

The story of Japanese FDI in the textile and apparel industries is very different from the preceding stories of the automobile and electronics industries. The actors are all Japanese companies; Japanese companies run the factories and sell their products to Japan, and Chinese people appear only as workers. But more and more Chinese companies will be involved in the trade in the future. First, Japanese apparel factories in China have begun to look for sources of fabrics among Chinese textile makers, as the quality of fabrics made by domestic firms is improving. The increase in domestic sourcing by apparel exporters is reflected in the recent drop of yarn and fabric imports of China (Table 9.9). Yarn and fabric imports per one dollar of apparel exports of China were 48 cents in 1996, but fell to 37 cents in 1999.

Secondly, the role of makers in the two-step division of labour may be assumed more and more by Chinese apparel makers; some Japanese companies such as Uniqlo are already utilizing Chinese domestic firms. In the past, Japanese companies had to manage production sites in China by themselves, because the quality standards of the Japanese market were very strict compared to those of China and it was difficult for Chinese apparel makers to meet Japanese standards. But as the quality standards in China's domestic market rise and as Chinese makers assimilate production management techniques, the necessity for Japanese companies to manage factories in

Table 9.9   Structure of China's textile and apparel trade, 1980–99 (US$ millions)

	Exports			Imports		
	Textile materials	Yarn and fabric	Apparel	Textile materials	Yarn and fabric	Apparel
1980	544	2 756	1 653	2 040	835	21
1984	929	3 692	2 653	693	954	6
1988	1 672	6 456	4 872	1 946	2 388	28
1992	669	8 587	16 748	3 042	6 695	402
1995	753	13 919	24 049	4 108	10 914	969
1996	713	12 113	25 037	3 770	11 980	1 044
1998	609	12 822	30 060	2 404	11 082	1 072
1999	980	13 044	30 078	1 938	11 081	1 102

Source: China's customs statistics.

China by themselves, sending an expensive Japanese manager, has dimi-nished. Japanese companies may gradually retreat to the realm where they have their core competence: developing and selling clothing that suits the taste of Japanese consumers.

Conclusion

Japanese firms in different industrial sectors have different cultures, so we must be careful in generalizing our observations from the above industries. But as these three sectors account for 49 per cent of Japanese manufacturing FDI to China in the 1990s, we can fairly say that the observations above are important aspects of Japanese FDI.

First, Japanese firms may be slow and risk-averse in deciding FDI, but once they have decided, they will not change their minds so easily and will build up supplier networks in the host country. This kind of behaviour makes them forfeit first-comer advantages, but they may achieve large production in the very long run.

Secondly, as Chinese domestic firms are good at assimilating production technology, and as European and American firms are aggressively approaching the Chinese market, Japanese firms are having a hard time in the end-product market in China in many sectors. But as competition intensifies, Japanese firms are revealing their core competence: production of key components. In the industries that require sophisticated manufacturing of key compo-nents, such as the automobile and electronics industries, Japanese firms will still have roles to play in China.

Thirdly, as China's investment environment improves, more and more Japanese firms will use China as a production base to supply products to Japan in order to benefit from cheap labour costs and an abundant labour supply. The role of manufacturers in this division of labour, however, will be gradually taken over by Chinese domestic firms.

References

Chen, J. (2000) *Chûgoku jôyôsha kigyô no seichô senryaku* [Growth Strategies of the Chinese Automotive Manufacturers], Tokyo: Shinzansha.

Editorial Commitee (ed.) (1999) *China Electronics Industry Yearbook*, Beijing: Publishing House of Electronics Industry.

Hiraoka, L. S. (2001) *Global Alliances in the Motor Vehicle Industry*, Westport: Quorum Books.

Kaburagi, S., H. Noda and S. Ikehara (2000) 'The Outlook of Foreign Direct Investment by Japanese Manufacturing Companies: Prospects of Overseas Business Operations after the Asian Economic Crisis', *JBIC Review*, vol. 1, pp. 3–50.

Lee, C. (1997) *Gendai chûgoku no jidôsha sangyô* [The Automobile Industry of Modern China], Tokyo: Shinzansha.

Mann, J. (1989) *Beijing Jeep*, New York: Simon & Schuster.

MOF (Ministry of Finance, Japan) (2000) *Statistics. Foreign Direct Investment*, http://www.mof.go.jp/english/e1c008.htm

MOFTEC (Ministry of Foreign Trade and Economic Cooperation, China) (2000) *1986–1999 Riben touzi qingkuang yilan* (<http://www.moftec.gov.cn/moftec_cn/tjsj/wztj/2000_9-22-15.html> 31 August 2001).

National Bureau of Statistics (2000) *China Statistical Yearbook*, Beijing: China Statistical Press.

Tôyô Keizai (1999) *Kaigai Shinshutsu Kigyô Sôran* [Japanese Multinationals: Facts and Figures], Tokyo: Tôyô keizai shinposha.

Wang, L. (ed.) (2000) *2000 Zhongguo waishang touzi baogao* [Report on Foreign Direct Investment in China], Beijing: Zhongguo caizheng jingji chubanshe.

Watanabe, M. (1996) *2000 nen no chûgoku jidôsha sangyô* [Chinese automobile industry in the year 2000], Machida: Sososha.

WTO (World Trade Organization) (2000) *International Trade Statistics*, Geneva: WTO.

Zhongguo xianxiangguan hangye minzhu guanli xiehui (1992) *Zhongguo xianxiangguan gongye fazhan shi* [A History of the Development of Chinese CRT Industry], Beijing: Dianzi gongye chubanshe.

10
The Role of the Overseas Chinese in the Sino–Japanese Economic Relationship
Yan Zhu

Introduction

The Sino–Japanese economic relationship has greatly intensified over the past 20 years since China began its reform and open-door policies. Today Japan is China's biggest trading partner. In 2000, China's trade value with Japan amounted to US$ 83.2 billion: US$ 41.7 billion for exports and US$ 41.5 billion for imports (China's Customs Statistics, 2000). Japan's total trade value with China was US$ 85.7 billion: US$ 30.4 billion for exports and US$ 55.3 billion for imports; and China is Japan's second largest trading partner after the United States (MOF, 2000) (for Sino–Japanese trade see Chapter 2). In terms of investment, Japan ranks third in foreign direct investment (FDI) to China after Hong Kong and the United States. By the end of 2000, the cumulative total of Japanese direct investment to China on contract value was US$ 38.8 billion, while the actually used value was US$ 27.8 billion (China's Latest Economic Indicators, 2001) (for Japanese FDI into China see Chapter 3).

However, compared to Japan, regional economies such as Hong Kong, Taiwan and Southeast Asian countries, where the overseas Chinese play a dominant role in the economy, established closer relationships with China at an earlier period. These regional economies also play an important role in the Sino–Japanese economic relationship.

In the following, we shall discuss the role of the overseas Chinese in the Sino–Japanese economic relationship, focusing on the cooperation between Japanese and overseas Chinese (as companies and economic regions) in mainland China on business know-how, foreign direct investment and trade.

The economic relationship between overseas Chinese and China, and overseas Chinese and Japan

Before entering into a discussion of the role of the overseas Chinese in the Sino–Japanese economic relationship, we must first define overseas Chinese and examine their economic relationship to China and to Japan.

Irrespective of nationality, the overseas Chinese are those people of Chinese descent who live in countries or regions other than mainland China. Besides Hong Kong and Taiwan, overseas Chinese mainly live in Southeast Asian countries where most of them have local citizenship but belong to minority groups and are referred to as ethnic Chinese.

Because of their business competence, the overseas Chinese are also a strong economic factor in Southeast Asian countries where they are minorities, not to mention Hong Kong and Taiwan, and Singapore, where they form the majority of the population. Overseas Chinese business communities (their companies and business groups) have a great weight in these economies, their economic strength often sufficient to dominate the local economies. Also considering the global expansion of overseas Chinese business in Asia, the overseas Chinese economy is the greatest economic power in Asia (outside of Japan). In this sense, one might even go so far as to say that this region is an overseas Chinese economic region.

They are linked to one another through the overseas Chinese network, and also cooperate in business. There are relations among overseas Chinese by blood (kinship and cognominal relations), by bands (relations between those whose ancestors hail from the same province in China) and by trade (relations between those who engage in the same trade or business transactions). There is a feeling of familiarity and a tradition of mutual aid among them based on the similarity of culture, language (or dialect), custom and sense of values. The overseas Chinese network has been formed on the basis of these relations and various organizations originating from such relations (that is clan societies, compatriot associations and groups of entrepreneurs such as Chinese chambers of commerce & industry). The network is primarily business-oriented, and overseas Chinese companies in different countries often use the network to form joint ventures, even on a global scale (Zhu, 1995, pp. 6–13).

Overseas Chinese, in general, have a close connection to the land of their ancestors. In the 1980s when China started its reform and open-door policies, overseas Chinese companies in Asia began to invest there. Large-scale investments were actively started by companies in Hong Kong in the early 1980s, by those in Southeast Asian countries in the latter half of the 1980s, and by those in Taiwan in the 1990s. Their investments have achieved remarkable success, and overseas Chinese companies now have a large presence in China. However, since 1997 when the Asian financial crisis broke out, investments from Southeast Asian countries have slowed down. In any case, overseas Chinese companies have invested in various industries in China including manufacturing, trade and distribution, real estate and infrastructure. Since most of the overseas Chinese hail from Guangdong and Fujian provinces in the southern part of China, investments tended to concentrate initially on these two provinces but later extended throughout all of China.

It is impossible to obtain exact statistics of the total foreign direct investments in China by overseas Chinese companies. However, the scale of the investments can be estimated by assuming that the investments from Hong Kong, Taiwan and Southeast Asian countries with concentrations of overseas Chinese are by overseas Chinese companies. With an estimate using this method, the cumulative total of direct investments up to 1999 by overseas Chinese companies on contract value amounted to more than US$ 410 billion, while the actually used value was more than US$ 200 billion. A little under 70 per cent of all foreign direct investments in China was made by overseas Chinese companies (see Table 10.1). Although these figures include a small amount of investments by non-Chinese companies, state enterprises and foreign capital, almost all of them can be regarded as investments by overseas Chinese companies. Investments from Hong Kong are especially large because overseas Chinese companies in Taiwan and Southeast Asian countries invest through Hong Kong for various reasons. In contrast, investments from Japan account for less than 10 per cent.

Why are the direct investments from overseas Chinese economies predominant and why are most of them successful? In addition to the benefit of cheap labour and a large market, which all investors in China share, overseas Chinese companies have a decided advantage over others: they have the same background of race, language, customs, mentality and values. Firstly, overseas Chinese, thanks to their racial and cultural background, have a quite reliable understanding of the political and economic systems of China and therefore of the long-term trend of the Chinese economy. Secondly, they have personal connections and have a better understanding

Table 10.1   Foreign direct investments in China from overseas Chinese economies (cumulative amounts in 1999)

	Contract value		Actually used value	
	US$ mn	%	US$ mn	%
Total foreign direct investment	613 717	100.0	307 631	100.0
Overseas Chinese economies	410 446	66.9	202 515	65.8
Hong Kong	310 957	50.7	154 797	50.3
Macao	9 309	1.5	3 636	1.2
Taiwan	43 774	7.1	23 863	7.8
Singapore	33 349	5.4	14 820	4.8
Thailand	4 802	0.8	1 789	0.6
Malaysia	4 547	0.7	2 002	0.7
Philippines	2 202	0.4	918	0.3
Indonesia	1 506	0.2	690	0.2
Japan	35 134	5.7	24 886	8.1

Source: Investment statistics by the Ministry of Foreign Trade and Economic Cooperation (MOFTEC), China.

of business practices and style in China, and can thus obtain government support more easily. In addition, they have a cost advantage because of the relative ease of communication, training of employees and labour management. These advantages that contributed to the success of foreign direct investments have been utilized in Japanese companies' entry into the Chinese market. They are a basis of the role of the overseas Chinese in the Sino–Japanese economic relationship.

On the other hand, Japan and overseas Chinese also have a close economic relationship. Economies where overseas Chinese are predominant have close economic relations with Japan in terms of trade, investment and finance. Considering the fact that overseas Chinese companies have a great weight in these economies, it can be inferred that business with Japan is mainly carried out by these companies. Moreover, when Japanese companies make direct investments, they tend to tie up with leading overseas Chinese companies and carry out joint investment projects (Zhu, 2000a, pp. 81–2). This is especially the case in Southeast Asian countries where, until the late 1980s, foreign direct investments were only possible in the form of joint ventures with domestic companies. When many overseas Chinese companies and joint ventures with Japanese companies encountered difficulties after the Asian financial crisis, Japanese companies supported them by buying their stocks under buyback agreements.

For overseas Chinese companies, entering into joint ventures with Japanese companies carries the advantage of acquiring the necessary capital and technology. Almost all the new, large-scale ventures in manufacturing industries by overseas Chinese companies have obtained technology from Japanese companies. These close relations between the two have been brought advantages in foreign investment; Japanese companies tend to invest in other countries, and in China, in partnership with overseas Chinese companies or through their existing joint ventures.

The role of overseas Chinese in Japanese direct investment in China

As we have seen, Japanese companies have fallen behind successful overseas Chinese companies in implementing direct investments in China, and the overall scale of investment and profits are smaller. For this reason, many Japanese companies have enlisted the cooperation of overseas Chinese companies that have had a head start in making investments in China. In the following, we shall investigate their mutual cooperation in direct investments in China.

Firstly, Japanese companies have studied overseas Chinese companies' management techniques that have led to successful investments in China. Especially in the early 1990s, when Japanese companies failed to forecast the long-term trend of the Chinese economy and suffered from the deficient investment environment including legal systems and from the frequent institutional changes due to the shift from a planned economy to a market economy, they were encouraged by the success of overseas Chinese companies and received many valuable suggestions from them. The lessons they learned were how to deal with the Chinese government, strategies for moving labour-intensive industries from the homeland to China, methods of income recognition and investment recovery, sales in the Chinese domestic market, and labour management.

Secondly, Japanese companies have made use of the overseas Chinese network by investing in China in various forms of collaboration with overseas Chinese companies. By doing so, they have been able to diversify risk, utilize overseas Chinese companies' personal connections and relations with other companies in China, and manage businesses in China in close liaison with their manufacturing and sales bases in Hong Kong, Taiwan and Southeast Asian countries. They have joined together in China with overseas Chinese groups from Hong Kong, Taiwan and Southeast Asian countries as well as with locally established joint ventures with overseas Chinese.

Another feature of Japanese companies' entry into China is that their investments are made not by Japan-based companies, but by their affiliates in Hong Kong or Taiwan (Wong, 1998, pp. 98–101). In addition, Japanese companies have invested in industrial complexes developed by overseas Chinese companies and have utilized the favourable investment environment. For instance, many Japanese companies have sited their factories in Suzhou Industrial Park, developed by the government of Singapore and partly bankrolled by overseas Chinese companies from Singapore and Indonesia. Since the industrial park was developed as a national project by the Singapore and Chinese governments, a joint venture in charge of the management of the park undertakes such tasks as negotiations with the Chinese government and incorporation procedures, providing 'one-stop' services. This has enabled Japanese companies to delegate burdensome work to overseas Chinese and concentrate on production (Zhu, 2000b).

There are also cases where Japanese companies have purchased overseas Chinese businesses in China. For instance, in 1994 Asahi Breweries, Ltd purchased three Chinese beer companies that had been bought out and restructured by China Strategic Holdings. This company, established in Hong Kong by overseas Chinese from Indonesia, made large-scale investments in China and purchased more than 200 companies, restructured them and listed their stocks on stock exchanges in China and other countries, or sold them to foreign companies. Such operations are possible only for overseas Chinese, who have connections and management know-how in China. The sale of the three beer companies was advantageous to both China Strategic Holdings and Asahi Breweries. The former was able to recover investment at an early stage while the latter was able to make an efficient investment in China by buying out established companies instead of investing in new ventures

(Zhu, 1995, pp. 112–3). The purchased beer factories are now the core of Asahi Breweries' business in China.

Thirdly, Japanese companies investing in China are making use of overseas Chinese talent in business management. Japanese companies in foreign countries are said to be behind companies of other nationalities in localization, especially in assigning local employees to executive posts. Although this is also the case in China, there are noteworthy exceptions. But many Japanese companies have sent overseas Chinese managers, engineers and executives to China from subsidiaries and joint ventures that they established in Hong Kong, Taiwan and Southeast Asian countries. They can naturally adapt to the Chinese environment more easily than Japanese delegated from Japan, because they can speak Chinese and have a better understanding of the culture and society. Especially in Fujian Province, which is near Taiwan and has almost the same culture, customs and dialect as Taiwan, there are many Japanese companies that have been established by investment through subsidiaries in Taiwan and whose 'foreign' executives, managers and engineers are all Taiwanese.

Fourthly, Japanese subsidiaries have teamed up with overseas Chinese companies in China on the basis of agreements on business activities or as component suppliers and assemblers. They often procure parts from overseas Chinese companies or supply components to the latter. Such relations are most conspicuous in the machine and electronics industries, especially in the personal computer industry.

On the other hand, overseas Chinese companies have sought out Japanese companies' cooperation in investments in China. Especially in manufacturing industries, most of them have imported manufacturing technology from Japan. For instance, the biggest overseas Chinese company in Thailand, CP (Charoen Pokphand) Group, established a joint venture for the production of motorcycles in Shanghai introducing Honda's technology in the 1980s. The joint venture, EK Chor China Motorcycle Ltd Corp. has developed into a major motorcycle manufacturer in China, and listed its stock on the New York Stock Exchange in 1992 (Zhu, 2000a, pp. 389–402). Another example is South-East Motor, which was established in 1996 in Fujian Province by China Motor, the second largest auto-maker in Taiwan. The company was given overall technological support by Mitsubishi Motors Corp., which is China Motor's partner in Japan. South-East Motor's new station wagon, which the company put into production in 1999, is a model localized for the Chinese market by Mitsubishi on behalf of China Motor.

Fifthly, Japanese funds are invested in China via Hong Kong. Investments in China from abroad, especially those from Taiwan and Southeast Asian countries, are mostly made through Hong Kong. This is partly for political reasons, that is for the purpose of circumventing government bans and public censure of investment in China, and partly because the financing of investment funds can be facilitated by Hong Kong's status as an international financial centre.

The functions of Hong Kong's financial market, especially of its banks, are closely related to Japan. The basic pattern of Hong Kong's market for loanable funds, that is for banking operations, is to raise funds from foreign banks through the interbank capital market and then make loans to customers in Hong Kong and other regions in the forms of financing and syndicated loans. In this regard, Japanese banks are the greatest lender to Hong Kong banks.

Japanese funds (Japanese banks could take capital from Japan to Hong Kong, to utilize in the Hong Kong financial market, for investment and to make profit) consistently account for about 60 per cent of the interbank funding from foreign banks to banks in Hong Kong. Most of the funds are borrowed by local companies and investors in Hong Kong, that is by overseas Chinese companies, and it is estimated that a substantial part of the funds obtained from the banks have been invested in China. In other words, the investments in China by companies in Hong Kong or by overseas Chinese companies via Hong Kong are essentially financed by Japanese funds. On the other hand, Hong Kong's financial market offers great advantages to Japanese banks. For one thing, it gives them opportunities for funding operations in Hong Kong. Secondly, Japanese banks can offer financial services to Japanese companies in China via Hong Kong. A considerable percentage of the aggregate loans by the banks in Hong Kong are to Japanese companies. Most of these loans have been made by branch offices of Japanese banks in Hong Kong to Japanese subsidiaries in China, with their headquarters in Japan as guarantors (Zhu, 1997, pp. 54–6, 228–32).

Such cooperation between Japanese and overseas Chinese companies in direct investments in China is an extension of the partnership already built up in countries where overseas Chinese companies are based. It has been beneficial to both parties. The economic relationship between Japan and overseas Chinese economies has also been capitalized on in direct investments in China and has become closer in the process.

The role of overseas Chinese in Sino–Japanese trade

The trade between Japan and China has expanded rapidly over the past 20 years, with the overseas Chinese playing various and important roles in that trade. Firstly, a considerable portion of the trade is carried on via Hong Kong, which is an international trade centre equipped with necessary facilities such as harbours. The most important part of the trade in Hong Kong is what is called entrepôt trade, which includes activities mostly intended for China. Hong Kong imports various goods from China and re-exports them to all the countries of the world, and re-exports to China diverse commodities imported from the world. Trade between Japan and China, which has been growing steadily every year, is also supported by the entrepôt activities in Hong Kong, and it accounts for a big share of Hong Kong's total re-exports (see Table 10.2). In 2000, Japan exported US$ 13.5 billion worth of goods to

Table 10.2 Sino–Japanese trade via Hong Kong (US$ billions, %)

	1993	1995	1997	1998	1999	2000
Sino–Japanese trade via Hong Kong	14.7	19.6	21.6	19.4	19.3	22.8
Japan → Hong Kong → China	10.1	12.0	12.7	12.1	11.8	13.5
China → Hong Kong → Japan	4.6	7.6	8.8	7.3	7.5	9.3
Share of the re-export from Hong Kong (%)	13.8	13.7	13.4	13.0	12.7	12.7

Source: Compiled by the author from *Hong Kong External Trade* (monthly).

China via Hong Kong, accounting for 21.4 per cent of the re-exports from Hong Kong to China and 32.5 per cent of all imports to China from Japan. China exported to Japan via Hong Kong US$ 9.3 billion worth of goods, accounting for 87.8 per cent of the re-exports from Hong Kong to Japan and 22.4 per cent of all exports from China to Japan (see also Chapter 2).

In contrast to the re-exports from Hong Kong, which require customs formalities, there is a form of Sino–Japanese trade via Hong Kong that does not need customs clearance and therefore is not counted as a re-export. This is called transhipment, which is direct Sino–Japanese trade that only uses the port facilities in Hong Kong. Exports from China to Japan are cleared by customs in China, transported to Hong Kong by trucks and ships, and loaded there into large container ships for Japan. Recently, such transhipment between China and Japan via Hong Kong has been gradually increasing (Zhu, 1997, pp. 47–9).

In such a manner, Hong Kong has contributed greatly to the growth of Sino–Japanese trade as an international trade and shipping centre, and such trade via Hong Kong will continue to increase in the future. Especially export goods to Japan produced in Guangdong province and other southern parts of China are more advantageous via Hong Kong, in terms of time, cost and location.

Secondly, overseas Chinese companies in China are directly engaged in Sino–Japanese trade. Most of the manufacturers in China established by overseas Chinese from Hong Kong, Taiwan and Southeast Asian countries are export-oriented enterprises which export a major portion of their products to Japan. Especially companies in labour-intensive industries such as textiles, food and parts of machinery and electronics, are heavily dependent on exports to Japan. Apparel and shoe-makers from Hong Kong and Taiwan, electronics companies from Taiwan, and food manufacturers from Southeast Asian countries have actively exported to Japan. The previously mentioned CP Group, an overseas Chinese company from Thailand, has established many companies in China in agribusiness, of which poultry farming and the food processing business is specifically targeted for export to Japan.

Taiwanese companies' local production of personal-computer-related goods in China has greatly influenced the import of such goods to Japan

(Zhu, 2001, pp. 34–42, 60–1). According to an estimate by the Institute for Information Industry (III) in Taiwan, the personal-computer-related companies in Taiwan produced a total of US$ 18.6 billion worth of products in China in 2000, accounting for 38.6 per cent of the total output (including overseas production) of Taiwan's personal computer industry, and 71.8 per cent of that of China. Through local production in China, the Taiwanese personal computer industry was able to ensure stable supplies of inexpensive parts and improve its export competitiveness, which resulted in the rapid increase of exports to Japan, especially of notebook computers. Direct investments from Taiwan and local production in China brought about rapid growth of the Chinese personal computer industry, which enormously increased its export of peripherals and parts to Japan.

According to Japanese trade statistics, imports from Taiwan of personal-computer-related products increased from yen 256 billion in 1998 to yen 599 billion in 2000, climbing to the top spot ahead of the United States. Imports from China also increased from yen 137 billion in 1998 to yen 271 billion in 2000, emerging from fifth to third position (see Figure 10.1). Lists of imports from Taiwan and China of personal-computer-related products by item show that the amounts and shares of almost all items concerning personal computers imported from Taiwan and China have increased (see Table 10.3). To be more specific, Taiwan's share of input–output devices has decreased, while China's share has increased correspondingly. This is due to the fact that Taiwanese companies relocated the production facilities of

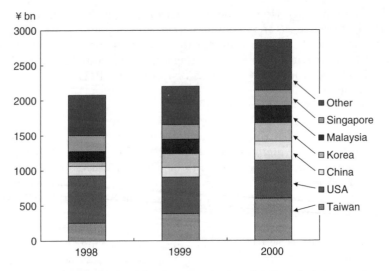

Figure 10.1 Japanese imports of personal-computer-related products by country

Source: Interchange Association: 'Interchange', 28 February 2001 (originally from trade statistics of the Ministry of Finance, Japan).

Table 10.3   Japanese imports of personal-computer-related products by item

	Amount (¥ billion)			Year-on-year increase (%)		Share (%)		
	1998	1999	2000	'99/'98	'00/'99	1998	1999	2000
Total	2075.3	2200.7	2858.4	6.0	29.9	100.0	100.0	100.0
Taiwan	256.0	387.6	599.1	51.4	54.6	12.3	17.6	21.0
China	137.0	140.8	270.8	2.8	92.3	6.6	6.4	9.5
Processors	542.7	620.0	819.1	14.3	32.1	100.0	100.0	100.0
Taiwan	101.2	175.5	281.6	73.5	60.4	18.6	28.3	34.4
China	0.4	1.6	21.2	347.8	1225.5	0.1	0.3	2.6
I/O devices	200.6	278.7	374.1	38.9	34.2	100.0	100.0	100.0
Taiwan	46.1	57.5	77.5	24.8	34.8	23.0	20.6	20.7
China	35.5	42.9	76.5	20.8	78.4	17.7	15.4	20.5
Storage devices	414.5	386.2	463.4	− 6.8	20.0	100.0	100.0	100.0
Taiwan	9.3	7.7	9.2	− 17.8	20.3	2.2	2.0	2.0
China	14.5	14.7	20.0	1.8	35.8	3.5	3.8	4.3
Other devices	125.6	138.9	226.0	10.6	62.7	100.0	100.0	100.0
Taiwan	12.2	13.7	18.1	12.5	32.1	9.7	9.8	8.0
China	0.8	1.3	3.2	56.0	147.9	0.7	0.9	1.4
Parts	791.9	776.9	975.7	− 1.9	25.6	100.0	100.0	100.0
Taiwan	87.3	133.3	212.7	52.7	59.6	11.0	17.2	21.8
China	85.9	80.3	149.8	− 6.4	86.5	10.8	10.3	15.4

Source: Interchange Association: 'Interchange', 28 February 2001 (originally from trade statistics of the Ministry of Finance, Japan).

monitors to China and started to export them to Japan. A similar tendency can be observed concerning storage devices; in fact the production of floppy disc drives (FDDs) and CD-ROMs has been transferred from Taiwan to China.

Most of the local production facilities in China managed by overseas Chinese companies have imported manufacturing equipment and vital parts from Japan. The above-mentioned electronics and personal computer companies from Taiwan have also imported from Japan to China several billions of dollars of vital parts such as integrated circuits products and hard disc drives (HDDs) in order to launch local production. The import of parts from Japanese manufacturing bases in Southeast Asian countries has also increased.

Prospects for the future

We have seen that the overseas Chinese have played a most important role in the Sino–Japanese economic relationship. On the basis of these analyses, we shall now discuss possible future changes in this relationship.

In the near future, radical change may occur in the Sino–Japanese economic relationship and the economic relationship between the overseas Chinese and China. The WTO entry of China in 2001 is a factor that may cause such a change. Once China has entered the WTO, it will have to implement various policies that the government has agreed to in the process of negotiations. First, China has to open its market, reduce tariffs in stages, and gradually abolish non-tariff barriers. Restrictions on foreign investment must be gradually eased; the door must be opened to foreign investment in the service sector; and equal national treatment must be given to foreigners. These deregulation measures will greatly reduce restrictions on trade and foreign direct investment in China, making Japanese entry into the Chinese market much easier. On the other hand, China will be able to enjoy various privileges as a WTO member. China will be automatically given most-favoured-nation trading status by other members, and will no longer be discriminated against in matters relating to international trade in goods and services and to outward foreign direct investment. This will lead to a large increase in exports from China and a gradual expansion in foreign direct investment by Chinese companies.

On the basis of such likely changes, we may be able to predict the following changes in the role of the overseas Chinese in the Sino–Japanese economic relationship:

- Firstly, Japanese investments in China will grow in scale and reach a higher level. Japanese companies will become less dependent on overseas Chinese companies' connections and know-how in China owing to deregulation (especially the easing of regulations on foreign direct investment) and the improvement of the investment environment that WTO entry will bring about.
- Secondly, the cooperation between Japanese and overseas Chinese companies in China, especially the component supplier–assembler interrelationship, will be sustained and intensified.
- Thirdly, with the increase in exports of goods produced in China that WTO entry will bring about, the role of overseas Chinese in China's trade will become more important. They will be able to contribute not only to Sino–Japanese trade, but also to the exports of Japanese companies' products from China to overseas Chinese economies.
- Lastly, the cooperation between Japanese and overseas Chinese companies will spread out on a greater level from China throughout Asia, including the economies in which overseas Chinese companies are based. As we have already seen, the relationship between Japanese companies and overseas Chinese companies in China is an extension of their cooperation built up in the latter's bases, that is in overseas Chinese economies. Their mutual cooperation in China has had the effect of further developing the relationship, which will be enhanced on a more intense level throughout

all of Asia in the future. To be more specific, Japanese companies will expand direct investment in China and, by doing so, further the specialization of the production systems built up in Asia (most of which are joint ventures with overseas Chinese) and local production in China. In this way, the production structures of Japanese companies will be reorganized more efficiently throughout Asia.

References

China's Customs Statistics (2000) *China's Customs Statistics, Monthly Export & Import*, Beijing: General Administration of Custom of People's Republic of China.

China's Latest Economic Indicators (2001) National Bureau of Statistics of PRC (ed.), Beijing: All China Marketing Research Co. Ltd.

MoF (Ministry of Finance, Japan) (2000) <http://www.mof.go.jp/1c015f1.htm> 31 August 2001.

To, T.-E. [Twu, Jaw-yann] (1998) *Kajin keizai-ken to Nihon* [The Overseas Chinese Economic Zone and Japan], Tokyo: Yûshindô.

Wong, Z. (1998) *Riben qiye zai Zhongguo de touzi* [Japanese Corporation's Investment in China], Beijing: Zhongguo Jingji Chubanshe.

Yu, C. (2000) *Ethnic Chinese, Their Economy, Politics and Culture*, Tokyo: The Japan Times.

Zhu, Y. (1995) *Kajin nettowâku no himitsu* [The Characteristics of Overseas Chinese Network], Tokyo: Tôyô Keizai Inc.

— (1997) *1997 Kawaru Honkon keizai kawaranai Honkon keizai* [1997: The Changeable and Unchangeable Factors in Hong Kong Economy], Tokyo: Tôyô Keizai Inc.

— (2000a) *Tettei kenshô: Ajia Kajin kigyô gurûpu no jitsuryoku* [A Thorough Study: the Economic Power of overseas Chinese Enterprise Group in Asia], Tokyo: Diamond Inc.

— (2000b) Interview conducted at Suzhou Industrial Park, December 2000.

— (2001) 'Mutual Reliance and Division of Labour Between China and Taiwan in the IT Industry', *Economic Review* (Fujitsu Research Institute), vol. 5 (1), pp. 34–63, <http:// www.fri.fujitsu.com/hypertext/fri/review/rev051/review03.html> 31 August 2001.

Index